REVISED EDITION

PUBLISHED BY

THE EPOCH TIMES

229 W 28TH ST, 7TH FLOOR

NEW YORK, NY 10001

PRINTED BY

CAI HONG PRINTING & PUBLISHING

60 COMMERCE WAY, SUITE A&B

TOTOWA, NJ 07512

TWO-VOLUME SET: ISBN: 978-1-63702-001-2

VOLUME I: ISBN: 978-1-63702-002-9

VOLUME II: ISBN: 978-1-63702-003-6

How The
SPECTER OF COMMUNISM IS RULING OUR WORLD

From The
Editorial Board of
"NINE COMMENTARIES ON
THE COMMUNIST PARTY"

VOLUME I

An Epoch Times Special Publication

Table of Contents

The specter of communism did not disappear with the disintegration of the Communist Party in Eastern Europe

Preface

THOUGH THE COMMUNIST REGIMES of Eastern Europe have disintegrated, the specter of communism has not disappeared. On the contrary, this evil specter is already ruling our world, and humanity must not harbor a mistaken sense of optimism.

Communism is neither a trend of thought, nor a doctrine, nor a failed attempt at a new way of ordering human affairs. Instead, it should be understood as a devil — an evil specter forged by hate, degeneracy, and other elemental forces in the universe.

In another dimension, not visible to us, it took the form of a serpent, then that of a red dragon, and it keeps company with Satan, who hates God. It exploits low-level beings and demons to wreak havoc on humankind. The goal of the specter is to ruin humanity. While the divine offers salvation, communism tells people not to believe in the divine, attacks human morality so as to make people abandon tradition, and causes people to disregard the divine's instruction and, ultimately, to be destroyed.

The communist evil specter, with its countless mutations, is full of guile. Sometimes it uses slaughter and violence to destroy those who refuse to follow it. Other times, it takes recourse in the language of "science" and "progress," offering a wonderful blueprint of the future in order to deceive people. Sometimes it presents itself as a profound field of learning and makes people believe that it is the future direction of mankind. Other times, it uses the slogans of "democracy," "equality," and "social justice" to infiltrate the fields of education, media, art, and law, bringing people under its banner without their awareness. At yet other times, it calls itself "socialism," "progressivism," "liberalism," "neo-Marxism," and other leftist terms.

Sometimes it holds up seemingly righteous banners such as pacifism, environmentalism, globalism, and political correctness. Other times, it supports vanguard art, sexual liberation, legalization of drugs, homosexuality, and other indulgences in human desires, giving the mistaken impression that it's part of a popular trend.

Extremism and violence aren't its only expressions — sometimes it pretends to care for the welfare of society. Yet its root purpose is to destroy, by whatever means, everything that is traditional, whether it be faith, religion, morality, culture, the institution of the family, art, pedagogy, or law — whatever it takes to have man fall into a moral abyss and be damned.

Communism and its various mutations are now found around the world. China and Cuba publicly proclaim themselves to be led by communist regimes. Even the United States — the leader of the free world — has fallen prey to attacks by the evil specter. Europe embraces socialism, and Africa and Latin America are enveloped in communist influence. This is the startling reality humankind now faces: The evil specter's conspiracy to destroy humankind is on the verge of success.

Humans instinctively desire to benefit themselves and avoid

danger. Instinct urges them to escape from suffering, to make a name for themselves, to establish prosperous enterprises, or merely to enjoy life. It is human to have these thoughts. However, if humans distance themselves from the divine, the evil specter can latch onto and intensify these thoughts to control them.

The hubris of the specter's revolt against divinity also makes those it controls experience a sense of hubris. These individuals then try to play God through the wielding of power, capital, and knowledge, with the aim of ruling the fates of millions and influencing the course of history through social movements.

Humans are created by the divine and have both good and evil in their nature. If people abandon evil and choose compassion, they can return to the divine. What awaits on the opposite side is evil personified — the devil. The choice resides solely with the individual.

Many fundamentally kindhearted people have unknowingly become the communist specter's agents or the targets of its manipulation — what Vladimir Lenin called "useful idiots." Though society as a whole has ended up on the verge of destruction because of the specter's inducements and temptations, very few people have willingly pledged their souls to the devil and chosen to deliberately corrupt mankind. For most, the kindness innate in human nature remains, giving them an opportunity to rid themselves of the specter's influence.

The purpose of this book is to set out this complex and tangled issue in plain language as truthfully as possible. Then people will be able to see the communist specter's tricks. More importantly, this book seeks to present the moral, cultural, and artistic traditions that the divine laid down for mankind. Individuals may then choose between the divine and the evil specter for themselves.

When a person's kind thoughts emerge, the divine will help free him from the devil's control. But the process of seeing the devil for what it is requires that one think deeply and discern clearly. This book seeks to reexamine the tides of history over the last several centuries and, from a high level and with a broad perspective, assess the multifarious masks and forms the devil has adopted in order to occupy and manipulate our world.

The goal of this effort is not to simply recount history, but to understand how we can stop the devil from ever ruling the world again. This relies on each individual's enlightenment, proactive abandonment of evil, and return to the traditions and way of life that the divine laid down for man.

The divine will triumph over the devil. Which side we stand on will determine our eternal destiny.

Introduction

THE COLLAPSE OF THE COMMUNIST regimes in the Soviet Union and Eastern Europe marked the end of a half-century-long Cold War between the capitalist and communist camps in the West and the East. At the time, many were optimistic, believing that communism had become a relic of the past.

The sad truth, however, is that a transmogrified communist ideology has taken hold and entrenched itself around the world. In China, North Korea, Cuba, and Vietnam, there are outright communist regimes; in Eastern European countries, communist ideology and customs still exert a significant influence; and in African and South American countries, socialism is practiced under the banner of democracy and republicanism. Then there are the nations of Western Europe and North America, which have become host to communist influences without people even realizing it.

Communism breeds war, famine, slaughter, and tyranny. These in themselves are terrifying enough, but the damage dealt by communism goes far beyond this. It has become increasingly clear that, unlike any other system in history, communism declares war on humanity itself — including human values and human dignity.

After establishing massive dictatorships in the Soviet Union and China, communism came to rule billions of people and caused more than one hundred million unnatural deaths in less than a century. In its overt attempts at world revolution, the communist bloc brought the world to the brink of nuclear war; meanwhile, leftist thinkers and activists have promoted the deliberate and widespread destruction of the family, social order, and traditional morality.

What is the nature of communism? What is its objective? Why does it take mankind as its enemy? How can we escape it?

1. Communism: A Devil Bent on the Destruction of Humanity

The Communist Manifesto begins with the sentence "A specter is haunting Europe — the specter of communism." The use of the term "specter" was not a whim on the part of Karl Marx. As we argue in this book, communism should not be understood as an ideological movement, a political doctrine, or a failed attempt at a new way of ordering human affairs. Instead, it should be understood as a devil — an evil specter forged by hate, degeneracy, and other elemental forces in the universe.

Following the Cold War, the poison of communism not only continued to harm formerly communist countries, but also spread throughout the world. Since then, the ideological infiltration of communism has enabled the specter to influence human society on a global scale. Under the influence of communist ideas, countless people have lost their ability to discern right from wrong, to differentiate good from evil. The devil's conspiracy has been carried out to an advanced stage of completion.

2. The Devil's Ways and Means

Man was created by the divine, and divine compassion has long protected man. The devil knew this, and so it set about severing this connection, in order to corrupt man and ensure that the divine would no longer take care of him. The devil's approach has been to subvert the culture given to mankind by the divine, in order to undermine human morality and thus warp man, making him unworthy of salvation.

Both good and evil, the divine and the devil, reside in the heart of every person. A life can sink into immoral decadence or elevate through moral cultivation. Those who believe in the divine know that by striving for moral conduct and thought, one's righteous thoughts can be strengthened by the divine, and the divine then will allow miracles to happen. The divine will also help one's morality rise in level so as to help one become a nobler person, in the end allowing one to return to heaven.

A person of low morality, however, is filled with selfishness: desire, greed, ignorance, and hubris. While the divine will never recognize such thoughts and actions, the devil will magnify them, intensifying his selfishness and wickedness. Manipulated to commit wrongdoing, he thus creates more karma and causes further moral decay, until, in the end, only Hell awaits him.

If the moral standards of human society as a whole decline, the devil will hasten this trend with the goal of causing more sins, more karma, and humanity's eventual destruction. The turbulence of Europe beginning in the eighteenth century and the attendant moral decline gave the devil such an opportunity. It set about subverting, step by step, the criteria of discernment between good and evil. It promoted atheism, materialism, Darwinism, and the philosophy of struggle.

The devil chose Marx as its envoy among men. In *The Communist Manifesto,* published in 1848, Marx and his associate Friedrich Engels advocated the violent destruction of private enterprise, social classes, nations, religions, and the family. The destructive Paris Commune of 1871 was the communist specter's first direct attempt at seizing power.

Marx's followers argue that political power is the central question of Marxian political science. This is both true and not true. When we clearly see communism's ultimate aims, we can recognize that political power is both important and unimportant to the communist project. It's important in that access to political power allows for a rapid means of corrupting humankind. With control over the levers of power, communists can promote their ideology with violence and eradicate a traditional culture in mere decades or less. Yet it's also unimportant, in that even without the apparatus of the state, the devil has other means of exploiting the weaknesses and shortcomings of man: even when communists do not hold political power, the specter's earthly agents can deceive, co-opt, coerce, and confuse society, subverting order and creating upheaval to overturn traditional thought. Communism uses such "divide and conquer" tactics in its efforts to gain global control.

3. Communism: The Devil's Ideology

The divine established a rich culture for human society based on universal values, paving the way for humans to return to heaven. Communism and the traditional culture of the divine are irreconcilable.

At the core of the evil specter are atheism and materialism — a confluence of elements from German philosophy, French social revolution, and British political economics, assembled as a secular religion meant to replace the position previously occupied by the divine and orthodox beliefs.

Communism turns the world into its church, bringing all aspects of social life under its purview. The devil occupies people's thoughts, causing them to revolt against the divine and discard tradition. This is how the devil leads man to his own destruction.

The devil chose Marx and others as its agents to oppose and destroy the principles laid down by the divine for human society. In the East, it launched a violent revolution and established a totalitarian state that united politics and secular religion. In the West, it establishes progressive, nonviolent communism through high levels of taxation and wealth redistribution. On a global scale, it seeks to spread communist ideology to political systems everywhere, with the goal of undermining nation-states and establishing a global ruling body. This is the "paradise on earth" promised in communism, a supposed collective society without classes, nations, or government, based on the principle of "from each according to his ability and to each according to his need."

Communism uses its program of creating a "paradise" on earth to promote an atheistic conception of "social progress." It uses materialism to undermine the spiritual pursuits of mankind in order to enable communist ideology to spread to every sphere, including not only social studies and philosophy but even natural sciences and religious teaching. Like a malignant tumor, communism metastasizes, eliminating other beliefs — including the belief in the divine — as it spreads. In turn, it destroys national sovereignty and identity, and humanity's moral and cultural traditions, thus leading man to destruction. In *The Communist Manifesto*, Marx proclaimed, "The communist revolution is the most radical rupture with traditional property relations; no wonder that its development involves the most radical rupture with traditional ideas." Marx thus accurately summarized the practice of communism over the past two centuries.

The divine is the source of moral order, and the divine's morality is eternal and unchanging. Moral standards are not for man to determine for himself, nor can they be changed by man. Communism sentences morality to death and attempts to have the communist New Man establish a fake revolutionary morality. It uses negative methods to expel all the positive factors from human traditions, with the goal of having negative factors occupy the world.

Traditional laws come from morality and are intended to uphold it. Communism tries to separate morality from the law, then destroy morality by concocting malicious new laws and subjecting existing law to twisted interpretations.

The divine calls upon man to be kind; communism incites class struggle and advocates violence and killing.

The divine established the family as the basic social unit; communism believes that the family is a manifestation of private property and capitalism, and aims to eliminate it.

The divine gives man the freedom to obtain wealth and the right to improve his lot in life; communism seeks to control all aspects of economic life by eliminating private property, expropriating assets, raising taxes, and monopolizing credit and capital.

The divine established the forms that morality, government, law, society, and culture should take; communism seeks the violent overthrow of existing social structures.

The divine transmitted to man the unique form of traditional art as a means of passing on the divine image. Traditional art recalls to mankind the beauty of heaven, reinforces faith, elevates morality, and nurtures virtue. Communism, on the other hand, would have man worship warped modern creations — artistic productions that stifle our divine nature, give full rein to the demonic impulse toward chaos and disorder, and manipulate the art world by spreading base, ugly, malformed, evil, and decadent ideas.

The divine wants man to be humble and full of reverence and wonder at heavenly creation. Communism connives at the demonic and arrogant side in man, encouraging him to revolt against the divine. By amplifying the evil inherent and inescapable in human nature, it exploits the idea of "freedom" to encourage conduct that is unrestrained by morality and unfettered by a sense of duty or honor. The slogan of "equality" is used to stir up envy and vanity, stoking man's desire for fame and material interests.

After World War II, the communists expanded their military and economic empire, and the communist bloc and the free world contended for decades. In countries ruled by overt communist regimes, its doctrine became a secular religion — an unchallengeable dogma written into textbooks. But elsewhere, communism took root under other guises.

4. A Metaphysical Understanding of the Devil

The idea of the devil referred to in this text is that of a supernatural power. To understand the chaos sown by the devil throughout the world, one must come to fully grasp the true nature of communism.

Simply put, the specter of communism is composed of hate; it draws its energy from the hatred that wells up in the human heart.

The communist specter is tied to Satan. Often the two are indistinguishable, thus we will not make an effort to consider them separately.

The devil's arrangements are present in both the East and the West, in every profession, and in every walk of life. Sometimes its power is divided, sometimes integrated; sometimes it uses this tactic, sometimes that. It follows no simple pattern. The communist specter is the initiator of an unrestricted war on mankind that has created battlefields out of every conceivable sphere, from academia to popular culture, from social affairs to international relations.

The specter's dark energy can migrate at will from one vehicle to the next. For instance, after the anti-war movement faded in the West in the 1970s, the devil manipulated rebellious adolescents to channel their energies into agitating for feminism, environmentalism, and the legalization of homosexuality. The devil then used these efforts to subvert Western civilization from within.

The devil recruits those of villainous character to serve as its agents and representatives in the human world. Under the specter's power, they use deceptive appeals to humanity and other fallacious narratives to draw compassionate and innocent people into the fold. Their sense of justice and morality hijacked by communism, they become some of the specter's most loyal apologists.

The devil's agents — most of whom are unaware of their role — are everywhere in society, from the elite, to the middle class, to the lower classes. Thus, its activities manifest sometimes as bottom-up revolutions, sometimes as top-down conspiracies, and sometimes as reforms from the center.

The devil can change forms and exist in multiple places at once. It uses lowly beings and specters in other dimensions to do its work. These beings feed on man's negative energies, including hate, fear, despair, arrogance, rebelliousness, jealousy, lust, rage, frenzy, idleness, and more. Pornography and drug addiction are tools the devil uses.

The devil is secretive and full of guile. It uses man's avarice, wickedness, and darkness to achieve its ends, and as long as a person's thoughts align with these qualities, the devil can control that person.

Many times, people think they are acting according to their own thoughts, failing to realize they are being manipulated.

5. The Devil's Many Faces

Just as the devil goes by many names, communism manifests in many ways. The demon uses contradictory positions to deceive: a totalitarian regime or a democracy, a planned economy or a market economy, control of the press or no restraints whatsoever on speech, opposition to homosexuality in some countries or legalization of homosexuality in other countries, wanton environmental destruction or clamor for environmental protection, and so on.

It can advocate violent revolution or embrace peaceful transition. It may manifest as a political and economic system or as an ideological trend in art and culture. It may take the form of pure idealism or cold-blooded scheming. Communist totalitarian regimes are just one of the demon's manifestations. Marxism-Leninism and Maoism form just one aspect of the devil's pernicious deceit.

Since utopian socialism developed in the eighteenth century, the world has seen the emergence of numerous ideological currents: scientific socialism, Fabian socialism, syndicalism, Christian socialism, democratic socialism, humanitarianism, eco-socialism, welfare capitalism, Marxism-Leninism, and Maoism. These ideologies are of two broad and sometimes overlapping types: violent communism or nonviolent communism. The nonviolent strains take the approach of infiltrating and gradually eroding the status quo.

One of the many ways the devil deceives is by making arrangements in the two opposing camps of the East and the West. As it carried out a vast invasion of the East, it also took on a new guise and stole into the West. The Fabian Society of Britain, the Social Democratic Party of Germany, the Second International of France, the Socialist Party in the United States, and many other socialist parties and organizations spread the seeds of destruction throughout Western Europe and North America.

During the Cold War, the concentration camps, slaughter, famines, and purges in the Soviet Union and China made some Westerners count themselves lucky that they still lived in luxury and freedom. Some socialists publicly condemned the violence of the Soviet Union on humanitarian grounds, which led many to let down their guard around them.

The demon of communism inhabits a variety of complex guises in the West and operates under many banners, making it almost impossible to counter. The following schools or movements were either derived from communism or used by communism to reach its ends: liberalism, progressivism, the Frankfurt School, Neo-Marxism, critical theory, the counterculture of the 1960s, the anti-war movement, sexual liberation, legalization of homosexuality, feminism, environmentalism, social justice, political correctness, Keynesian economics, avant-garde art, and multiculturalism.

6. Socialism: The Preliminary Stage of Communism

In the West, many view socialism and communism as being separate, which provides fertile ground for socialism to flourish. In fact, according to Marxist-Leninist theory, socialism is simply communism's preliminary stage.

In 1875, in *Critique of the Gotha Programme*, Marx put forward the idea that there is an initial phase of communism, which is followed by a "higher" phase. Friedrich Engels, compelled by changes in the international situation in his later years, also proposed "democratic socialism," in which votes were used to obtain political power.

Democratic socialism was adopted by social democratic party leaders and theorists of the Second International and led to the left-wing parties in many capitalist countries around the world today. Later, Lenin set down clear definitions of socialism and communism: He considered socialism to be the preliminary phase of communism, and communism to be developed on the basis of socialism. The state ownership and planned economy of socialism are part of the initial preparation for communism.

Socialism has always been part of Marxism and the international communist movement. While branches of socialism or left-wing doctrines popular in the West seem superficially unrelated to communism, they are nonviolent forms of the same root ideology. Left-wing parties come to power in Western countries through elections, rather than violent revolution. High taxation serves the same role as the outright state ownership seen under communist regimes, and excessive social welfare is used in place of planned economics. Creating a welfare state is an important aspect of realizing socialism in Western countries.

It is thus impossible to understand the dangers of communism or socialism by focusing solely on the violence and slaughter committed by regimes that espouse those ideologies. Totalitarian communism and seemingly nonviolent forms of socialism go hand in hand, as communism requires this preliminary phase of development, just as a living organism needs a period of gradual maturation. If a free country turned into a totalitarian regime overnight, the drastic contrast between propaganda and reality would leave most people shocked. Many would rebel or at least passively resist. This would lead to high costs for totalitarian rule, and the regime would likely need to commit mass slaughter to eliminate the resistance, as happened in the Soviet Union and China.

Unlike under totalitarian rule, socialism in democratic states slowly eats away at people's freedoms through legislation, without their notice — like the metaphor of the boiling frog. The process of establishing a socialist system takes decades or generations, leaving people gradually numb, oblivious, and accustomed to socialism, all of which enhance the deceit. The endgame of socialist movements implemented gradually and through "legal" means is no different from that of their violent counterparts.

Some left-leaning states in the West today use the idea of the "common good" to convince the populace to sacrifice their individual freedoms. Citizens in these countries retain what appears to be a high degree of political liberties only because socialism has yet to become a strong political system. But socialism is not a static concept. Socialist countries set equality of outcome as the primary goal and thus are bound to deprive people of their freedom in the name of progress. Socialism inevitably undergoes a transition to communism, with people continually stripped of their rights until what remains is a tyrannical authoritarian regime.

Socialism uses the idea of guaranteeing equality of outcome through legislation, while in actuality, it drags down moral values and deprives people of the freedom to incline toward goodness. Under normal circumstances, people of all kinds naturally vary in their religious beliefs, moral standards, cultural literacy, educational backgrounds, intelligence, fortitude, diligence, sense of responsibility, aggressiveness, innovation, entrepreneurship, and more. Of course, it's impossible to enforce equality by suddenly elevating those at lower levels, so instead, socialism artificially restrains those at higher levels. Especially in terms of moral values, the socialism of the West uses pretexts like "anti-discrimination," "value-neutrality," or "political correctness" to attack basic moral discernment. This is equivalent to an attempt to eliminate morality as such. This has come along with the legalization and normalization of all manner of anti-theist and profane speech, sexual perversions, demonic art, pornography, gambling, and drug use. The result is a kind of reverse discrimination against those who believe in God and aspire to moral elevation, with the goal of marginalizing and eventually getting rid of them.

7. Romantic Notions About Communism

To this day, there are numerous Westerners who harbor romantic fantasies about communism, yet have never lived in a communist country and borne the suffering there, and thus have no understanding of what communism actually means in practice. During the Cold War, many intellectuals, artists, journalists, politicians, and young students from the free world went to Russia, China, or Cuba as tourists and travelers. What they saw — or, rather, were allowed to see — was completely different from the lived reality of the people of those countries.

Communist countries have perfected their ability to deceive foreigners: Everything the foreign visitors were shown was carefully crafted to their tastes, including the model villages, factories, schools, hospitals, daycare centers, and prisons. The receptionists and guides they encountered were members of the Communist Party or others considered politically reliable. The tours were rehearsed. The visitors were greeted with flowers, wine, dancing and singing, banquets, and smiling young children and officials. Then they were taken to see people who appeared to be hard at work yet able to talk freely and as equals, students studying hard, and lovely weddings.

What they did not get to see were the sham trials, mass sentencings, mob lynchings, struggle sessions, kidnappings, brainwashing, solitary confinement, forced labor camps, massacres, theft of land and property, famines, shortages of public services, lack of privacy, eavesdropping, surveillance, monitoring by neighbors and informants everywhere, brutal political struggles in the leadership, and extravagant luxuries of the elite. They especially were not allowed to see the suffering of ordinary people.

The visitors mistook what had been staged for them as the norm in communist countries. They then promoted communism in the West through books, articles, and speeches, and many of them didn't know they had been deceived. A small number did see cracks in the edifice, but then fell into another trap: They saw themselves as "fellow travelers" and adopted the Chinese attitude of "not airing dirty laundry in front of outsiders." They reasoned that the slaughter, famine, and suppression in communist countries were simply part of the cost of transitioning to communism. They were confident that while the path to communism was crooked, the future was bright. They refused to tell the truth because that would be blackening the name of the "socialist project." Lacking the courage to tell the truth, they chose a shameful silence.

According to the communist fantasy, everyone is free and equal, there's no oppression or expropriation, there's great material abundance, and everyone gives according to his ability and receives according to his need — a heaven on earth, where every individual is able to develop freely. A human society of this sort is only a fantasy, one that the devil has used as bait to deceive man.

In reality, power falls into the hands of a small elite. Real communism is a totalitarian apparatus controlled by a small group of leaders, who use their monopoly on power to suppress, tyrannize, and deprive the majority. The time has not yet arrived for this in some socialist countries, and so they appear to be moderate. When the

conditions are ripe, all of that will change, and the naïve supporters of a socialist utopia will find it's too late for regret.

8. The Destruction of Culture and Morality

The devil's placement of its agents into every field and nation has
led the ignorant and credulous to hasten their journey toward
destruction.

Communism teaches people to oppose belief in God and to cast
out the divine. It simultaneously launches attacks on religions from
the outside while manipulating people to corrupt religion from
the inside. Religions have been politicized, commercialized, and
turned into entertainment. Numerous morally corrupt clergymen
put forward fallacious interpretations of religious texts, misleading
their followers and going so far as to commit adultery with their
lay members or even engage in pedophilia.

This chaos has left sincere religious believers bewildered and bereft
of hope. Just a century ago, an unwavering belief in the divine was
a sign of moral decency. Now, religious believers are considered
foolish and superstitious. They keep their beliefs to themselves, not
even discussing their faith among friends for fear of being mocked.

Another important goal of communism is the destruction of the
family through ideas like gender equality and "sharing wealth and
wife." The twentieth century, in particular, was host to modern
feminist movements that promoted sexual liberation, the blurring
of gender differences, attacks against "patriarchy," and the weakening of the father's role in the family.

These movements changed the definition of marriage, promoted
the legalization and legitimization of homosexuality, promoted the
"rights" to divorce and abortion, and used social welfare policies to
effectively encourage and subsidize single parenthood. All of this

resulted in the collapse of families and led to higher incidences of poverty and crime. This has been one of the more startling transformations of society over the last several decades.

In the political sphere, while communist regimes have continued with their rigid dictatorships, party politics in free societies have come to a point of crisis. Communism has exploited loopholes in the legal and political systems of democratic nations by manipulating major political parties. To secure electoral victory, politicians have resorted to dirty tricks and made promises that they could never fulfill. The result of communist influence in democratic countries is that political parties around the world today tend to fall on the left of the political spectrum, advocating higher taxes, higher social welfare expenditures, bigger government, and economic interventionism. The government plays an enormous role in molding society; a left-leaning government allows variants of Marxism to spread throughout society, indoctrinating the youth to elect progressively more left-wing candidates.

Higher education, which is supposed to play the role of transmitting the essence of the wisdom and culture of the ages, has also been subverted. In the first half of the twentieth century, the communist specter arranged for the systematic destruction of the education system. China, famous for its profound ancient civilization, was subjected to the New Culture Movement even before the Chinese Communist Party was formally established. This was part of the effort to disconnect the Chinese people from their traditions. After the communists seized power, they nationalized the education system and filled the textbooks with Party ideology, transforming generations of young Chinese into ferocious "wolf cubs," a Chinese term for those who grow up under communism and are indoctrinated to hate and kill class enemies.

In the West, the specter launched the progressive education movement, using the banner of "science and progress" to gain control of philosophy, psychology, pedagogy, and eventually the entire education system, thus indoctrinating teachers and school administrators. High school education began excluding orthodox ideas and traditional morality. Academic standards were lowered to make students less literate and numerate, and less able to form their own judgments or use common sense. Atheism, the theory of evolution, materialism, and the philosophy of struggle were all instilled in students.

Following the counterculture movement of the 1960s, advocates of political correctness have become thought police, forcing teachers to indoctrinate students with all manner of twisted ideas. Students now graduate from school without a strong moral compass, with no foundation in their own culture, and with little common sense or sense of responsibility. They are left to blindly follow the crowd, thus joining society's downward trend.

Out in society, there is widespread drug abuse, rising rates of crime, a media sphere full of sex and violence, an art world that treats grotesquerie as beauty, and all manner of evil cults and occult groups. Young people blindly adore film and television stars, waste their time on online games and social media, and end up dispirited and demoralized. People worry desperately about the security of the world and what the future holds, in the face of senseless violence and terrorism.

9. Returning to the Divine and Tradition

Human civilization was transmitted to man by the divine. Chinese civilization has seen the prosperity of the Han and Tang dynasties, and Western civilization reached its peak during the Renaissance.

If human beings can maintain the civilization given to them by the divine, then man will be able to maintain his divine connections and understand the Law taught when divinity returns to the human realm. If humans destroy their culture and tradition, and if the morality of society collapses, then they will fail to understand the divine teachings because their karma and sins will be too great and their thinking will have departed too far from the instructions of the divine. This is dangerous for mankind.

This is an era of both despair and hope. Those who don't believe in the divine pass lives of sensuous pleasure. Those who believe await the return of the divine in confusion and disquiet.

Communism is a scourge on humanity. Its goal is the destruction of mankind, and its arrangements are meticulous and specific. The conspiracy has been so successful that it has almost been carried out to completion, and now the devil is ruling our world.

The ancient wisdom of mankind tells us this: One righteous thought can conquer one hundred evils, and when a person's Buddha-nature emerges, it shakes the world of ten directions. The devil seems powerful but is nothing before the divine. If human beings can maintain their sincerity, kindness, compassion, tolerance, and patience, they will be protected by the divine, and the devil will have no dominion over them.

The mercy of the Creator is limitless, and every life has a chance to escape catastrophe. If humankind can restore tradition, elevate morality, and hear the compassionate call of the Creator and the Heavenly Law that provides salvation, man will be able to break through the devil's attempt at destruction, embark on the road to salvation, and move toward the future.

CHAPTER ONE

The Specter's Strategies for Destroying Humanity

THE SPECTER OF COMMUNISM has been working for centuries to corrupt and destroy humanity. It began by crippling man spiritually, divorcing him from his divine origins. From here, the specter has led the peoples of the world to cast out their millennia-old cultural traditions that the divine had meticulously arranged as the proper standards for human existence.

Bereft of its ancient heritage, the whole of human society is breaking down at an unprecedented pace. Meanwhile, the specter's earthly agents have exploited this societal havoc to push their nefarious agendas, masking them as "liberation" and "progress."

Over the past two hundred years or more, the specter's influence has overtaken the labyrinth of social affairs and historical development. Its demonic influence takes myriad and seemingly contradictory forms, from the overt brutality of communist rule found in the East, to the piecemeal subversion of Western politics, culture, and mainstream society.

1. The Corruption of Human Thought

In today's world, the criteria for discerning good and evil have been inverted. Righteousness is cast as wickedness and vice as compassion. Sinister concepts are disguised as science, and gangster logic is masked as "social justice." "Political correctness" is used to impose thought control, and the notion of "value neutrality" is used to render people insensitive to brutal atrocities.

Man was created by the divine, and the faithful receive divine protection. The specter's first and primary aim, therefore, is to sever the connection between man and the divine.

The socialist anthem, "The Internationale," claims that there has never been any Creator. In the 1850s, German materialist philosopher Ludwig Feuerbach said that God was merely a projection of man's inner nature. But humanity's traditional morality, culture, society, and reason all come from the divine. In the tumultuous currents of history, spiritual faith may be described as a strong anchor line keeping mankind from being lost to the waves.

Atheism lures the arrogant into playing God and attempting to control the fates of others and society; the leaders of communist movements are prone to self-deification. British philosopher Edmund Burke, reflecting on the bloodshed of the French Revolution, said, "When men play God, presently they behave like devils." A concept closely linked to atheism is materialism, which denies the existence of the soul. Materialism took root during the Industrial Revolution, when rapid progress in science, technology, and production fueled a cult of empiricism and atheism. People lost faith in divine miracles and rejected divine commandment. The concept of dialectical materialism is the core tenet of Marxism and other radical ideologies. In recent history, the dialectical theory was first articulated by German philosopher Georg Hegel as a general set of principles for logical thought. Marxism then absorbed select aspects of Hegel's work, while exaggerating the nature of dialectical conflict.

In the hands of the specter, materialism and atheism serve as demonic weapons used to overthrow man's spiritual faith, undermine human morality, and destroy traditional culture. Materialism and atheism have established the basis for a whole host of warped intellectual pretensions. The corruption of philosophy has gone hand in hand with the corruption of science. A cult of "scientific rationality" has replaced normal reason with a type of secular religion used to repress faith and deny morality, reinforcing the atheistic worldview.

The contemporary scientific community dismisses all phenomena it cannot explain or verify using its methods as superstition and pseudoscience, or ignores them entirely. Aiming to dominate academic thought and the education system, it inundates those fields with atheistic theories such as Darwinism. Darwin's flawed theory of evolution has been widely adopted as an instrument for distancing man from the divine. It equates man with beasts, undermining both his self-respect and his reverence for divine creation. In the twentieth century, the theory took over the spheres of research and education; today, those who believe in creationism are ridiculed. Apart from their impact on the natural sciences, atheism and materialism spawned many philosophical and ideological trends rooted in the concept of struggle. The theory of evolution now not only dominates the study of biology, but also holds sway in the social sciences. From Darwin's original theory came the pernicious philosophy of social Darwinism, with its concepts of "natural selection" and "survival of the fittest" reducing the community of nations to a jungle of barbaric struggle.

The demonic philosophy of struggle also has invaded the field of language. The definitions and nuances of words have been twisted to conform with atheistic and materialist thought. In British writer George Orwell's dystopian novel *Nineteen Eighty-Four*, Newspeak is an artificial language created to reinforce the Party's control over the people. In many ways, Orwell's visions have become reality. "Freedom" has been twisted to mean a state unrestrained by morality, law, or tradition. Principles such as "all men are created equal" and "all men are equal before the law" have been distorted to mean absolute egalitarianism. "Tolerance" has been deviated to mean acceptance of all sorts of warped thought and conduct. Rational thinking has been made a tool of narrow-minded empirical science. In the pursuit of equality of outcome, justice has become "social justice."

The goal of communism is not to resolve problems, but rather, as Chinese republican leader Chiang Kai-shek once said, "to expand global contradictions to the greatest extent possible and cause human struggle to continue forever."

This has been observed time and again throughout modern history. Communism incites hatred among the people, creates and escalates conflicts, and seizes power through violent revolution or subterfuge. In every case, the "liberation" promised by the revolutionaries results in brainwashing, killing, and tyranny.

2. The Subversion of Traditional Culture

Mankind's orthodox culture was imparted by the divine. In addition to maintaining the normal functioning of human society, the most important role of divinely inspired culture is to provide a means for humanity to understand the divine law taught in the final epoch and to be saved from elimination.

Divinely inspired culture provides for strong moral protection against evil. The specter of communism thus aims to destroy human culture by turning people against their own traditions.

The spread of atheism and materialism weakened the religious roots of civilization, giving rise to new ideological movements grounded in struggle. In secular society, the specter's representatives undermined traditional education, created degenerate modern art, promoted sexual promiscuity and pornography, and popularized drug use. The sinful and the revolting are now glorified as liberating and expressive.

For thousands of years, traditional education played a key role in developing and passing on mankind's exquisite culture. Students learned to work diligently to master professional, artistic, or academic skills, and to be good people and citizens.

Western countries started establishing free public education in the nineteenth century. By the start of the twentieth century, atheistic and anti-traditional thought had begun gradually seeping into the curricula, facilitated by leftist pedagogical experts who had infiltrated academia and held sway over educational policy. The theory of evolution became required learning, while political correctness was made the norm in social studies. Textbooks were gradually filled with atheism, materialism, and class struggle. Traditional culture, exemplified by the great literary classics, was at odds with the demonic ideological current. Thus, the classics were incrementally marginalized or reinterpreted according to modern social theory, leaving bright and gifted students without any deep understanding of the wisdom contained in humanity's most important literary works.

Students' creativity and curiosity now are squandered in the pursuit of meaningless causes, while they remain unversed in the fundamentals of work and life. Math and literacy standards have fallen. Long school hours separate children from their parents and families, ensuring continuous exposure to the degenerated education system. Under the slogan of "independent thinking," students are educated to be anti-tradition and anti-authority and are encouraged to despise society and their elders. They are fed leftist narratives on history and social studies and are immersed in vulgar entertainment.

In countries ruled by communist regimes, children are actively indoctrinated in Marxist political studies from the time they enter preschool or kindergarten. Traditional culture and faith are completely replaced by an atheistic communist culture of hatred and struggle. Growing up with a constant barrage of ideological brainwashing, children raised in these countries learn to think using the same twisted logic as the communist party.

Eccentric and deviated trends fill today's consumer culture, while age-old trades have died out. Traditional standards of workmanship and business ethics have been lost. Alienated from their traditional culture and ways of life, people drift further from the divine. Today's society worships sexual freedom and perversion. Youth are addicted to video games, social media, and pornography.

Art also has come under relentless attack. Upright, traditional arts came from the divine and first appeared in temples, churches, and other places of worship. True art presents truthfulness, kindness, beauty, and honor, thus helping humanity to maintain an orthodox moral culture. Garbage now occupies the halls of art. Dark, sinister paintings depict things of the netherworld. Impressionism, surrealism, and other grotesque styles have replaced the exquisite works of antiquity and the Renaissance. In literature, the ancient classics that embodied the wisdom of entire civilizations have been cast out in favor of shallow and convoluted modern writing.

Music, once composed and performed in awe of divine glory, is today dominated by obscenity and noise. Pop culture is full of demonic themes celebrating violence and drugs. Celebrities with hundreds of millions of fans promote degenerate and immoral lifestyles. The sublime, noble, and pure are ridiculed, while the vulgar and shameless are lauded.

3. Communism in the East and the West

Communism is characterized by the atheistic philosophy of struggle and derives its political organization and ideology from those of gangs and cults. In the East, communism is represented by totalitarian regimes and ruthless leaders, such as Vladimir Lenin, Joseph Stalin, Mao Zedong, Jiang Zemin, and their followers. The situation in the West is more complex, as powerful elites in fields such as government, business, academia, and religion scheme to undermine society.

Once-upright religions have been infused with the secular religion of socialism. Whether due to political control by communist regimes, or the misguided interpretations of unfaithful clergymen, traditional teachings and holy scripture have been altered. Liberation theology has infused an otherwise upright faith with Marxist ideology and class struggle, and moral perversion has spread among priests. Consequently, many believers have lost hope in the church and have given up faith in divine salvation.

Along with religion and the nation, the family is among the divine cornerstones of human civilization. It is an important bastion of morality and tradition and serves as a conduit for culture to be passed from one generation to the next. Leftist movements around the world promote feminism, sexual liberation, and homosexuality, undermining the traditional family structure and harmonious gender roles. These ideological trends legitimize and encourage promiscuity, adultery, casual divorce, and abortion, breaking down healthy relationships and the basic standards for human existence. Destroying the family is a key factor in how the devil is destroying humankind.

Totalitarianism in the East

Russia was weakened by its defeats in World War I, forcing the czar to abdicate. Taking advantage of the political chaos, communist revolutionaries launched the 1917 October Revolution to overthrow the constitutional government. Following a devastating civil war, the communists founded the world's first socialist regime — the Soviet Union — and used its vast resources to export revolution abroad via the Communist International.

The Chinese Communist Party (CCP) was created in 1921 with direct Soviet backing. Over the following decades, the communists waged a violent and treacherous rebellion against the Republic of China. The CCP benefited greatly from the Japanese invasion in World War II and continued fighting against the ruling Nationalist Party during and after the war. In 1949, the communists took over all of mainland China, establishing a totalitarian People's Republic.

Both the Soviet and the Chinese communist parties ruthlessly slaughtered tens of millions of their own people in times of peace. To enforce its malicious Marxist ideology, the CCP launched the unprecedented Cultural Revolution, declaring war on China's five thousand years of traditional culture and exquisite ancient civilization.

Beginning in the 1980s, the CCP introduced economic reforms to stave off its own collapse, while keeping the political sphere under its strict totalitarian control. To this day, the Party maintains its tight grip on power through campaigns of suppression, such as the crackdown on the democracy movement and the persecution of Falun Gong.

Infiltration in the West

China's imperial court, the Western divine right of kings, and the American system of checks and balances are forms of government established by the divine for humans according to their unique cultures and environments. Though communist revolutions have failed to take power in Western countries, the specter of communism has nonetheless established covert control over the free world via subversion and infiltration. Without violent revolution, Western countries have abandoned upright methods of statecraft and broadly adopted various characteristics of the communist system, such as heavy taxation, bloated welfare states, excessive and self-serving bureaucracies, and political correctness.

The law, originally founded on religious morality and divine commandment, has been altered to accommodate deviant understandings of ethics and freedom. In the communist countries of the East, the law exists to do the regime's bidding. In the West, the law is interpreted through leftist ideology and modified to uproot moral concepts of good and evil. Legislation is passed to show leniency toward serious crime, encourage adulterous sexual lifestyles, undermine the family, and curb the rights of upstanding citizens through heavy regulation.

Governments and citizens alike have been dragged into a culture of avaricious overconsumption. Financial elites have done away with the traditional wisdom that governed sustainable economics, replacing the gold standard with a fluctuating fiat currency. Banks and the state encourage the accumulation of endless debt, leading to perennial economic crises and eroding national sovereignty.

The communist specter has used globalization as a tool to gradually break down the sovereignty of individual nations through organizations such as the League of Nations and the United Nations. Billed as utopian solutions to international conflict and disputes, these global authorities have in reality come to serve nefarious agendas. The United Nations, despite receiving most of its funding from Western democracies, has increasingly come under the sway of communist regimes like the People's Republic of China. International organizations are used to spread leftist ideology and undermine legitimate national interests. The ultimate aim is to bring the whole world under one totalitarian regime with tight controls on politics, ideology, and population.

Leftist and other pernicious agendas have been able to acquire so much mainstream influence in Western countries largely due to the help of mass media. In countries run by communist regimes, all outlets are subject to state censorship, if not directly controlled by the communist party. Elsewhere, the media has been brought under the sway of financial and partisan bias. Honest reporting and discourse are buried by an avalanche of sensationalism, political virtue-signaling, and outright fake news.

4. The Breakdown of Society

In order to topple traditional human society, the specter has driven social movements, mass immigration, and other upheavals on a global scale. This process has been underway for several centuries.

Warfare and Revolution

Seizing political power is one of the key steps in communism's plan to destroy humanity. Karl Marx, in summarizing the lessons learned from the Paris Commune, wrote that the working class must overthrow the original governmental apparatus and replace it with its own state. Power is always the core issue in Marxist political theory.

War is one of the specter's most effective tools for breaking down the old international order, destroying bastions of tradition, and accelerating the development of communist ideology. Many wars were waged under demonic influence. World War I brought about the collapse of several European empires, chiefly czarist Russia. This paved the way for the Bolshevik Revolution.

World War II provided the conditions for the CCP to seize power and for the Soviet Union to take over Eastern Europe, thereby establishing the postwar socialist camp. The war also created the disorder of decolonization, which the Soviet and Chinese communist regimes exploited to support the worldwide communist movement. National liberation movements brought many countries across Asia, Africa, and Latin America under authoritarian socialism.

The instigation of revolution can be divided into the following steps:

1. Foment hatred and discord among the people.

2. Deceive the public with lies and establish a revolutionary united front.

3. Defeat the forces of resistance one at a time.

4. Use violence to create an atmosphere of terror and chaos.

5. Launch a coup to seize power.

6. Suppress the reactionaries.

7. Build and maintain a new order using the terror of revolution.

The communist countries attempted to launch a world revolution via the Communist International, exporting revolutionary activism and creating unrest by supporting local leftists in non-communist states.

Communism exploits divisions between people and channels the rage of individuals into collective hatred. Communist revolutions succeed through acts of terror, and communist regimes implement policies of state terrorism. Most terrorist movements take inspiration from the Leninist organizational model, and the Soviet and Chinese communists supported terrorist groups as a kind of task force to damage public order and fragment society throughout the rest of the world.

Economic and Social Crises

All around the world, socialist and communist movements have taken advantage of economic unrest to edge themselves into positions of influence, with the eventual goal of overthrowing the existing social order.

Economic crises can be created and utilized as a means of encouraging revolution or casting socialist movements as saviors. When politicians in democratic countries find themselves desperate for solutions, they make Faustian bargains, gradually steering their countries toward big government and high-tax socialism. As Saul Alinsky wrote in *Rules for Radicals,* "The real action is in the enemy's reaction."

The Great Depression of the 1930s was the key juncture at which Europe and the United States embarked on the path toward big government and widespread interventionism. The financial crisis of 2008 continued tipping the scales in favor of expanding leftist policies.

With the rise of industrialization and globalization came mass migration, first from the countryside to cities, then across borders and continents. People have moved from one place to another since antiquity. However, the rapid domestic and international population movements seen in modern times are the result of the specter's manipulation.

Mass migration dissolves national identity, borders, sovereignty, cultural traditions, and social cohesion. As masses of people are removed from their traditional identities, they are more easily absorbed into the drift of modernity. It is difficult for immigrants living in an unfamiliar environment to secure their livelihood, let alone participate deeply in their host countries' political processes or cultural traditions. Newly arrived immigrants are thus easily recruited as free votes for leftist parties and social causes. Meanwhile, immigration creates ripe conditions for stirring up racial and religious animosities.

Communism makes use of social trends to inflame and agitate people, escalate conflicts, mobilize movements to destabilize society, bludgeon the political opposition, dominate discourse, and appear to seize the moral high ground. Examples include the anti-war movement and environmentalism, which communists hijacked for their own purposes.

5. The Divide-and-Conquer Strategy

The communist specter handles people according to their different characteristics and motivations. It takes the lives of some while taking advantage of others' greed. It can put human idealism and emotion to work, indoctrinating individuals to serve as the pawns of revolution and rebellion.

Eliminating Dissent

Some people are wiser and more perceptive than others. Some are closer to the divine and not susceptible to the devil's trickery. In countries with long and rich historical experiences, it is difficult to get people to go along with the deception. The communist specter does not hesitate to physically liquidate the discerning members of society who see through its conspiracy and are brave enough to stand out by resisting. To this end, it arranges political campaigns, religious persecutions, show trials, and assassinations.

In China, which boasts five thousand years of divinely inspired civilization, the CCP could only break down the cultural order by launching a series of political campaigns that killed tens of millions of people. It paid special attention to murdering the scholars, gentry, and spiritual practitioners who served as the custodians of traditional Chinese culture.

Elites across all nations and industries have taken up a demonic way as the specter plays to their interests and endows them with power according to how closely they follow its agenda. For those who seek fame and influence, the specter gives them a reputation and authority. For the greedy, it arranges profit. It inflates the egos of the arrogant and maintains the bliss of the ignorant. The gifted are seduced with science, materialism, and unrestricted freedom of expression. Individuals with lofty ambitions and good intentions have their ideals turned into self-glorification, making them feel the warm glow of accomplishment in becoming presidents, prime ministers, think-tank scholars, policymakers, administrators, big-shot bankers, professors, experts, Nobel laureates, and the like, with outstanding social status, political influence, and vast fortunes. Once established, these great personalities are co-opted, each according to his or her circumstances. Many of them become the specter's ignorant agents and, in the words of Lenin, "useful idiots."

Dumbing Down the Masses

Communist ideology manipulates public knowledge by employing false narratives, deluding people with its warped educational system, and controlling the mass media. It uses people's sense of security and shallow interests to make people care only about their immediate interests, vulgar entertainment, competitive sports, social gossip, and indulgence in erotic and carnal desires. At the same time, politicians cater to the lowest common denominators to undermine voters' vigilance and judgment, and thus capture the electorate.

In totalitarian communist countries, the people are never allowed to have anything to do with politics. In democratic countries, those concerned with the public good have their attention diverted to trivial issues (such as transsexual rights), echoing the famous stratagem from ancient Chinese military history: "advancing via a hidden route while repairing the plankways in the open." Viral news, social sensations, and even terrorist attacks and wars are arranged as cover for communism's ultimate goal.

The public is inculcated with a modern consciousness and mobilized to overpower the minority of people who stubbornly hold to tradition. Intellectuals levy heavy criticism of folk cultures around the world, fostering narrow-minded prejudice among their undiscerning audiences. The concepts of critical and creative thinking are abused to pit those of the younger generation against authority, preventing them from absorbing the knowledge and wisdom of traditional culture.

In communist countries, after the bearers of traditional culture were slaughtered, the bulk of the population was indoctrinated to

33

participate in revolution. After the CCP seized power, it took two and a half decades to nurture a generation of "wolf cubs," a Chinese term for those who grew up under communism and were indoctrinated to hate and kill class enemies. They were encouraged to fight, smash, rob, and burn indiscriminately.

The CCP actively cultivates murderous sentiment. During the Cultural Revolution, teenage girls readily beat their teachers to death in Mao's ideological crusade. Today, internet trolls known as the "Fifty Cent Army" infest Chinese social media sites, constantly writing about beating and killing, with typical posts reading, "Recover the Diaoyu Islands even if China is laid to waste," and, "We would rather China be peppered with graves than fail to exterminate the last Japanese."

In the West, communist parties proudly harken to the experience of the French Revolution and the Paris Commune. Every revolution and insurrection has been introduced by mobs that had no scruples, no shame, and no compassion.

Fragmenting Society

Today, the older generation is being marginalized and removed from society at an accelerated pace. As young people are given ever more rights, political power, and privileges, the elderly lose their positions of authority and prestige, speeding up mankind's break with tradition. Contemporary literature, arts, and popular culture are all geared toward the tastes and values of the young, who are under pressure to follow endlessly changing trends, lest they be ostracized by their peers.

Rapid scientific and technological progress renders the elderly unable to keep up and adapt to the massive social changes that occur as a result. The transformation of urban and rural spheres combined with mass migration work together to alienate the elderly and estrange them from the present. The torment and helplessness of their solitude are exacerbated by the realities of modern life, where the young are in a constant state of professional or social competition and have little time to spare for their parents and elders.

In traditional human society, people help each other. When there are conflicts, they have religion, morality, laws, and folk customs to facilitate resolution and cooperation. Such an organic society cannot be made to collapse all at once. It must first be broken up into atomized units, dissolving the traditional reliance between individuals and alienating them from each other.

Virtually every conceivable standard has been used to divide society into opposing groups and instigate hatred and struggle among them. Class, sex, race, ethnicity, and religious denomination can all serve as bases for division. Communism and other ideologies influenced by the specter magnify the animosity between the bourgeoisie and the proletariat, the rulers and the ruled, progressives and "regressives," liberals and conservatives — all while the government expands its powers to build an unstoppable totalitarian state.

6. Deception and Defense

The communist specter has concealed itself well. It is difficult to fathom the scale of its deception, which it created through a vast array of stratagems running the spectrum from hidden to overt.

The specter's most diabolical schemes are carried out in broad daylight, where they are presented as sensible, reasonable, and legal. They are so pervasive that it is difficult to expose these schemes for what they are. At times, certain aspects of the specter's agenda are revealed, but only to deflect attention and scrutiny away from a greater conspiracy. For example, during the Cold War, the world was divided between two military and political camps. Yet, while their social systems appeared to be diametrically opposed, the same demonic process was taking place on both sides in different forms. Many revisionist Western-style communists, socialists, Fabianists, liberals, and progressives publicly rejected the Soviet and Chinese models, but their efforts led society on a path toward a social structure no different from those of the Soviet Union and China. In plain terms, the communist specter used the totalitarian East as a diversion for the active infiltration of the West.

Those who dare to expose the specter's scheme are labeled "conspiracy theorists," "extremists," "far-right," "alt-right," "sexists," "racists," "warmongers," "bigots," "Nazis," "fascists," and other terms of abuse meant to isolate and marginalize them from academia and the broader society. Reduced to objects of ridicule and fear, their ideas gain no audience and exert no influence. People are simultaneously conditioned to oppose and hate certain ethnicities, groups, and individuals, thus drawing attention away from the fundamental evil that is the communist specter.

It is impossible for all of humanity to be taken in by the specter's deception. But communism in its myriad forms has gained influence over the majority of people and their leaders around the globe. It is no exaggeration to say that the specter of communism is ruling our world. In view of the general strategies outlined above, the following chapters examine in detail how this specter's rule came to be, and what mankind must do to avoid ultimate destruction at its hands.

CHAPTER TWO

Communism's European Beginnings

MANY OF THE PROPHECIES FORETOLD in orthodox religions have come to pass, as have the predictions made by Nostradamus and those passed down in cultures around the world, from Peru to Korea. In Chinese history, from the Han to the Ming dynasties, there have been surprisingly accurate prophetic texts.

These prophecies show us the important truth that history is not a coincidental process, but rather a drama in which the sequence of major events has been pre-established. In the end times, which also could herald the beginning of a new historical cycle, all of the world's religions are awaiting one thing: the arrival of the Creator in the human realm.

All dramas have a climax. Though the devil has made arrangements to destroy humankind, the Creator has means of awakening the world's people, helping them to escape the devil's bondage, and offering them salvation. The ultimate battle between good and evil is unfolding today.

Orthodox religions the world over have foretold that in the era of the Creator's return, the world would be awash with demons, abominations, and ominous events as humanity lost its moral restraints. This is the world today.

The state of degeneration we face today has been long in the making. It began hundreds of years ago, with the rise of its core driving forces: atheism and the deception of humanity. It was Karl Marx who created an ideology to encompass the deception in all its permutations, and it was Vladimir Lenin who put the theory into brutal practice.

Marx, however, was not an atheist. He was a Satanist and became the demon whose mission it was to prevent man from recognizing the Creator in the end times.

1. Karl Marx's Satanic Works

Marx wrote many books throughout his life, the best-known being the 1848 *Communist Manifesto* and the three volumes of *Das Kapital*, published between 1867 and 1894. These works form the theoretical basis of the communist movement.

It is less widely known that over the course of his life, Marx turned over his soul to the devil and became its agent in the human realm. In his youth, Marx had been a devout Christian. He was an enthusiastic believer in God before he was overcome by his demonic transformation. In his early poem "Invocation of One in Despair," Marx wrote of his intent to take revenge on God:

So a god has snatched from me my all
In the curse and rack of Destiny.

All his worlds are gone beyond recall!
Nothing but revenge is left to me!
On myself revenge I'll proudly wreak,
On that being, that enthroned Lord,
Make my strength a patchwork of what's weak,
Leave my better self without reward!
I shall build my throne high overhead,
Cold, tremendous shall its summit be.
For its bulwark — superstitious dread,
For its Marshall — blackest agony. [1]

In a letter to his father, dated November 10, 1837, Marx described the changes he was experiencing: "A curtain was fallen, my holiest of holies was ripped apart, and new gods had to be set in their place. ... A true unrest has taken mastery of me and I will not be able to calm the excited spirits until I am in your dear presence." [2]

In Marx's poem "The Pale Maiden," the lyrical voice is that of a young woman who abandons her love of Christ and meets a ghastly end. Marx wrote:

Thus heaven I've forfeited, I know it full well.
My soul, once true to God, is chosen for hell. [3]

Marx's family clearly noticed the change in him. In an earlier letter, dated March 2, 1837, his father wrote to him: "Your advancement, the dear hope of seeing your name someday of great repute, and your earthly well-being are not the only desires of my heart. These are illusions I had had a long time, but I can assure you that their fulfillment would not have made me happy. Only if your heart remains pure and beats humanly and if no demon is able to alienate your heart from better feelings, only then will I be happy." [4]

One of Marx's daughters wrote that when she was young, Marx told her and her sisters many fairy tales. Her favorite was the meandering story of Hans Röckle, a magician who was always short on cash and had no choice but to sell off his lovely puppets to the devil. [5] What Marx sold to the devil in exchange for his success was his very soul.

As seen in the preceding examples, abandoning God and associating with Satan is a common theme in Marx's poetry. In "The Fiddler," Marx speaks via the lyrical voice:

How so! I plunge, plunge without fail
My blood-black saber into your soul.
That art God neither wants nor wists,
It leaps to the brain from Hell's black mists.
Till heart's bewitched, till senses reel:
With Satan I have struck my deal.
He chalks the signs, beats time for me,
I play the death march fast and free. [6]

In the biography *Marx,* author Robert Payne wrote that the stories Marx told can be taken as allegories for his own life, and that he seemed to be knowingly acting on the devil's behalf. [7]

Marx's soul turned to evil. In his rage against God, he saw the divine as something to be overthrown. The American political philosopher Eric Voegelin wrote: "Marx knew that he was a god creating a world. He did not want to be the creature. He did not want to see the world in the perspective of creaturely existence. ... He wanted to see the world from the point of the coincidentia oppositorum, that is, from the position of God." [8]

In his poem "Human Pride," Marx expressed his will to break away from and replace God:

Then the gauntlet do I fling
Scornful in the World's wide open face.
Down the giant She-Dwarf, whimpering,
Plunges, cannot crush my happiness.
Like unto a God I dare
Through that ruined realm in triumph roam.
Every word is Deed and Fire,
And my bosom like the Maker's own. [9]

In another verse, he wrote, "I long to take vengeance on the One Who rules from above," and, "The idea of God is the keynote of a perverted civilization. It must be destroyed." [10]

Soon after Marx died, his housemaid Helene Demuth said she had observed him performing some kind of prayer ritual before a line of candles during his illness. Marx clearly believed in the supernatural. [11]

Throughout human history, great sages taught sentient beings the way to enlightenment and laid the foundations of the world's civilizations. Jesus Christ established the bedrock of Christian civilization, and Lao Tzu's wisdom is the foundation of Taoism, a central pillar of Chinese philosophy. In ancient India, Shakyamuni's teachings led to Buddhism. The origins of their wisdom are a wonder — they obtained their insights from enlightenment on the path of spiritual cultivation, not by ordinary learning.

Marx's theories referenced the work of previous intellectuals but ultimately originated from the evil specter. He wrote in the poem "On Hegel":

Since I have found the Highest of things
and the Depths of them also,
Rude am I as a God, cloaked by the dark like a God. [12]

By the specter's arrangement, Marx entered the human world and established the cult of communism to corrupt human morality, with the intention that humankind would turn against the divine and doom itself to eternal torment in Hell.

2. Marxism's Historical Context

In order to spread Marxism, the specter laid down various intellectual and social foundations. We will examine these as the context for the rise of communism.

Scholars believe that Marx's theory was deeply influenced by Ludwig Feuerbach, who was an early denier of God's existence. Feuerbach believed that religion was no more than one's awareness of "the infinity of consciousness" — that is to say, that people invented God by imagining their own abilities writ large. [13] Feuerbach's theory sheds some light on how communism emerged and spread. Advances in science, mechanization, material goods, medicine, and leisure created the impression that happiness is a function of material wealth. Therefore, any dissatisfaction must arise from social limitations. It seemed that with material advancement and social change, people would have the means to build a utopia without any need for the divine. This vision is the principal means by which people are lured and then initiated into the cult of communism.

Feuerbach was not the first to reject Christianity and God. David Friedrich Strauss questioned the authenticity of the Bible and the divinity of Jesus in his 1835 book *The Life of Jesus Critically Examined*.

We may trace such atheistic ideas back to the Enlightenment in the seventeenth and eighteenth centuries or, if need be, to the time of the ancient Greeks. But that is not the purpose of this book.

Although Marx's *Communist Manifesto* was written over a decade prior to the publication of Charles Darwin's *On the Origin of Species*, the theory of evolution provided Marx with an ostensibly scientific grounding. If all species evolved as a result of "natural selection," and human beings are merely the most advanced of organisms, then there is no room for the divine.

In December 1860, Marx wrote to Engels about Darwin's theory, praising On the Origin of Species as "the book that contains the natural-history foundation for our viewpoint [historical materialism]." In a letter to the socialist philosopher Ferdinand Lassalle in January 1862, Marx said, "Darwin's book is very important and serves me as a natural-scientific basis for the class struggle in history." [14]

The theory of evolution in the field of natural science and materialism in the field of philosophy provided Marxism with two powerful tools for misleading and recruiting followers.

Society underwent profound changes in Marx's lifetime. During the first Industrial Revolution, artisanal craftsmanship was replaced with mass production. Technological advancement in agriculture freed up surplus labor to move to cities and toil in factories. Free trade created innovation in sales and marketing. Industrialization fostered the rise of cities and the movement of people, information, and ideas.

Following Marx's exile from Germany, he moved to France, Belgium, and then England, where he settled down in the Dickensian environment of the London slums. The second Industrial Revolution began in Marx's later years, bringing electrification, the internal combustion engine, and chemical manufacturing. The invention of the telegraph and the telephone revolutionized communications.

Each change threw society into upheaval as people scrambled to adapt to the new reality amid technological shifts. Many could not keep up, leading to the polarization of haves and have-nots, economic crises, and the like. At the same time, as technology made it possible to transform the natural world on a large scale, humanity's arrogance grew.

This upheaval created ripe conditions for spreading Marx's view that societal norms and traditions were oppressive relics to be destroyed. But Marxist influence is most appropriately understood in terms of the devil's long-term scheme to destabilize humanity and sever the connections between man and the divine.

3. The French Revolution

The impact of the 1789 French Revolution was massive; it destroyed the monarchy, overturned the traditional social order, and gave rise to a system of mob rule.

Engels said: "A revolution is certainly the most authoritarian thing there is; it is the act whereby one part of the population imposes its will upon the other part by means of rifles, bayonets, and cannon — authoritarian means, if such there be at all; and if the victorious party does not want to have fought in vain, it must maintain this rule by means of the terror which its arms inspire in the reactionists." [15]

The Jacobin Club, which took power after the French Revolution, knew this well. Following the execution of French King Louis XVI, Jacobin leader Maximilien Robespierre's Reign of Terror brought the executions of another seventy thousand people, most of whom were completely innocent. Later generations wrote a posthumous epitaph for Robespierre, who was buried in a common grave:

Who'er thou art who passest, pray
Don't grieve that I am dead;
For had I been alive this day,
Thoud'st been here in my stead! [16]

The Jacobin Club's policies of economic, political, and anti-religious terror in the French Revolution, were a prelude to the tyranny of communist parties. Foreshadowing the political killings under Lenin and Stalin, the French revolutionaries instituted the Revolutionary Tribunal and set up guillotines in Paris and other communities. Revolutionary committees decided whether a prisoner was guilty, while special agents of the National Convention held authority over the military and administrative subdivisions. The sans-culottes, or proletariat, were considered the most revolutionary class.

According to the Law of 22 Prairial, enacted on June 10, 1794, pretrial and defense counsel were banned, and all convictions were required to result in the death penalty. Rumors, inference, and personal judgment, in lieu of evidence, were all considered valid for the purpose of obtaining a verdict. The law's promulgation greatly expanded the Reign of Terror, with an estimated three hundred thousand to five hundred thousand people jailed as suspects. [17] Likewise, the economic terror of the Jacobins seemed to foreshadow the "war communism" that would be implemented in Russia by Lenin. On July 26, 1793, hoarding grain became an offense punishable by death. The paramilitary forces known as the armées révolutionnaires were empowered to ransack towns and villages, searching for stored grain in houses, barns, and warehouses. Those who were accused of hoarding would be torn apart by mobs or sent to the guillotine. [18]

One of the greatest adversaries of the French revolutionaries was the Catholic faith. During the Reign of Terror, revolutionaries including Pierre Gaspard Chaumette established a form of atheism called the Cult of Reason. It was based on Enlightenment trends and was intended to replace Catholicism. [19] On October 5, 1793, the National Convention abolished the Christian calendar and instituted the Republican Calendar. On November 10, the Notre-Dame de Paris was rechristened the Temple of Reason, in a ceremony featuring a young actress who was styled as the Goddess of Reason, an object of worship for the masses. The dictates of the Cult of Reason were quickly enforced throughout Paris. Within a week, only three Christian churches remained in operation. Anti-religious terror filled Paris. Priests were arrested en masse, and some were executed. [20]

The French Revolution not only provided a model for the Soviet regime established by Lenin, but also was closely connected to the development of Marxism.

François-Noël Babeuf, a utopian socialist who lived through the French Revolution and was executed in 1797 for his involvement in the Conspiracy of the Equals, advocated the abolition of private property. Marx considered Babeuf to be the first revolutionary communist.

Socialist ideologies continued to make headway in French politics during the nineteenth century. The League of Outlaws, which took Babeuf as its spiritual founder, developed rapidly in Paris. German tailor Wilhelm Weitling joined the league in 1835. Under his leadership, the secret society renamed itself the League of the Just.

In a meeting held in June 1847, the League of the Just merged with the Communist Correspondence Committee led by Marx and Engels to form the Communist League. In February 1848, Marx and Engels published the foundational work of the international communist movement, *The Communist Manifesto.*

Revolutions and insurrections took place one after another following the end of Napoleonic rule, affecting Spain, Greece, Portugal, Germany, various parts of Italy, Belgium, and Poland. By 1848, revolution and war had spread throughout Europe, providing the optimal environment for the spread of communism.

In 1864, Marx and others established the International Workingmen's Association, also known as the First International, positioning Marx as the spiritual leader of the communist workers' movement. As leader, Marx worked to create a core group of strictly disciplined revolutionaries who would rally the workers to revolt. At the same time, he found reasons to banish from the organization anyone who disagreed with him. Mikhail Bakunin, the first major Russian Marxist, gathered many recruits for the communist movement, but Marx accused him of being a czarist agent and expelled him from the First International. [21]

In 1871, the French branch of the First International launched the first communist revolution: the rise to power of the Paris Commune.

4. Communism's Debut in Paris

The Paris Commune was established following France's defeat in the Franco-Prussian War of 1870. Though French Emperor Napoléon III had surrendered, the Prussian armies laid siege to Paris before withdrawing. The humiliation of surrender, combined with long-standing unrest among the French workers, led to a general uprising in Paris, and the newly established French Third Republic withdrew to Versailles, leaving a power vacuum in the capital.

In March 1871, the Paris Commune began with the rebellion of armed mobs and bandits from the lowest rungs of society, led by socialists, communists, anarchists, and other activists. The movement was affiliated with and heavily influenced by the First International. It aimed at using the proletariat as the agents of revolution to destroy traditional culture and transform the political and economic structure of society.

What followed was killing and destruction on a mass scale as the rebels laid waste to the exquisite relics, monuments, and art of Paris. "What good does it do me for there to be monuments, operas, café-concerts where I have never set foot because I don't have the money?" wrote French writers Edmond and Jules Goncourt, summarizing the sentiments of those who partook in the destruction. American diplomat Wickham Hoffman, who was stationed in Paris at the time of the Commune, said, "It is bitter, relentless, and cruel; and is, no doubt, a sad legacy of the bloody Revolution of 1789." American writer and publisher William Pembroke Fetridge described the Commune as "the most criminal [act] the world has ever seen" and "a revolution of blood and violence." Its leaders were "ruthless desperadoes, ... the refuse of France ... madmen, drunk with wine and blood." [22]

The struggle between tradition and anti-tradition begun in the French Revolution were now further played out, eight decades later. Louis-Auguste Blanqui, the honorary president of the Paris Commune, said: "Two principles share France: that of legitimacy and that of popular sovereignty. ... The principle of popular sovereignty rallies all men of the future, the masses who, tired of being exploited, seek to smash the framework that suffocates them." [23]

The extremism of the Commune originated in part from the hate-filled ideas of Henri de Saint-Simon, a utopian socialist who considered the welfare of a country proportionate to its number of workers. He advocated the death of the rich, whom he believed to be parasites.

In *The Civil War in France,* Marx described the Commune as a communist state: "The direct antithesis to the empire was the Commune. The cry of 'social republic,' with which the February Revolution was ushered in by the Paris proletariat, did but express a vague aspiration after a republic that was not only to supersede the monarchical form of class rule, but class rule itself. The Commune was the positive form of that republic." Additionally, he wrote, "The Commune intended to abolish that class property which makes the labor of the many the wealth of the few." [24]

The Paris Commune pioneered the methods of communist revolution. Monuments including the Vendôme Column commemorating Napoléon were destroyed. Churches were looted, clergy slaughtered, and religious teachings banned from schools. The rebels dressed the statues of saints in modern clothing and affixed smoking pipes to their mouths.

Women as well as men participated in the savagery. Zhang Deyi, a Chinese diplomat who was in Paris at the time, described the situation in his diary: "The rebellious not only included male thugs; women also joined in the rampage. ... They took up lodging in high buildings and feasted on delicacies. But their pleasure was short-lived, as they were unaware of the danger coming to them. On the verge of defeat, they looted and burned buildings. Priceless treasures were reduced to ashes. Hundreds of female rebels were arrested and admitted that it was mainly the women who led the arson." [25]

The Paris Commune lasted a little over two months before it was suppressed by the French military. On May 23, 1871, before the last line of defense had fallen, the Commune leaders ordered the burning of the Luxembourg Palace (the seat of the French Senate), the Tuileries Palace, and the Louvre. The Paris Opera House, the Paris City Hall, the Ministry of the Interior, the Ministry of Justice, the Palais Royal, and the luxury restaurants and apartment buildings on both sides of the Champs-Elysées were also to be destroyed rather than allowed to fall into the hands of the government.

That evening, Commune members, carrying tar, asphalt, and turpentine, started fires at multiple locations across Paris. The magnificent Tuileries Palace was lost to the flames. Fortunately, the arsonists' attempt to torch the nearby Louvre was foiled by the arrival of Adolphe Thiers's troops. [26]

Marx quickly adjusted his theory in the wake of the Paris Commune, revising *The Communist Manifesto* to clarify that the working class should not simply take over the state mechanism, but rather completely break it down and destroy it.

5. First Europe, Then the World

Marx's updated manifesto made communism even more potent. On July 14, 1889, six years after Marx's death, thirteen years after the dissolution of the First International, and one hundred years after the French Revolution, the International Workers Congress was revived. Marxists rallied again in what historians refer to as the Second International.

The European workers' movement established itself rapidly, guided by communist slogans like "liberate humanity" and "abolish social classes." Lenin later said: "The services rendered by Marx and Engels to the working class may be expressed in a few words thus: they taught the working class to know itself and be conscious of itself, and they substituted science for dreams." [27]

Lies and indoctrination were used to infect popular movements with communist ideology, leading more and more people to accept it. By 1914, there were close to thirty global and local socialist organizations, and countless more trade unions and cooperatives, with more than ten million union members and more than seven million cooperative members. Their ranks were often heavily infiltrated by socialists.

In *How to Change the World: Reflections on Marx and Marxism*, historian Eric Hobsbawm wrote, "The radiation of Marxism was particularly important and general in some countries of Europe in which virtually all social thought, irrespective of its political connections with socialist and labour movements, was marked by the influence of Marx." [28]

Communism was also spreading via Europe to Russia and East Asia. In the 1880s, Lenin studied *Das Kapital* and began his translation of *The Communist Manifesto* into Russian. He was imprisoned and exiled by the czarist Russian authorities for his political activities.

World War I led to the triumph of communism in Russia. At the time of the 1917 revolution that toppled Czar Nicholas II, Lenin was living in Western Europe. By the end of the year, he was back in Russia and had seized power in the October Revolution. Russia was a nation of rich ancient heritage, with a vast population and abundant natural resources. The establishment of the Soviet regime on the territory of the world's largest country was a huge boon for the world communist movement.

Just as World War I assisted the rise of the Russian communists, World War II prompted the communist movement to proliferate across Eurasia and swallow up China. After World War II, the Soviet Union became a superpower armed with nuclear weapons, giving it the means to promote communism on a global scale.

In the notes for his famous "Iron Curtain" speech, Winston Churchill said: "A shadow has fallen upon the scenes so lately lighted by the Allied victory. Nobody knows what Soviet Russia and its Communist international organization intends to do in the immediate future, or what are the limits, if any, to their expansive and proselytising tendencies." [29]

During the Cold War, the free world engaged in a fierce confrontation with the communist camp, which had spread across four continents. But even as the nations of the free world remained democratic in form, they gradually turned socialist in essence.

CHAPTER THREE

Tyranny in the East

A CENTURY HAS PASSED SINCE the Communist Party seized power in the Soviet Union. According to records compiled by the US Congress, communist regimes have been responsible for the deaths of at least one hundred million people. [1] *The Black Book of Communism* details this history of murder, drawing on documents declassified by the governments of nations in the former Soviet Union and Eastern Europe, as well as records on the victims of communist political campaigns in China, North Korea, and other communist countries. [2]

Communist totalitarianism is often compared to that of the Nazis during World War II. While there are many parallels between the two, one crucial distinction is often overlooked: The Nazis committed genocide, but the ultimate goal of communism goes beyond physical slaughter.

People of faith do not consider physical demise to be one's true death since they believe the soul goes to heaven or is born again in the cycle of reincarnation. For communism, killing is a tool to destroy the basic moral foundations of humanity; it aims to kill not just the physical body, but also the soul.

Communist regimes are given to committing the worst atrocities. They tend to select the most ruthless and unscrupulous leaders, and carry out intense political purges among their own ranks. It is difficult for many to understand the rationale behind the barbarity inflicted by communist parties upon their own cadres, particularly when it comes to those who are persecuted simply for deviating on specific issues while otherwise being wholly loyal to the party and its leadership. One reason is that the communist specter, in its rebellion against the divine and humankind, possesses an instinctual fear that its doom is always around the corner. To reinforce itself, the specter needs individuals who have no regard for moral right and wrong. These individuals are identified by their brutality during mass killings, and their elevation to positions of party leadership enables the specter to ensure the perpetuation of its earthly tyranny.

In 1989, the Chinese Communist Party officials who refused to participate in the June 4 Tiananmen Square massacre were purged or denied promotion. Jiang Zemin, who demonstrated his cruelty during the massacre, was promoted to become leader of the CCP. After Jiang began the persecution of Falun Gong in 1999, he promoted officials such as Luo Gan and Zhou Yongkang to high positions, as they had demonstrated their ability to commit the most brutal of crimes during the persecution.

Another of its motives for killing is to recruit participants from general society, as was done during the Cultural Revolution. By committing murder and other crimes amid the chaos, these people acted as accomplices to the CCP's savagery, and the most brutal perpetrators became the staunchest followers of the Party. Even today, many former Red Guards who committed assault and murder during the Cultural Revolution express no remorse for the events of their youth.

Furthermore, by killing its victims openly and deliberately, the Communist Party terrorizes the general population into obedience.

Throughout history, rulers and tyrants have killed out of a perceived need to safeguard their power or their empires by defeating an enemy. Communist parties, however, cannot do *without* enemies. Even where no enemies exist, they must be invented so that the killing can continue. In a country like China, with its long history and rich culture, communism could not achieve its aims without continuous killing. The Chinese people, steeped in a cultural heritage of five thousand years, believed in and revered the divine. They would not bend to the will of the barbaric and blasphemous CCP unless they were brutalized. The Party's fundamental means of maintaining its rule, as learned from the Soviet trial run, is through mass murder.

1. The Rise of Totalitarian Communism

Being the embodiment of an evil specter, communism's starting point could not be anything other than dishonorable. After Karl Marx proclaimed that "a specter is haunting Europe — the specter of communism," bandits and ruffians established the Paris Commune, laying waste to the French capital and its unparalleled works of art and culture. Later, the communist parties in Russia and China seized power through despicable acts of conspiracy and bloodshed.

Marxist theory and the various ideological tracts penned by communist regimes are replete with promises to support and represent the interests of proletarian workers and peasants. But in practice, the working class is quickly betrayed and suffers the worst abuses under communism.

a. The Soviet Communists' Rise to Power

In February 1917, as the Russian Empire lost ground to German and Austro-Hungarian forces in World War I, food shortages and deteriorating working conditions drove Russian industrial workers to go on strike. As the turmoil spread across the country, Czar Nicholas II was forced to abdicate, and the Russian Provisional Government was established to manage the country until democratic elections could be held.

But on November 7, 1917 — or October 25 by the traditional Julian calendar — a group of communist revolutionaries led by Vladimir Lenin launched an armed insurrection in the Russian capital of Petrograd (today's St. Petersburg). In what is known as the October Revolution, Lenin's Bolshevik Party overthrew the provisional government and established the world's first communist regime.

Less than three weeks later, during the democratic election for the Constituent Assembly, the Party of Socialist Revolutionaries won a plurality of the national vote and a majority of the seats. The Bolsheviks won less than 25 percent of the vote and only a handful of delegates.

After this setback, Lenin trampled on his early promise to respect the outcome of the elections. When the Constituent Assembly convened in Petrograd on January 18, 1918, Lenin declared the assembly an enemy of the people. Having prepared in advance to enact martial law, and having seized the government administration from the Provisional Government, the Bolsheviks mobilized troops to disband the assembly by force, destroying the democratic process in Russia.

Like the Russian Marxist movement itself, Lenin's rise was not entirely a Russian phenomenon. Despite the end of czarist rule, Russia continued to fight in the war on the side of France and Great Britain against the German-led Central Powers. Calculating that the Bolsheviks could throw Russia into political chaos — and thus remove a major threat from Germany's eastern front — Kaiser Wilhelm II arranged for the exiled Lenin's safe passage back to Russia via Germany and Sweden into Finland, a territory of the Russian Empire at the time. Wilhelm II also provided Lenin with money, weapons, and munitions. By the end of World War I, the Bolsheviks had received at least 50 million marks from Germany. [3]

Winston Churchill had this to say about Germany's role in Lenin's return: "They turned upon Russia the most grisly of weapons. They transported Lenin in a sealed truck like a plague bacillus from Switzerland to Russia." [4]

The October Revolution, and subsequent Leninist takeover, was the origin of all violent communist movements throughout the world in the twentieth century. It triggered the international rise of communism and the countless catastrophes that followed.

Immediately after seizing power from the Constituent Assembly, the Bolsheviks turned on the Russian workers, who in early 1918 were the first to resist the communist dictatorship. Tens of thousands of workers from Petrograd and Moscow held parades and demonstrations to protest the dissolution of the democratically elected assembly. Bolshevik soldiers cracked down on the unrest with lethal force, filling the city streets with the workers' blood.

The country's largest labor union, the All-Russian Union of Railwaymen, announced a strike to protest the Bolshevik coup and gained the broad support of many other labor organizations. The Bolsheviks put down the strike with its armed forces, just as it had done to the workers of Petrograd and Moscow. The All-Russian Union and other independent unions were then banned.

In March 1918, the Bolsheviks rebranded themselves as the All-Russian Communist Party. (In 1925, following the 1922 establishment of the Union of Soviet Socialist Republics, the party was again renamed the All-Union Communist Party. Finally, in 1952, it formally became the Communist Party of the Soviet Union.) Those labor organizations that remained were gradually forced under the control of the Communist Party.

In the summer of 1918, Russia faced a massive food shortage due to the ongoing civil war between various communist factions (including the Bolsheviks), regional independence movements, and the White movement, led by anti-communist Russian military officers. In June, with the country on the verge of famine, Lenin dispatched Joseph Stalin to Tsaritsyn to seize grain from the Volga basin, traditionally a breadbasket of Russian agriculture.

The Communist Party's tyranny prompted resistance from the peasants. In August 1918, peasants in the Penza region rose up in an armed revolt, which quickly spread to the surrounding areas. The Party sent troops to suppress the uprisings, and Lenin sent a telegram to the Penza Bolsheviks:

Hang (and make sure that the hanging takes
place in full view of the people) no fewer than 100
known landlords, rich men, bloodsuckers.
Publish their names.
Seize all their grain from them.
Designate hostages in accordance with yesterday's telegram.

Do it in such a fashion that for hundreds of kilometers
around, the people might see, tremble, know, shout. ... [5]

In the spring of 1919, starving workers in cities across Russia went on strike several times to demand the same rations as Red Army soldiers, as well as the right to free speech, democratic elections, and the abolition of political privileges afforded to the communists. All these movements were handled by the Cheka secret police (the forerunner of the KGB), who jailed or shot the workers.

Tambov, southeast of Moscow, had been one of the richest provinces in Russia prior to the October Revolution. After the Soviet Union sent "grain-requisitioning teams" to seize the region's stores, more than fifty thousand Tambov farmers formed local militias to fight the requisitioning teams, in what came to be known as the Tambov Rebellion. In June 1921, the Soviet regime authorized military commander Mikhail Tukhachevsky to fight the farmers with poison gas. [6] Tukhachevsky's use of chemical weapons, combined with fires that burned across the region, rendered much of Tambov completely desolate. An estimated one hundred thousand Tambov peasants who took part in the resistance and their relatives were imprisoned or exiled. About fifteen thousand people died in the insurgency. [7] Later, Tukhachevsky himself was tortured and executed during Stalin's purge of the Red Army in the 1930s.

The Soviet regime's establishment of totalitarian dictatorship, utter betrayal of the Russian workers, and later mass murder of millions of ordinary citizens would be repeated by the CCP in textbook fashion. Starting with its own seizure of power in the late 1940s, the CCP would bring about catastrophes unprecedented in Chinese history.

b. The Chinese Communist Party's Power Grab

Marxism and other left-wing ideologies were introduced to China from abroad prior to the fall of the Qing Dynasty in 1911 and gained currency among radical scholars and youth desperate for solutions to the perils facing their nation.

In the 1910s, communist Chinese activists led the New Culture Movement to criticize traditional culture, which they blamed for China's backwardness. In 1919, supported with funding provided by the new Soviet regime, Chinese communists assumed a guiding role in the May Fourth Movement, a series of student protests that had grown out of the New Culture Movement and which targeted both foreign powers and the Chinese political elites.

In April 1920, the Bolsheviks dispatched Grigori Voitinsky to China to establish a local communist organization. In July 1921, the CCP was founded in Shanghai by Chen Duxiu, Li Dazhao, and other Chinese Marxists.

The newly formed CCP operated through subterfuge. In 1923, Lenin dispatched Mikhail Borodin to broker an alliance between the Chinese Nationalist Party (Kuomintang) and the Soviet Union. Under the terms of the partnership, the Kuomintang took in the nascent CCP as a branch party, giving the communists further opportunities to subvert the Nationalist cause.

Aware that the CCP was trying to co-opt the Kuomintang in order to seize power, Nationalist leader Chiang Kai-shek launched a purge of the communists in 1927. Over the next few years, the Kuomintang mounted several military campaigns intended to destroy the CCP's "Soviet regions" in southern China. These operations were partially successful, but the communists managed to escape to a new base area in Yan'an, northwestern China. In the 1930s, the growing threat from Imperial Japan forced the Kuomintang to pause its campaigns against the CCP rebellion.

The CCP took full advantage of China's instability in the face of Japanese expansionism. As Nationalist forces bore the brunt of the fighting, the CCP grew its strength. In 1937, the year that Japan launched its all-out invasion of China, the CCP's Red Army had been on the verge of defeat by the Kuomintang. By the time of China's victory in 1945, the communists boasted 1.32 million regular troops and a militia force of 2.6 million. [8] Following Japan's surrender, the CCP used the cover of peace talks with the Kuomintang to position its forces for the coming civil war.

Millions of people gave their lives on the battlefields of World War II, yet the unexpected result was the meteoric expansion of totalitarian communism. The CCP's diplomatic efforts during and after the war led the United States and the Soviet Union to abandon their policies of support for the Nationalists. In 1949, the CCP defeated the Kuomintang and founded what would become the most brutal totalitarian communist regime on earth, the People's Republic of China (PRC).

At their peak, communist powers controlled one-third of the world's population, as they comprised Russia and China, the world's largest nations by size and population. Communist governments extended across large swaths of Europe and Asia, and many countries in Africa, South America, and Southeast Asia became clients or allies of the Soviet Union or the PRC.

China has a broad and profound culture with a history of five thousand years. Its people are steeped in a tradition of worshipping gods and revering the divine. The communist specter could not destroy traditional Chinese culture via conspiracy alone.

After seizing power and establishing the PRC in mainland China, the CCP targeted the elites of society, who had served as the bearers of traditional culture; it destroyed the physical artifacts of Chinese civilization; and it severed the connections between the Chinese people and their gods. Through mass killing, China's traditional heritage was replaced with Communist Party culture. With each passing generation, Party culture has only become more deeply ingrained in the mainland Chinese worldview.

The CCP began to invent enemies as soon as it took power, beginning with the elites. In the countryside, it slaughtered landlords and gentry. In the cities, it killed businessmen, creating an atmosphere of terror as it looted the wealth of civil society.

To rouse the peasants to kill landlords and "rich farmers" in support of the new communist regime, the CCP implemented a so-called land reform that promised the peasantry their own land. But after the landowners were murdered, the CCP claimed the land would be turned over to the peasants in the form of cooperatives. This meant the land still did not belong to the peasants.

In March 1950, the CCP issued the "Directive on the Strict Suppression of Counter-Revolutionary Elements," also known as the Campaign to Suppress Counterrevolutionaries, which focused on killing landlords and rich peasants in the countryside. The CCP declared that by the end of 1952, more than 2.4 million "counterrevolutionaries" had been eliminated. In fact, more than five million people had been murdered. [9]

After killing the landlords and rich peasants in the countryside, the CCP launched the Three-Anti and Five-Anti campaigns to slaughter wealthy urbanites. Under this pressure, many capitalists chose to commit suicide with all of their family members.

The CCP did not stop with the extermination of landlords and capitalists. It also robbed the wealth of peasants, small merchants, and craftsmen. After this class genocide, the vast majority of the working class remained impoverished.

2. The Brutality of Communist Rule

Though communist regimes come to power through deception and violence, their worst atrocities are committed in times of peace. In both the Soviet Union and the PRC, the revolution was immediately followed by bloody political campaigns to eliminate "class enemies," mass famines, the establishment of concentration camps, and ruthless purges of Party cadres as well as terror among the general populace. Similar brutality was ubiquitous across the communist bloc, and the world's surviving communist states all remain repressive authoritarian regimes.

a. Soviet Communist Atrocities

In 1922, after the conclusion of major military campaigns left the Bolsheviks the *de facto* victor in the Russian civil war, the Soviet Communist Party faced immediate crises of its own making. Enthusiastically implemented Marxist policies had led to widespread famine across Russia, killing millions of people. The communist leadership was forced to roll back much of its political program — retroactively termed "war communism" — and institute the New Economic Policy (NEP). This was an effective truce with the Russian peasantry, as they were allowed to work their own land and sell crops without intervention from the state.

However, the Soviet communists never intended the NEP as anything other than an emergency measure to stave off imminent rebellion. During the famine caused by war communism, a friend of Lenin's remarked that the disaster he'd orchestrated was good in that it would "destroy faith not only in the tsar, but in God too." [10]

Communist regimes use terror and mass murder as a means of reinforcing their dictatorships. In 1928, the NEP was scrapped and replaced with collective farms controlled by the regime. Russian peasants, who objected to having their land and grain seized, put up stiff resistance to the Communist Party. They would pay dearly for their disobedience.

Killing by Famine

Most of communism's victims were killed by man-made famines. Between 1932 and 1933, mass starvation caused by the Soviet Communist Party killed millions of people, mostly peasants, across the regions of Ukraine, southern Russia, and Central Asia. The famine in Ukraine, known as the Holodomor, claimed the lives of about four million people.

After the civil war ended in 1922, the Communist Party's imposition of collective farming met with widespread resistance from the Ukrainian peasantry. To deal with this, the Soviet regime classified a majority of skilled farmers under the derogatory term "kulaks" and exiled them to Western Siberia and the republics of Central Asia. The removal of these farmers was a huge loss to Ukrainian agriculture, and in 1932, production plummeted.

In the winter of 1932–1933, the Soviet government cut off food supplies to Ukraine and set up security fences along the borders. At first, Ukrainians survived on the stored vegetables and potatoes in their homes, but these were soon requisitioned by Party authorities. A large number of farmers starved to death. The authorities prevented villagers from traveling to the cities in search of food. Many people starved to death as they walked along the railways. In desperation, people turned to eating the dug-up carcasses of cats, dogs, and livestock. Some even resorted to cannibalism. [11]

The Holodomor famine left more than one million Ukrainian children orphaned. Many of them became homeless and had no choice but to beg for food in the cities. To eliminate this embarrassment, Stalin signed orders authorizing police to shoot children as young as 12. During the famine, bodies of starvation victims could be seen all over the streets of Kharkov, the capital of Soviet Ukraine at the time.

The Gulags: Europe's First Concentration Camps

On September 5, 1918, Lenin ordered the establishment of the first Soviet concentration camp on the Solovetsky Islands for the incarceration of political prisoners and dissidents who opposed the October Revolution. In the following years, the Communist Party built a constellation of concentration camps across the Soviet Union — the notorious gulag labor camps of the Stalinist era. (The term "gulag" is an abbreviation in Russian for "Chief Administration of Corrective Labor Camps.")

The gulag system grew to a monstrous scale under the leadership of Stalin as the Communist Party intensified its political terror and carried out ever-greater purges. By the time of Stalin's death in 1953, there were 170 gulag administrations containing more than thirty thousand individual camps scattered across the Soviet Union, in what Aleksandr Solzhenitsyn would famously describe as "the Gulag Archipelago" in his book by the same name. Solzhenitsyn listed thirty-one different methods that the Soviet secret police used to exhaust their prisoners' strength and force them to confess to any crime. [12]

Those sent to the gulags suffered from a constant shortage of food and clothing while being forced to perform heavy labor for twelve to sixteen hours a day in the freezing cold of the Russian winter. The death toll was enormous. Many people were imprisoned along with their entire families, with husbands incarcerated and wives exiled. Not even the elderly, some already in their 80s, were spared. The condemned ranged from high-ranking Party elites, state leaders, and military commanders, down to completely ordinary citizens from every walk of life, including religious believers, engineers, technicians, doctors, students, professors, factory workers, and peasants.

According to conservative estimates, more than half a million prisoners perished in the gulag system between 1930 and 1940, during the years of Stalin's prewar terror. The system was formally disbanded in 1960. While the true numbers remain unknown, it is thought that 18 million people were imprisoned in the gulags and more than 1.5 million died.

Concentration camps are usually thought to be a Nazi creation, but it was the Soviet gulag system that preceded similar forms of repression around the world, in both communist and non-communist regimes. According to former Soviet military intelligence officer and popular historian Viktor Suvorov, before World War II, Adolf Hitler sent Gestapo officers to Russia to tour the gulags and learn from the experience the Soviets accumulated in operating them.

The Great Terror Against the Soviet Elite

Followers of the communist specter are also bound to become its victims. This played out during the Stalinist era, as the Communist Party carried out bloody purges throughout its own ranks. Following Lenin's death, Stalin targeted the upper echelons of the communist leadership.

The repressions reached a height between 1936 and 1938, when millions of Party members and Soviet officials were put on show trial for ludicrous charges, in a brutal episode known as the Great Terror. Hundreds of thousands were shot, often after making full confessions under torture.

Out of the 1,966 delegates to the Seventeenth Congress of the All-Union Communist Party in 1934, more than half (1,108) were arrested on charges of counter-revolutionary activity. Of the 139 members and candidate members of the Central Committee elected at the Seventeenth Congress, 110 were killed. [13] Lavrenty Beria, Stalin's secret police chief, once said, "Show me the man and I'll find you the crime." Except for Stalin, all of the Politburo members remaining at the time of Lenin's death in 1924 — Lev Kamenev, Grigory Zinovyev, Aleksey Rykov, Mikhail Tomsky, and Leon Trotsky — were executed or assassinated by 1940.

No section of society was spared in the Great Terror and other Stalinist purges. Repression in the religious, scientific, educational, academic, and artistic fields preceded the purges that gutted the military and political elite. But the main victims of Stalin's terror were ordinary people, including not just relatives and friends of the accused, but workers and other rank-and-file Soviet citizens accused of and punished for completely fictitious crimes.

Nor did the executioners themselves escape the Terror: Genrikh Yagoda, chief of secret police until 1936, was arrested in 1937 and shot the next year. His replacement, Nikolai Yezhov, fell from power in 1939 after overseeing the bloodiest round of internal purges. He was shot in an execution chamber designed according to his own specifications.

Even today there are no answers concerning how many were arrested, killed, imprisoned, or exiled during the terror of the Stalin era. In June 1991, on the eve of the dissolution of the Soviet Union, KGB secret police chief Vladimir Kryuchkov said that between 1920 and 1953, about 4.2 million people were "suppressed" — including 2 million during the Great Terror alone. [14] Alexander Yakovlev, a reformist politician in the Soviet and Yeltsin eras, said in a 2000 interview that the victims of the Stalinist repression numbered at least 20 million. [15]

b. The CCP's Deadly Campaigns

Deadly and traumatic political inquisitions have been a feature of the Chinese communist movement since even before it seized power over mainland China in 1949. In 1942, when the CCP was holed up in northwestern China, Mao Zedong launched the Yan'an Rectification Movement. Party cadres were subject to harrowing treatment, including torture, detention, and "thought reform," ostensibly to root out those with insufficient ideological loyalty. Thousands were killed during the movement, which was the CCP's first mass political campaign.

From 1949 — the year the PRC regime was established — to 1966, tens of millions of Chinese lost their lives in the Campaign to Suppress Counterrevolutionaries, the Three-Anti and Five-Anti campaigns, the Anti-Rightist Campaign, and the great famine caused by the Great Leap Forward campaign.

This period of mass killing was followed by bloody struggles within the CCP's ranks. As a new generation of Chinese — raised to be atheistic "wolf cubs" indoctrinated in the education and Party culture of communism — came of age, the communist specter launched a campaign of even more rampant killing and destruction to wipe out five thousand years of traditional Chinese culture.

The Cultural Revolution was the last and in some regards the most destructive political campaign of the Mao era. Beginning in 1966 and spanning the final decade of Mao's life, its objective was the violent replacement of traditional Chinese culture with Party culture.

The Great Chinese Famine

Between 1959 and 1962, China experienced the world's deadliest famine. To deceive the world, the CCP still claims that it faced three years of "natural disasters."

In fact, in 1958, the CCP had rashly begun the People's Commune movement and the Great Leap Forward. These wild schemes, which depleted grain stocks and decimated Chinese agricultural production, were supported by a deluge of false reports claiming bumper harvests produced by officials across all levels of leadership, from rural regions to the cities. The CCP used these reports as justification for collecting grain from the peasants, who were forced to turn in their food, seeds, and animal feed to the regime.

The CCP's administrative organs at all levels sent teams to the countryside. They used torture and interrogations to squeeze the last morsels of food from the hapless peasants. Following the example set by the Soviet communists, the CCP prevented villagers from entering cities in search of food, causing the mass death of families and even whole villages. The corpses of famine victims littered the countryside. When peasants were caught stealing to survive, they were killed. Cannibalism was widespread.

The grain seized by the government was traded for large amounts of Soviet weaponry or for gold that the CCP used to pay off debts as it turned a blind eye to the loss of Chinese lives. In just three years, the Great Famine had wiped out tens of millions of people.

The Cultural Revolution: Slaughter and Cultural Genocide

The Cultural Revolution repeated the frenzy of the Yan'an Rectification Movement on a national scale, with fanatical youth encouraged to smash, beat, torture, and murder for the sake of destroying the so-called "four olds" — old customs, old culture, old habits, and old ideas — of China.

On May 16, 1966, the CCP published what came to be called the "May 16 Notice," which marked the beginning of the Cultural Revolution. In August, with the children of high-ranking CCP cadres leading the way, students from secondary schools in Beijing formed a band of Red Guards. The mob went on a rampage across Beijing, in a frenzy of ransacking, assault, and killing. By the end of the month, known as Red August, thousands of people in Beijing had been murdered.

In the Beijing district of Daxing, 325 people were killed between August 27 and September 1, across forty-eight production brigades of thirteen people's communes. The victims varied in age from just thirty-eight days old to eighty years old, and twenty-two families were wiped out completely. The Red Guards bludgeoned, stabbed, or strangled their victims. They killed infants and toddlers by stepping on one leg and tearing the child in two. [16]

As the specter of communism directed people to beat and kill, it erased their human compassion, brainwashing them with slogans like "treat the enemy with the numb cruelty of the harsh winter." With every crime against humanity, the CCP displaced the traditional culture and moral virtue of the Chinese. Envenomed by Party culture, many people became tools of murder.

When confronted with the bloodthirsty deeds of the totalitarian communist regime, most people are at a complete loss as to how anyone could descend into such inhuman barbarism.

Estimating the casualties of the Cultural Revolution is a daunting task. Most studies suggest a minimum death toll of two million. R. J. Rummel, an American professor who has researched mass killing, wrote in his book *China's Bloody Century: Genocide and Mass*

Murder Since 1900 that the Cultural Revolution claimed the lives of 7.73 million people. [17]

Dong Baoxun, an associate professor of China's Shandong University, and Ding Longjia, deputy director of the Shandong Party History Research Office, co-authored the 1997 book *Exonerate the Innocent: Rehabilitate the Wrongly Accused and Sentenced*. It quoted Ye Jianying, then vice-chairman of the CCP Central Committee, as making the following statements during the closing ceremony of the Central Working Conference on December 13, 1978: "Two years and seven months of comprehensive investigation by the Central Committee have determined that twenty million people died in the Cultural Revolution, over one hundred million suffered political persecution, ... and 800 billion yuan was wasted." [18]

In August 1980, CCP leader Deng Xiaoping gave two interviews with Italian journalist Oriana Fallaci in which he described the difficulty of quantifying the Cultural Revolution's ravages:

"People were divided in two factions that massacred each other. ... It is hard to estimate because they died of all kinds of causes. Besides, China is such a vast country. But listen: So many died that, even if other tragedies had not taken place during it, the number of dead would be enough to say that the Cultural Revolution was the wrong thing to do." [19]

Deng described a typical case: Kang Sheng, the head of the CCP's secret police, accused the party secretary of Yunnan Province, Zhao Jianmin, of treason and of being an agent of the Kuomintang. Not only was Zhao imprisoned, but his downfall also impacted 1.38 million people throughout the province, of whom 170,000 were persecuted to death and 60,000 were beaten to the point of disability. [20]

Unprecedented Evil: The Persecution of Falun Gong

Decades of murderous violence and atheistic indoctrination by the CCP have taken a massive toll on the moral fabric of society, bringing it far below the standards required of humanity by the divine. Even many of those who still believe in the divine are ignorant of genuine faith, since they are trapped in the sham religious organizations controlled by the CCP. Should the situation continue to degenerate, humanity will face certain extinction, as prophesied in the holy texts of every ancient civilization.

But the specter of communism is bent on preventing man from being saved by the Creator. For this reason, it destroyed traditional cultures and corrupted human moral values.

During the spring of 1992, to restore human morality and provide a path to salvation, Mr. Li Hongzhi began to teach Falun Gong — a spiritual practice based on belief in the principles of truthfulness, compassion, and tolerance — to the public.

Falun Gong, also called Falun Dafa, spread across China in a few short years. As practitioners, their relatives, and their peers experienced miracles of improved health and character, tens of millions of people took up the practice in China and around the world. With so many people practicing cultivation in Falun Gong and holding themselves to higher standards, society began to rediscover its moral bearings.

The CCP, since it first seized power, has never relaxed its persecution of spiritual faiths. Naturally, it regards Falun Gong as its greatest adversary.

In July 1999, then-CCP leader Jiang Zemin unilaterally ordered the systematic persecution of Falun Gong and its practitioners. In a brutal campaign that reached every corner of China, the CCP applied every method imaginable in its efforts to fulfill Jiang's directive to "kill them physically, bankrupt them financially, and ruin their reputations."

Party mouthpieces subjected the Chinese people to constant propaganda filled with hatred and slander of Falun Gong, rejecting its principles of truthfulness, compassion, and tolerance in favor of falsehood, wickedness, and struggle. The specter brought society to new lows in moral degeneration. In an atmosphere of reactivated hatred and repression, the Chinese people turned a blind eye to the persecution happening around them, betraying Buddhas and the divine. Some abandoned their conscience and participated in the campaign against Falun Gong, ignorant of the fact that they were damning themselves in the process.

The communist specter did not limit the persecution to China. It silenced the nations of the free world while the Chinese regime engaged in the frenzied jailing, murder, and torture of Falun Gong practitioners. Sated with economic incentives, the free world remained silent or even accepted the Party's lies, giving the persecutors free rein to commit the worst crimes.

In the persecution of Falun Gong, the CCP introduced an evil never before seen: live organ harvesting. As the largest group of people imprisoned for their faith in China, Falun Gong practitioners are killed on demand, vivisected on the operating tables of state and military hospitals, and their organs sold for tens of thousands or even hundreds of thousands of dollars.

On July 6, 2006, Canadian lawyers David Matas and David Kilgour (former Canadian secretary of state, Asia-Pacific) published a report titled *Report Into Allegations of Organ Harvesting of Falun Gong Practitioners in China*. Examining eighteen types of evidence, they shed light on the CCP's monstrosity, calling it "a grotesque form of evil ... new to this planet." [21]

Matas and Kilgour, along with investigative journalist Ethan Gutmann, worked with a team of international investigators to publish *Bloody Harvest/The Slaughter: An Update* in June 2016. Running over 680 pages and containing more than 2,400 references, the report proved beyond any doubt the reality and scale of the live organ harvesting carried out by the Chinese communist regime.

On June 13, 2016, the US House of Representatives unanimously passed Resolution 343, demanding the CCP bring an immediate end to forced organ harvesting from Falun Gong practitioners and other prisoners of conscience. [22]

In June 2019, after a yearlong investigation, an independent people's tribunal in London unanimously concluded that prisoners of conscience have been — and continue to be — killed in China for their organs "on a significant scale." [23] The tribunal was chaired by Sir Geoffrey Nice QC, who previously led the prosecution of former Yugoslavian President Slobodan Milošević for his war crimes in Kosovo. The tribunal further concluded that adherents of Falun Gong have been one of the main sources of organs to fuel the Chinese regime's transplant industry. This lucrative business has sustained support for the persecution of Falun Gong and attracted clients from China and around the world, making them complicit in the CCP's mass murder.

3. A Century of Killing

The introduction to *The Black Book of Communism* provides rough estimates of the death tolls of communist regimes around the world. It verified a figure of ninety-four million, including the following:

- 65 million in China

- 20 million in the Soviet Union

- 2 million in North Korea

- 2 million in Cambodia

- 1.7 million in Africa

- 1.5 million in Afghanistan

- 1 million in Vietnam

- 1 million in Eastern Europe

- 150,000 in Latin America (mainly Cuba)

- 10,000 due to "the international Communist movement and Communist parties not in power." [24]

Apart from Russia and China, lesser communist regimes have shown themselves no less willing to engage in absolute evil. The Cambodian genocide was the most extreme incident of mass murder carried out by a communist state. Various estimates place the number of Cambodians killed by Pol Pot's Khmer Rouge regime between 1.4 million and 2.2 million — up to one-third of Cambodia's population at the time.

Between 1948 and 1987, the North Korean communists killed more than 1 million of their own people through forced labor, executions, and internment in concentration camps. In the 1990s, famines killed at least 220,000 people, according to estimates based on North Korean census data. In total, based on the North Korean data, between 600,000 and 850,000 people died unnatural deaths between 1993 and 2008. [25] Other estimates place the real figure of those killed by the famine alone at between 1 million and 3.5 million. After Kim Jong Un came to power, he committed more overt murders, with the victims including high-ranking officials and his own relatives. Kim also has threatened the world with nuclear war.

In just one century, since the rise of the first communist regime in Russia, the specter of communism has murdered more people in the nations under its rule than the combined death toll of both world wars. The history of communism is a history of murder, and every page is written with the blood of its victims.

CHAPTER FOUR

Exporting Revolution

THE COMMUNIST CULT'S SPREAD across the world is fueled by violence and deception. While communist superpowers, like the Soviet Union or China, have used military force to impose their political system upon weaker countries, it should not be forgotten that communist regimes' violent conquests were aided — and, to a great extent, made possible by — their effective use of propaganda. In recent years, the Chinese Communist Party has continued this strategy by pouring billions into its Grand External Propaganda Program. [1]

This chapter provides an introduction to how the communist regimes of the East, particularly the People's Republic of China (PRC), spread their ideology and influence in Asia, Africa, South America, and Eastern Europe, chiefly during the Cold War.

1. Exporting Revolution to Asia

The Chinese communist movement owes its success to the Soviet Union. In 1919, the Bolshevik regime established the Third International (Comintern) as its vehicle to further revolution worldwide. In April 1920, Comintern representative Grigori Voitinsky traveled to China, and soon after, an office was set up in Shanghai to make preparations for the establishment of the CCP. For several years, the CCP was completely dependent on Soviet funding and served as an organ of the Soviet communist regime. [2] The CCP continued to further Soviet interests in China for the next three decades.

The CCP's victory in mainland China was indirectly related to leftist influence in the United States. US officials in the State Department and other institutions who were sympathetic to the Chinese communists colored Washington's understanding of the political situation in China during and after World War II. Their influence led the United States to cut off aid to Chiang Kai-shek's Nationalist government as the Soviet Union, meanwhile, stepped up its support of the CCP.

US President Harry Truman also made the decision to scale down America's presence in Asia following the war. In 1948, US troops began withdrawing from South Korea, and on January 5, 1950, Truman announced that the United States would not interfere with affairs in the Taiwan Strait. This included the cessation of military assistance — even in the event of war — to Nationalist China, which by that point had retreated to the island of Taiwan and faced invasion by the communist-held mainland. [3] US Secretary of State Dean Acheson reiterated Truman's policy and said that the Korean Peninsula lay outside the "defense perimeter" of the United States. [4] These anti-interventionist policies provided an opportunity for the communist bloc to expand its influence in Asia and were ended only after the United Nations voted to defend South Korea following its invasion by the North in June 1950.

The CCP made the exporting of revolution a cornerstone of its foreign policy. In addition to providing financial support, training, and weapons for left-wing insurrections, the PRC sometimes sent troops to directly assist guerrilla fighters against legitimate governments. In 1973, during the Cultural Revolution, PRC foreign aid spending peaked at nearly 7 percent of the national budget.

The CCP's extravagant project to export revolution was paid for by the wealth — and often the lives — of the Chinese people.

According to Qian Yaping, a Chinese scholar with access to confidential documents released by the PRC's Ministry of Foreign Affairs, "Ten thousand tons of rice were shipped to Guinea and fifteen thousand tons of wheat were sent to Albania in 1960. From 1950 to the end of 1964, total foreign aid expenditure was 10.8 billion yuan, during which time most spending took place ... in the midst of the Great Chinese Famine." From 1958 to 1962, tens of millions died of hunger during the famine. Yet foreign aid expenditures in these years totaled 2.36 billion yuan. Had this money been spent domestically, countless Chinese could have been saved from starvation. [5]

a. The Korean War

Communist parties seek world domination, making use of power-hungry leaders such as Joseph Stalin, Mao Zedong, Kim Il Sung, and Ho Chi Minh to bring more territory and people under their evil ideology.

On June 25, 1950, after extensive planning, North Korea invaded the South. Seoul fell in just three days, and after a month and a half of war, almost the entire Korean Peninsula was under Northern occupation. Mao had made his own preparations for the Korean War. In March 1950, Chinese armies had amassed along the Sino–Korean border, ready to aid the North. As UN forces pushed deep into North Korean territory, the CCP sent its People's Volunteer Army into action, saving Kim's communist regime from complete destruction. The war dragged on for three years, claiming millions of lives on both sides. Communist China suffered about one million casualties. [6]

In addition to rescuing the Kim regime, the CCP had another motive for participating in the conflict: During the Chinese civil war, 1.7 million soldiers had defected from the Kuomintang (Nationalist Chinese) forces to join the CCP's ranks. The Korean War provided a convenient opportunity to dispose of these politically unreliable troops. [7]

Since the PRC and the Soviet Union fought for influence over North Korea, the North benefited from both sides. For example, in 1966 when Kim visited China, he observed the construction of the Beijing subway system and requested that an identical subway be constructed in Pyongyang — for free. Mao immediately decided to halt the construction in Beijing and send equipment and personnel — including two divisions of the People's Liberation Army Railway Corps and numerous engineers, totaling several tens of thousands of personnel — to Pyongyang. The North didn't spend a penny or use any of its own people in the construction, yet demanded that the CCP guarantee the safety of the subway in times of war. In the end, Pyongyang's subway system became one of the deepest in the world, with an average depth of 90 meters (295 feet) and a maximum depth of 150 meters (492 feet) underground. After the construction was completed, Kim told the public that it had been designed and built by Koreans. Moreover, Kim often bypassed Beijing and went directly to the Soviet Union for money and materiel. After the Korean War, the CCP left representatives in North Korea with the mission of bringing the North into the PRC orbit. Instead, those friendly to the CCP were either killed or jailed in Kim's purges, and the PRC lost on all fronts. [8]

North Korea encapsulates the horrors of communism imposed from without. The Kim regime is one of the most brutal and repressive on earth, and the North Korean people live in crushing poverty.

After the collapse of the Soviet Union, the CCP drastically reduced aid to North Korea. In the 1990s, North Korea experienced a devastating famine. The nongovernmental organization North Korean Defectors' Association reported in 2007 that in the first 60 years of communist rule by the Kim dynasty, at least 3.5 million North Koreans died of hunger and related diseases. [9]

b. The Vietnam War

Before the Vietnam War, the CCP supported the Communist Party of Vietnam (CPV) against the French colonial government. In 1954, the French suffered a major defeat at Điện Biên Phủ, resulting in that year's Geneva Conference and the confrontation between North and South Vietnam. Following the French retreat from Indochina, North Vietnam invaded the South via the Ho Chi Minh Trail through Laos and Cambodia. From 1964 to 1973, the United States participated in the conflict in an effort to contain the spread of communism to the South. At the time, the Vietnam War was the largest military conflict in a single theater since World War II.

Mao sent advisers to the CPV as early as 1950. The head of the military advisory group was PLA Gen. Wei Guoqing. The CCP's land reform advisory group detained and executed tens of thousands of Vietnamese landlords and "rich peasants," triggering famine and agrarian riots in the North. The CCP helped the CPV suppress these uprisings and launched ideological rectification movements of the Party and army, similar to the CCP's Yan'an Rectification Movement of 1942–1944. Mao aided Vietnam on a large scale, despite the fact that tens of millions of people were starving to death in China. He did this in order to compete with the Soviets for influence in Vietnam, and also to boost his authority within the CCP.

In 1962, Liu Shaoqi, vice chairman of the CCP, ended Mao's disastrous Great Leap Forward policy at the Seven-Thousand People's Assembly and made preparations for economic restoration. This would have effectively marginalized Mao, so in order to keep his power, Mao pushed the PRC into greater involvement in the Vietnam War. Liu, who had no influence in the People's Liberation Army (PLA), had to shelve his economic recovery plans.

In 1963, Mao dispatched first Luo Ruiqing, then Gen. Lin Biao, to Vietnam. Liu Shaoqi promised Ho Chi Minh that the PRC would shoulder the costs of the North Vietnamese war effort, telling him, "You can take China as your home front if there's a war." The CCP made good on this promise. By 1975, the CCP's total aid to Vietnam reached $20 billion, and hundreds of thousands of Chinese troops had been deployed to North Vietnam, serving in various combat and support roles.

Ironically, the aid requested of the CCP by the CPV became a point of political fracture between the PRC and North Vietnam. To keep the North Vietnamese fighting the United States, the CCP steadily supplied them with weapons and other war materials. Meanwhile, the CPV hoped to end the war more quickly, and, starting in 1969, joined the US-led Paris peace talks. The talks excluded China, meaning that the CPV was undermining Beijing's desire to keep the United States tied down in Vietnam.

In the 1970s, following the attempted defection and death of prominent CCP military leader Lin Biao, Mao urgently needed to reassert his political authority. Furthermore, Sino–Soviet relations had reached a nadir after a series of military clashes between the two powers in 1969 along the Ussuri River. To counter the Soviet threat, Mao cooperated with the United States and invited US President Richard Nixon to visit China.

Facing opposition to the Vietnam War back home, the United States was loath to continue fighting, and in 1973 withdrew its troops from Vietnam. On April 30, 1975, North Vietnam occupied Saigon and took South Vietnam. Under the direction of the CCP, the CPV began suppressions similar to the CCP's Campaign to Suppress Counterrevolutionaries. More than two million people in South Vietnam risked death to flee the country, becoming the largest refugee wave from Asia during the Cold War.

c. The Khmer Rouge

After unifying the country and signing a peace agreement with Washington, the CPV distanced itself from Beijing's influence and developed stronger relations with the Soviet Union. Unhappy with this, Mao used the Cambodian Khmer Rouge regime, which was aligned with the CCP but at odds with Vietnam, to put pressure on Hanoi.

The CCP's support for the Communist Party of Kampuchea (broadly known as the Khmer Rouge) began in 1955, with Khmer leaders receiving training in China. Pol Pot, paramount leader of the Khmer Rouge, came to power with Mao's approval in 1963. In 1970 alone, the CCP provided the Khmer Rouge with enough weapons to equip thirty thousand people. Destabilized by the Vietnam War, Cambodia fell to the Khmer Rouge in 1975.

Pol Pot's rule was extremely brutal. He abolished the currency, ordered all urban residents to join collective forced-labor squads in the countryside, and slaughtered intellectuals to rid the country of

"Western" influence. In a little over three years, more than a quarter of the Cambodian population had perished from starvation or were murdered in the infamous "killing fields." Not content with terrorizing only its own subjects, the Khmer Rouge repeatedly sent troops across the border into southern Vietnam and committed multiple massacres in Vietnamese border villages. Supported by the Soviets, Vietnam invaded Cambodia in December 1978. Having experienced three years of living hell, the Cambodian people welcomed the Vietnamese army. Just one month into the war, the Khmer Rouge was driven from the capital city of Phnom Penh and forced to flee into the mountains to fight as guerrillas. Vietnam's punitive war against the Khmer Rouge infuriated then-Chinese leader Deng Xiaoping. In early 1979, Deng ordered the PLA to launch a "counterattack" against Vietnam, resulting in a three-week war that many historians say was decisively won by Vietnam. The CCP continued to launch attacks on Vietnam throughout the 1980s.

In 1997, Pol Pot's erratic behavior led to fierce disputes within the Khmer Rouge. He was arrested by Khmer commander Ta Mok and, in a public trial, was sentenced to life imprisonment. In 1998, he died from heart failure. In 2014, despite the CCP's repeated attempts at obstruction, the Extraordinary Chambers in the Courts of Cambodia sentenced two Khmer leaders, Khieu Samphan and Nuon Chea, to life in prison.

d. The Rise and Fall of CCP Infiltration in Southeast Asia

In addition to its actions in the former French colonies of Indochina, the CCP made great efforts to assist communist rebellions throughout Southeast Asia. These communist movements were especially active during the 1950s and 1960s, after which they were defeated or marginalized by the local governments.

The CCP's export of revolution had painful repercussions for the Chinese diaspora. Thousands of overseas Chinese in Southeast Asian countries were murdered in bouts of ethnic violence, and in many communities the Chinese had their rights to do business and receive an education restricted.

One typical example was in Indonesia. During the 1950s and 1960s, the CCP provided significant financial and military support to prop up the Communist Party of Indonesia (Partai Komunis Indonesia, or PKI). The PKI was the largest political group at the time, with three million direct members by 1965. Added to that, its affiliated organizations brought the combined total affiliates and members to twenty-two million scattered across Indonesia's government and society, including many close to the first Indonesian president, Sukarno.

Mao was criticizing the Soviet Union at the time for supporting "revisionism," that is, a departure from strict Marxist doctrine, and strongly encouraged the PKI to take the path of violent revolution. PKI leader D. N. Aidit was an admirer of Mao and was preparing to stage a military coup. On September 30, 1965, military leader Suharto crushed this attempted coup, cut ties with China, and purged a large number of PKI members. The cause of this purge is related to statements made by Zhou Enlai, the PRC premier. During one of the international meetings between the communist countries, Zhou promised the Soviet Union and representatives of other communist countries: "There are so many overseas Chinese in Southeast Asia. The Chinese government has the ability to export communism through these overseas Chinese, and make Southeast Asia change color overnight." In reaction to the CCP's attempts to foment a local revolution, large-scale anti-Chinese movements began in Indonesia. [10]

The anti-Chinese movement in Burma (also known as Myanmar) was similar. In 1967, soon after the start of the Cultural Revolution, the Chinese Consulate in Burma, as well as the local branch of the CCP's Xinhua News Agency, began heavily promoting the Cultural Revolution among overseas Chinese, encouraging students to wear Mao badges, study his Little Red Book, and confront the Burmese government. The Burmese military junta under the rule of Gen. U Ne Win gave orders to outlaw the wearing of badges with Mao's image and the study of Mao's writings, and to shut down Chinese schools. In June 1967, anti-Chinese riots took place in the capital city of Yangon, where dozens were beaten to death and hundreds injured.

In July 1967, the CCP's official mouthpieces called for "firmly supporting the people of Myanmar under the leadership of the Communist Party of Burma to wage armed conflict and start a major revolt against the Ne Win government." Soon after, the CCP sent out a military counsel team to assist the Communist Party of Burma (CPB), which had been forced into the forest by Burmese government forces. On Jan. 1, 1968, a large number of Chinese Red Guards and CPB forces attacked Burma from the Chinese province of Yunnan, defeating the Burmese government forces and taking control of the Kokang region. [11]

The CCP's attempts at exporting revolution around the time of the Cultural Revolution involved the promotion of violence and the provision of military training, weapons, and funding. When the CCP stopped trying to export revolution, communist parties in various countries all disintegrated and were unable to recover.

In 1961, the Malayan Communist Party (MCP) decided to abandon armed conflict and instead gain political power through legal elections. Deng Xiaoping summoned MCP leader Chin Peng and others to Beijing, demanding that they continue their efforts at violent insurrection, because at the time, the CCP believed that a revolutionary high tide centered around the Vietnamese battlefield would soon sweep Southeast Asia. The MCP thus continued its armed struggle and attempts at instigating revolution for another twenty years. [12] The CCP funded the MCP, having it procure arms on the black market in Thailand, and in 1969, the CCP established the Malaysian Sound of Revolution Radio Station in Yiyang City, Hunan Province, to broadcast in Malay, Chinese, Tamil, English, and other languages. [13]

In addition to the countries noted above, the CCP also attempted to export revolution to the Philippines, Nepal, India, Sri Lanka, Japan, and elsewhere, in some cases providing military training and in some cases spreading propaganda. Some of these communist organizations later became internationally acknowledged terrorist groups. For example, the Japanese Red Army, founded in 1971, had its roots in the radical movement of the 1960s and became notorious for its anti-monarchist and pro-violence revolutionary propaganda. The group was responsible for a range of terrorist attacks, including multiple aircraft hijackings and the Lod Airport massacre.

In the late 1970s, after the Cultural Revolution, the CCP scaled back its support to Southeast Asian communist movements. During a meeting between Singapore's Prime Minister Lee Kuan Yew and Deng Xiaoping, Lee requested that Deng stop the radio broadcasts by the MCP and the Communist Party of Indonesia. At the time, the PRC was surrounded by enemies and isolated, and Deng had just assumed power and required international support, so he agreed to Lee's request. Deng met with MCP leader Chin Peng and set a deadline to shut down the broadcasts agitating for communist revolution. [14]

2. Exporting Revolution to Latin America and Africa

Both the Soviet Union and the PRC mounted extensive campaigns to support communist movements in the Middle East, South Asia, Africa, and Latin America. However, in the late 1960s, finding itself under pressure from the United States' and NATO's containment strategy, the Soviet Union adopted a new ideological line of détente. This policy called for peaceful coexistence with Western capitalist countries, which led the Soviet Union to decrease its support for Third World revolutionary movements. The CCP, which preaches global revolution, accused the Soviets of "revisionism." In the early 1960s, Wang Jiaxiang, the minister of the International Liaison Department and a former PRC ambassador to the Soviet Union, proposed a similar policy but was criticized by Mao as being too friendly to the imperialists, revisionists, and reactionaries and not supportive enough of the world revolutionary movement.

During the Cultural Revolution, the CCP often used the slogan: "The proletariat can liberate itself only by liberating all of humanity." In 1965, Lin Biao, then-minister of national defense, claimed in his article "Long Live the Victory of the People's War!" that a high tide in world revolution was imminent. Following Mao's theory of "encircling the cities from rural areas" (which is how the CCP seized power in China), Lin compared North America and Western Europe to cities, and Asia, Africa, and Latin America to rural areas. Exporting revolution to Asia, Africa, and Latin America was regarded as an important political and ideological task for the CCP, as it would lay the groundwork for conquering the West. Therefore, in addition to exporting revolution to Asia, the CCP under Mao's leadership competed with the Soviet Union for influence in Africa and Latin America.

a. Latin America

Professor Yinghong Cheng of Delaware State University wrote in his article "Exporting Revolution to the World: An Exploratory Analysis of the Influence of the Cultural Revolution in Asia, Africa, and Latin America":

> *In Latin America, Maoist communists in the mid-1960s established organizations in Brazil, Peru, Bolivia, Colombia, Chile, Venezuela, and Ecuador. The main members were young people and students. With the support of China, in 1967 Maoists in Latin America established two guerrilla groups: The Popular Liberation Army of Colombia [which] included a female company that mimicked the Red Detachment of Women and was called the María Cano Unit [; and] Bolivia's Ñancahuazú Guerrilla, or National Liberation Army of Bolivia. Some communists in Venezuela also launched armed violence actions in the same period.*
>
> *In addition, the leader of the Peruvian Communist Party, Abimael Guzmán, was trained in Beijing in the late 1960s. Apart from studying explosives and firearms, more importantly was his grasping of Mao Zedong Thought, particularly ideas of "the spirit transforming to matter," and that with the correct route, one can go from "not having personnel to having personnel; not having guns to having guns."* [15]

Abimael Guzmán was the leader of the Peruvian Communist Party (also known as the Shining Path), which was identified by the governments of the United States, Japan, Canada, the European Union, and Peru as a terrorist organization.

Cuba was the first country in Latin America to establish diplomatic ties with the CCP. In order to win over Cuba and at the same time compete with the Soviet Union for leadership of the international communist movement, the CCP extended to Che Guevara a $60 million loan in November 1960 when he visited China. This was at a time when the Chinese people were dying of starvation from the Great Leap Forward campaign. Zhou Enlai also told Guevara that the loan could be waived through negotiations. Later, when Fidel Castro began leaning toward the Soviet Union after Sino–Soviet relations broke down, the CCP sent a large number of propaganda pamphlets to Cuban officials and civilians through the embassy in Havana in an attempt to instigate a coup against the Castro regime. [16]

In 1972, when Mexico and the CCP established diplomatic relations, the first Chinese ambassador to Mexico was Xiong Xianghui, a CCP intelligence agent. Xiong was given the tasks of collecting intelligence (including about the United States) and interfering with the Mexican government. Just before Xiong arrived, Mexico announced the arrest of a group of guerrillas that had been trained in China. Mexican President Luis Echeverrí was particularly incensed because in forming a diplomatic relationship with China, he had withstood fierce opposition from within Mexico and from the United States. Xiong suggested to Zhou Enlai that he smooth over the incident by inviting Echeverría to visit China. Echeverría accepted the invitation and further requested that the CCP give Mexico preferential treatment in trade, to which the CCP agreed. [17]

b. Africa

Cheng also described how the CCP influenced the independence of African countries and the path they took after independence:

According to Western media reports, before the mid-1960s, some African revolutionary youth from Algeria, Angola, Mozambique,

Guinea, Cameroon, and Congo received training in Harbin, Nanjing, and other Chinese cities. A member of the Zimbabwe African National Union (ZANU) described his one-year training in Shanghai. In addition to military training, it was mainly political studies, how to mobilize rural people and launch guerrilla warfare with the goal of people's war. [18]

In the 1960s, Tanzania and Zambia received the most assistance from the CCP's external revolution projects on the continent.

For example, the CCP sent a group of experts from the Shanghai Textile Industry Bureau to build a textile factory in Tanzania. The leader of the group injected a strong ideological tone into the aid project. Upon arrival at the construction site, he hung the five-star red flag of the PRC, erected a statue of Mao and Mao's quotations, played Cultural Revolution-era music, and recited Mao quotes. The construction site became a model of the Cultural Revolution overseas. He also organized a propaganda team to promote Mao Zedong Thought and actively spread rebellious views among the local workers. The Tanzanian authorities were incensed by the CCP's attempts to encourage a local revolution.

Then Mao decided to build a Tanzania–Zambia railway that would also connect East Africa with Central and southern Africa. From 1970 to 1976, China sent fifty thousand laborers and spent nearly ten billion yuan constructing the railway's 320 bridges and 22 tunnels. The equivalent cost of the railway today would have been in the hundreds of billions of yuan, or in the tens of billions in US dollars. However, due to poor management and corruption in both Tanzania and Zambia, the railway has never been profitable and is still dependent on Chinese aid to continue its operations.

3. Socialism in Eastern Europe

The Soviet Union occupied eastern Germany following the defeat of the Nazis in World War II, in accordance with the division of power laid out at the Yalta Conference. Moscow set up communist regimes in all the Eastern European countries under its control, forming the Warsaw Pact military alliance.

As the Cold War progressed, the Soviet Union struggled to maintain dominance over its satellite states. Following the Sino–Soviet split, the PRC made inroads with Eastern European regimes, particularly the Balkan nation of Albania.

a. Soviet Repression of Popular Movements in Eastern Europe

In February 1956, Soviet leader Nikita Khrushchev denounced Stalin in a secret speech given at the Twentieth Congress of the Communist Party of the Soviet Union (CPSU), beginning a period of limited political liberalization. The relaxed atmosphere led to revolts in Eastern Europe, first in Poland and then Hungary.

In Poland, after the death of de facto dictator Bolesław Bierut in March 1956, his successors began pushing for reform and a break with the Stalinist legacy. In June, tens of thousands of factory workers in Poznań went on strike. After the protesters were brutally repressed, the Party leadership, recognizing the rise of nationalist sentiment, took steps to placate the people. They elected as leader Władysław Gomułka, who was hawkish on the Soviet Union and willing to stand up to Khrushchev.

An attempted revolution in Hungary then took place in October 1956, beginning with a group of students who wrote a list of sixteen demands, including the withdrawal of Soviet troops. On October 23, protesters toppled the bronze statue of Stalin, leaving behind his boots, into which the crowd placed Hungarian flags. An estimated two hundred thousand protesters filled the streets. Soviet tanks and troops opened fire on the crowds, killing scores of unarmed demonstrators.

The Soviet Union initially wished to cooperate with the newly established opposition party and named Imre Nagy as prime minister and chairman of the Council of Ministers. But after Nagy came to power, he withdrew from the Warsaw Pact and pushed for further liberalization. In response, on Nov. 4, the Soviets sent sixty thousand troops and tanks to crush the independence movement, killing several thousand. Nagy was captured and eventually executed, along with hundreds of his supporters. Hundreds of thousands of Hungarians fled to the West. [19]

The Soviet invasion of Hungary was followed a decade later by Czechoslovakia's Prague Spring in 1968. The Czechoslovak Communist Party (KSČ), following Khrushchev's 1956 speech, had loosened regulations, allowing the growth of a relatively independent civil society. One representative figure of the time was Václav Havel, who later became the first president of today's Czech Republic.

In January 1968, reformist politician Alexander Dubček took over as first secretary of the KSČ. He strengthened reforms and promoted the slogan of "socialism with a human face." Soon afterward, Dubček began the large-scale rehabilitation of individuals who had been wrongly persecuted during the Stalin period. Dissidents were released, control over the media was relaxed, academic freedom was encouraged, citizens were allowed to travel abroad, and surveillance over the church was reduced. Most crucially, the KSČ allowed limited intra-party democracy.

The Soviet Union, remembering the 1956 Hungarian uprising, considered such reforms a betrayal of socialist principles and feared that other countries would follow suit. From March to August 1968, Soviet officials, including CPSU General Secretary Leonid Brezhnev, held five conferences with Dubček attempting to pressure him to abandon the democratic reforms. Dubček ignored Brezhnev's demands. That August, the Soviet Union and other Warsaw Pact nations invaded Czechoslovakia with hundreds of thousands of troops, catching the country by surprise. The Prague Spring was crushed and "socialism with a human face" was no more. [20]

The Soviet Union relied on its military strength to impose communist rule upon Eastern Europe and maintain its control over the region. Even the slightest moves toward liberalization led to rebellions against the socialist system. In the late 1980s, the Soviet leadership embarked on political and economic reforms, leading to the end of the Cold War, the fall of the Berlin Wall, and the collapse of all communist regimes in Eastern Europe. With the Soviet Union unwilling to maintain the costly policies that were necessary to continue its dominance, the people of Poland, Romania, Bulgaria, Czechoslovakia, and East Germany rose up in generally peaceful protest against the local regimes.

On June 4, 1989, the day of the Tiananmen Square massacre in China, Poland held its first round of free democratic elections. The second round, held on June 18, removed the communists and their coalition partners from parliament.

By October 1989, multiple cities in East Germany saw mass demonstrations against the ruling Socialist Unity Party (SED). In a visit to Berlin that month, Soviet leader Mikhail Gorbachev told SED General Secretary Erich Honecker that reform was the only way forward.

Immediately afterward, East Germany lifted travel restrictions to Hungary and Czechoslovakia, which were undergoing their own political liberalizations following the Soviet example. This allowed vast numbers of people to defect to Western Germany through Czechoslovakia, and the Berlin Wall could no longer stop the waves of fleeing citizens. On November 9, the SED gave up on controlling the inter-German border. Tens of thousands of East Germans poured into West Berlin, and the wall was dismantled. The symbol of the communist Iron Curtain that had stood for decades disappeared into history. [21]

b. Albania and China

The CCP expended a great deal of effort to gain influence over Albania, which early on had criticized Moscow and left the Warsaw Pact. Mao was pleased with Albania's break with the Soviets, and thus he began the program of giving "aid" to Albania, regardless of the cost.

Xinhua reported that "from 1954 to 1978, China provided financial aid to the Party of Labour of Albania seventy-five times; the sum in the agreement was more than ten billion Chinese yuan." At the time, the population of Albania was only around two million, which meant each person received the equivalent of five thousand yuan. Meanwhile, China's average annual GDP per capita was just two hundred yuan. During this period, China was also in the throes of the Great Leap Forward famine, as well as the economic collapse caused by Mao's Cultural Revolution. During the famine, the PRC used its small reserves of foreign currency to import food. In 1962, Reis Malile, the Albanian ambassador to China, traveled to China to demand agricultural aid. By order of Party Vice Chairman Liu Shaoqi, a Chinese ship carrying wheat purchased from Canada and bound for China changed course and unloaded the wheat at an Albanian port. [22]

Additionally, China helped Albania construct a textile factory, but Albania did not have cotton, so Beijing had to use its foreign reserves to buy cotton for Albania. On one occasion, Albanian officials asked Geng Biao, the PRC ambassador to Albania at the time, to replace major equipment at a fertilizer factory and demanded that the equipment come from Italy. China then bought machines from Italy and installed them for Albania. Meanwhile, Albania took Chinese aid for granted and often wasted it. Enormous amounts of steel, machine equipment, and precision instruments sent from China were left exposed to the elements. Albanian officials were unconcerned; they believed that if the material or equipment broke down or was lost, China would simply give them more.

In 1974, Albania pursued a loan of five billion yuan from China. Despite being in a state of near-total economic collapse due to the Cultural Revolution, the PRC approved a one billion yuan loan to Albania. However, the Albanian leadership was greatly dissatisfied and started an anti-Chinese movement with slogans like "We shall never bow our heads in the face of economic pressure from a foreign country." It also refused to accommodate the PRC's requests for petroleum and asphalt.

4. Communism After the Cold War

After the revolutions of 1989, the Soviet Union itself underwent drastic political changes. In August 1991, hardliners in the CPSU, KGB, and military who considered Gorbachev's reforms a betrayal of communism staged a coup, putting the Soviet leader under house arrest and sending tanks to occupy Moscow. But the plot had no support from the rank-and-file Party members or the general public, and the conspirators were arrested or committed suicide. On December 25, 1991, with independence movements growing throughout the country, Gorbachev announced the dissolution of the Soviet Union into fifteen independent republics.

The end of the Cold War, the collapse of the Soviet bloc, and the initiation of economic reforms in China appeared to signal the end of communism's threat to the free world and humanity. In reality, the standoff between the United States and the Soviet Union diverted people's attention away from the CCP's own machinations, giving it decades to bolster its totalitarian system and undermine the free world.

In contrast to the post-World War II de-Nazification movement, with its public trials of Nazi war criminals and broad education against the evils of fascist ideology, a full reckoning of communist crimes has yet to materialize. Russia and many other former Soviet republics have never made a clean break with their Soviet past or abolished the secret police apparatus. A former KGB agent served as Russia's secret police chief and is now in charge of the country. Communist ideologies and their followers are not only still active, but are spreading their influence to the West and around the world.

The anti-communist activists in the West — the older generations who have a deeper understanding of communism — are gradually dying out, while members of the newer generations are not being sufficiently educated about it. Communist and left-wing organizations around the world have been able to continue their radical or progressive movements to overthrow and destroy traditional values and social structures.

The first president of the Russian Federation, Boris Yeltsin, took a degree of action to purge Soviet ideology — laying off former Soviet civil servants, pulling down statues of Lenin and other communist leaders, and rebuilding Orthodox Christian churches destroyed by the CPSU — but these steps proved largely superficial in cleansing the country of a deeply rooted Party culture that had been instilled in people and institutions for nearly seven decades. Furthermore, the political turmoil and economic collapse that followed the end of the Soviet Union fueled nostalgia for the bygone era.

The resurgence of popular support for communism in Russia led to the formation of the Communist Party of the Russian Federation (CPRF). It became and remained a major political party until the rise of Vladimir Putin's United Russia.

In October 1993 — only two years after the citizens of Moscow had taken to the streets to demand their independence and democracy — tens of thousands of Moscovites marched in Red Square, shouting the names of Lenin and Stalin and waving the former Soviet flags. In recent polls, such as one conducted by Moscow's RBK TV in 2015, many respondents (about 60 percent in the RBK poll) said that the Soviet Union should be resurrected. In May 2017, the Communist Youth League, which was established as an affiliated organization of the CPSU, held an oath-swearing ceremony for youth in Moscow's Red Square before Lenin's tomb. At the rally, CPRF Chairman Gennady Zyuganov claimed that sixty thousand new recruits had joined the Party recently and that the Communist Party continued to survive and grow.

The specter of communism continues to haunt the world's largest country. In Moscow alone, there are more than eighty monuments to Lenin, whose tomb in Red Square continues to attract tourists and followers. The crimes of the KGB have never been thoroughly exposed and condemned by the world. Over the past century, overt communist influence in government has faded away in most countries. At the height of the communist movement in the Cold War, there were more than two dozen ruled by avowed communist regimes. Today, only four remain: China, Vietnam, Cuba, and Laos. While North Korea's ruling party has dropped references to Marxism-Leninism, it is still a totalitarian communist state. More than one hundred countries around the world have registered communist parties.

By the 1980s, there were more than fifty communist parties in Latin America, with a total membership of one million (of which the Communist Party of Cuba accounted for roughly half). In the early 1980s, the United States and the Soviet Union were in fierce competition in the hot spots of Latin America and Asia. With the collapse of Eastern Europe and the Soviet Union, communist parties that focused on violence to enforce their rule, like the Peruvian Communist Party, became fewer and fewer.

Nevertheless, the majority of Latin American countries still came under variants of socialism. Leftist political parties took on names like the Democratic Socialist Party and the People's Socialist Party. A number of communist parties in Central America removed the words "communist party" from their names but continued to promote communist and socialist ideologies, becoming even more deceptive in their operations.

Of the thirty-three independent countries in Latin America and the Caribbean, the majority have communist parties that are accepted as legitimate political players. In Venezuela, Chile, Uruguay, and elsewhere, the communist party and the ruling party have often formed coalition governments, while communist parties in other countries play the role of opposition.

In the West and in other regions around the world, communism did not resort to violent revolution as was done in the East. Instead, it took a hidden approach, with proponents of leftist ideologies infiltrating nearly every aspect of society. Decades later, Western forms of communism have largely succeeded in subverting traditional society and morality, disintegrating the culture imparted by the divine. In this sense, the specter of communism has asserted its control over the entire world.

CHAPTER FIVE

Infiltrating the West

THE 2016 US PRESIDENTIAL ELECTION was one of the most dramatic in decades. The campaign trail was full of twists and turns that persisted long after the election. The winner, Republican nominee Donald Trump, was besieged by negative media coverage and protests in cities around the nation. The demonstrators held signs emblazoned with slogans such as "Not My President" and declared that Trump was racist, sexist, xenophobic, or a Nazi. There were demands for a recount and threats of impeachment before he even assumed office.

Investigative journalism has revealed that many of these protests were instigated by certain interest groups. As shown in *America Under Siege: Civil War 2017*, a documentary directed by Florida-based researcher Trevor Loudon, a significant portion of the demonstrators were "professional revolutionaries" with ties to communist regimes and other authoritarian states, such as North Korea, Iran, Venezuela, or Cuba. The film also highlighted the role of two prominent American socialist organizations: the Stalin-ist Workers World Party and the Maoist Freedom Road Socialist Organization. [1]

Loudon, having researched the communist movement since the 1980s, determined that left-wing organizations have made the United States their primary target for infiltration and subversion. The fields of American politics, education, media, and business have increasingly shifted to the left under the influence of well-placed individuals. Even as people around the globe cheered the triumph of the free world after the Cold War, communism was stealthily taking over the public institutions of Western society, in prepara-tion for the final struggle.

Communism manifests as totalitarian governments in Eastern countries such as the Soviet Union or China, where it conducts mass killing and destroys traditional culture. However, it also has been silently and steadily gaining control over the West through subversion and disinformation. It is eroding the economy, political processes, social structures, and moral fabric of society to bring about humanity's degeneration and destruction.

America is the light of the free world and is tasked with the divinely given role of policing the globe. U.S. military intervention proved instrumental in determining the outcomes of both world wars. During the Cold War, facing the menace of a nuclear holo-caust, the United States successfully contained the Soviet bloc until the disintegration of the Soviet and Eastern European communist regimes. The success of the American experiment with liberty and enlightened governance has spared the world from mass destruc-tion and domination by tyrannical regimes.

America's Founding Fathers applied their knowledge of West-ern religious and philosophical traditions to write the Declaration of Independence and the Constitution of the United States. These documents recognize as self-evident the rights bestowed upon man by the Creator — starting with the freedoms of belief and speech — and established the separation of powers to guarantee the republican system of government.

The freedom of the West runs directly counter to the goal of communism. While masking itself with beautiful visions of a collective, egalitarian society, communism aims to enslave and destroy humanity.

As communist parties did not directly take power in Western countries, the specter aims to conquer the West through subversion, having its supporters infiltrate all organizations and institutions. There have been at least five major forces driving communist and left-wing subversion in the West.

The first force of subversion was the Soviet Union, which founded the communist Third International (Comintern) to spread revolution worldwide.

The second was local communist parties, which worked with the Soviet Communist Party and the Comintern.

The third was the economic crisis and social upheaval that encouraged many Western governments to adopt socialist policies in the past few decades, resulting in a steady shift to the left.

The fourth was those who sympathized with and supported the Communist Party and socialism. These fellow travelers have served communism as a fifth column of "useful idiots" within Western society, helping to destroy its culture, sow moral degeneracy, and undermine legitimate governments.

The Chinese Communist Party is a fifth force. After the Chinese communists implemented economic reform, which started in the 1980s, the CCP established political, business, and cultural exchanges that gave it an opportunity to infiltrate the West.

Given the sheer complexity of the communist specter's arrangements, it is beyond the scope of this work to provide a comprehensive account of its infiltration in the West. However, by understanding the broad strokes, readers can gain some awareness of how the devil operates and learn to see the common threads in its many layers of deception. For the sake of brevity, this chapter offers a general overview of communism's reach in the United States and Western Europe.

1. Communism via Violence and Nonviolence

In the popular imagination, the Communist Party is synonymous with violence, and with good reason. The fact that the communist regimes of Russia and China took power through violent revolution and used violence as a tool of repression drew attention away from communism's less visible forms. In *The Communist Manifesto*, Karl Marx and Friedrich Engels wrote: "The Communists disdain to conceal their views and aims. They openly declare that their ends can be attained only by the forcible overthrow of all existing social conditions." [2]

According to Marx, communist revolution would begin in advanced capitalist countries, but Vladimir Lenin believed that socialism could be built in Russia, which was comparatively backward in its economic development. Lenin's other significant contribution to Marxism was his doctrine of party-building, which consisted of adopting the techniques of coercion, deception, and violence found in criminal organizations and animating them with Marxist socioeconomic theory. According to Lenin, the working class is incapable of developing class consciousness or demanding revolution on its own and thus must be rallied to action by an external force. The agents of revolution would be organized in a highly disciplined proletarian "vanguard" — the Communist Party.

The British Fabian Society, founded in 1884, a year after Marx's death, took a different path in the struggle to impose socialism. The society's original coat of arms depicted a wolf in sheep's clothing, and its name is a reference to Quintus Fabius Maximus Verrucosus, the ancient Roman general and dictator, who earned fame for his delaying tactics in the war against Carthage. The first pamphlet produced by the group included a note that read, "For the right moment you must wait, as Fabius did most patiently, when warring against Hannibal, though many censured his delays; but when the time comes you must strike hard, as Fabius did, or your waiting will be in vain, and fruitless." [3]

To gradually bring about socialism, the Fabian Society invented the policy of "permeation" to infiltrate politics, business, and civil society. The society encourages its members to advance socialist aims by joining suitable organizations and ingratiating themselves with important figures, such as cabinet ministers, senior administrative officials, industrialists, university deans, and church leaders. Sidney Webb, a core member of the society, wrote:

> As a Society, we welcomed the adhesion of men and women of every religious denomination or of none, strongly insisting that Socialism was not Secularism; and the very object and purpose of all sensible collective action was the development of the individual soul or conscience or character. ... Nor did we confine our propaganda to the slowly emerging Labour Party, or to those who were prepared to call themselves Socialists, or to the manual workers or to any particular class. We put our proposals, one by one, as persuasively as possible, before all who would listen to them — Conservatives

whenever we could gain access to them, the churches and chapels of all denominations, the various Universities, and Liberals and Radicals, together with the other Socialist Societies at all times. This we called "permeation"' and it was an important discovery. [4]

Both the Fabian Society's nonviolent communism and Lenin's violent communism had the same ultimate aim, and Lenin did not reject nonviolent means. In his book *"Left-Wing" Communism: An Infantile Disorder*, Lenin criticized the communist parties of Western Europe that refused to cooperate with what he called the "reactionary" labor unions or to join the "capitalist" national parliament. Lenin wrote in his book: "For a Communist, with a correct understanding of his own ends, the art of politics lies in correctly calculating the conditions and the moment when the proletarian vanguard can take over power successfully. He must decide when, after this assumption of power, that vanguard will be able to obtain adequate support from sufficiently inclusive strata of the working-class and non-proletarian laboring masses, and when it will be able to maintain, consolidate and extend its supremacy, educating, training and attracting ever widening circles of the laboring masses." [5]

Lenin repeatedly stressed that communists must hide their real intentions. In the pursuit of power, no promise or compromise would be ruled out. In other words, to achieve their goals, they must be unscrupulous. Both Russia's Bolsheviks and the Chinese communist movement made liberal use of violence and deception on their way to gaining power.

The brutality of the Soviet and Chinese communist regimes has drawn attention away from the nonviolent communism found in the West. The Fabian Society specialized in disguise. It chose Bernard

Shaw, an Irish playwright, to put a prosaic spin on the true aims of nonviolent socialism with prosaic rhetoric. Shaw wrote, on the final page of his book *The Intelligent Woman's Guide to Socialism and Capitalism*: "I also made it quite clear that Socialism means equality of income or nothing, and that under socialism you would not be allowed to be poor. You would be forcibly fed, clothed, lodged, taught, and employed whether you like it or not. If it were discovered that you had not character enough to be worth all this trouble, you might possibly be executed in a kindly manner." [6]

Just as a Leninist regime may sometimes find it expedient to scale back the overt brutality of its rule, Western communist parties and their various front organizations are not above employing violence and other criminal acts when doing so advances their political agenda.

2. War of Espionage and Disinformation

Communism holds the nation to be an oppressive construction of class society, so it aims to do away with the concepts of patriotism and national loyalty. In *The Communist Manifesto*, Marx and Engels proclaim that "working men have no country." The manifesto ends on the note, "Workers of all countries, unite!"

Under Lenin's leadership, the Bolsheviks founded the world's first socialist regime and immediately established the Comintern to instigate socialist revolution around the globe. The goal of the Soviet Union and the Comintern was to overthrow the legitimate regimes of every nation on earth and establish a socialist world dictatorship of the proletariat.

Communist parties around the world sought guidance from the Comintern and accepted its funds and training. With the resources of a vast empire at its disposal, the Bolsheviks recruited activists worldwide and trained them to carry out subversive operations in their own countries.

Founded in 1919, the Communist Party USA (CPUSA) was one such organization that followed the Comintern and the Bolsheviks. Though the CPUSA itself never became a major political force, its influence on the United States was nevertheless significant. The CPUSA colluded with activists and activist organizations to infiltrate workers' and student movements, the church, and the government.

In the late 1950s, Fred Schwarz, a pioneer of American anti-communist thought, told the US House Un-American Activities Committee: "Any attempt to judge the influence of Communists by their numbers is like trying to determine the validity of the hull of a boat by relating the area of the holes to the area which is sound. One hole can sink the ship. Communism is the theory of the disciplined few controlling and directing the rest. One person in a sensitive position can control and manipulate thousands of others." [7]

It is now known that Soviet operatives were active within the US government during World War II. Despite the anti-communist efforts of Sen. Joseph McCarthy, the facts were hidden or obscured from the public by leftist politicians, academics, and the left-wing media.

In the 1990s, the US government declassified the Venona files, a collection of Soviet communications that were decoded by American intelligence during World War II. These documents showed that at least three hundred Soviet spies were working in the US government, including high-ranking officials in the Roosevelt administration who had access to top-secret information. Other agents used their positions to influence American policymaking and statecraft. Among those found to be Soviet spies were US Treasury official Harry Dexter White, State Department official Alger Hiss, and Julius and Ethel Rosenberg, the couple who were executed by electric chair for transmitting military and atomic secrets to the Soviet Union.

The communications intercepted and decrypted by the Venona project were just the tip of the iceberg; the full extent of Soviet infiltration into the US government remains unknown. As high-ranking American officials, some of the Soviet operatives had opportunities to influence important political decisions.

Hiss, who served as the director of the State Department's Office of Special Political Affairs, played a key role as President Franklin D. Roosevelt's adviser during the Yalta Conference at the end of World War II. He helped determine postwar territorial arrangements, draft the United Nations Charter, decide prisoner exchanges, and the like.

White was a trusted aide to Secretary of the Treasury Henry Morgenthau Jr. He helped create the 1944 Bretton Woods international financial agreement and was one of the architects of the International Monetary Fund and the World Bank. White encouraged the Chinese Nationalist Party (Kuomintang) to appoint underground CCP member Ji Chaoding to a high rank in the Republic of China's Ministry of Finance. Taking up the post in 1941, Ji was the architect of disastrous currency reforms that damaged the Kuomintang's reputation and benefited the CCP's rise. [8] Some historians argue that the influence of Soviet spies and their left-wing sympathizers in US foreign policy led the United States to end military aid to the Kuomintang during the Chinese Civil War after World War II. Mainland China was consequently lost to the CCP. [9]

Whittaker Chambers, a Soviet informant and CPUSA associate who later defected and testified against other spies, said: "The agents of an enemy power were in a position to do much more than purloin documents. They were in a position to influence the nation's foreign policy in the interest of the nation's chief enemy, and not only on exceptional occasions, ... but in what must have been the staggering sum of day to day decisions." [10]

Yuri Bezmenov, a KGB agent who defected to the West in 1970, discussed Soviet methods of subversion in his writings and interviews. According to Bezmenov, the James Bond-style spies of popular culture who blow up bridges or sneak around stealing secret documents couldn't be further from reality. Only 10 to 15 percent of the KGB's personnel and resources were allocated to traditional spy operations, with the rest going to ideological subversion.

Bezmenov, alias Tomas Schuman, said subversion happens in four stages: demoralization, destabilization, crisis, and "normalization." The first stage, lasting for the period of time needed to raise a generation, is to demoralize and subvert public perceptions of reality in the enemy country; the second focuses on throwing society into chaos; and the third instigates a crisis that leads to a civil war, revolution, or foreign invasion. These steps culminate in the fourth and final stage of "normalization" — that is, bringing the country under communist control.

Bezmenov listed three fields of subversion, or demoralization, under the first stage: ideas, structures, and life. Ideas cover religion, education, the media, and culture. Structures include government administration, the legal system, law enforcement, the armed forces, and diplomacy. Life encompasses families and communities, health, and relations between people of different races and social classes.

As an example, Bezmenov explained how the concept of equality was manipulated to create unrest. Agents would promote the cause of egalitarianism, making people feel discontent with their political and economic circumstances. Activism and civil unrest would be accompanied by economic deadlock, further exacerbating labor and capital relations in a worsening cycle of destabilization. This would culminate in revolution or invasion by communist forces. [11]

Another defector, Ion Mihai Pacepa, the highest-ranking intelligence officer to defect from the Soviet bloc, escaped to the United States in 1978. He further exposed how communist regimes adopted strategies of psychological warfare and disinformation against Western countries to bring about the first stage. According to Pacepa, the purpose of disinformation was to alter people's frame of reference. With their ideological values manipulated, people would be unable to understand or accept the truth even when presented with direct evidence. [12]

Bezmenov said the first stage of ideological subversion usually took fifteen to twenty years — that is, the time needed for the education of a new generation — while the second stage took two to five years and the third stage, only two to six months. In an interview he gave in 1984, Bezmenov said the first stage had been accomplished to a greater extent than even Soviet authorities had expected.

The accounts of many Soviet spies and intelligence officials and declassified documents from the Cold War suggest that infiltration and subversion tactics were the driving forces behind the counterculture movement of the 1960s.

In 1950, McCarthy began to expose the extent of communist infiltration across the US government and society. But four years later, the Senate voted to censure him, and the government's initiative to rid itself of communist influence was brought to a halt. Today, McCarthyism is synonymous with political persecution — an indication that the left wing has successfully established dominance in the ideological struggle.

Communist infiltration hasn't lessened since the collapse of the Soviet Union and the end of the Cold War. The left wing fights tooth and nail to protect adulterers, abortionists, criminals, and communists, while supporting anarchy and opposing civilization.

3. From the New Deal to Progressivism

On October 24, 1929, panic set in at the New York Stock Exchange and a record 12.9 million shares were traded. The crisis spread from the financial sector to the entire economy, and the ensuing Great Depression spared neither the industrialized nor the developing nations of the world. The US unemployment rate, which was three percent in 1929, shot up to a quarter of the labor force by 1933. Industrial production in major industrial countries, apart from the Soviet Union, dropped by an average of 27 percent. [13]

In early 1933, within one hundred days of Roosevelt's inauguration, many bills were introduced around the theme of solving the crisis. The policies increased government intervention in the economy, with Congress passing major reforms, including the Emergency Banking Act, Agricultural Adjustment Act, National Industrial Recovery Act, and Social Security Act. Though Roosevelt's New Deal essentially petered out upon the outbreak of World War II, many of the institutions and organizations that emerged during that period have continued to shape American society to the present day.

Roosevelt issued more executive orders on average per year than any other U.S. president. Nevertheless, the unemployment rate in the United States did not fall below the double digits until 1941 and the war was underway. The New Deal's real effect was to set the US government on a trajectory of high taxation, big government, and economic interventionism.

In his 2017 book *The Big Lie: Exposing the Nazi Roots of the American Left*, conservative thinker Dinesh D'Souza argued that the National Industrial Recovery Act, which formed the center-piece of Roosevelt's New Deal, essentially meant the end of the US free market. [14]

According to *FDR's Folly*, a 2003 book by historian Jim Powell, the New Deal prolonged the Great Depression rather than ending it: The Social Security Act and labor laws encouraged further unemployment, while high taxes encumbered healthy businesses, and so on. [15] Economist and Nobel Prize Laureate Milton Friedman praised Powell's work, saying: "Truth to tell — as Powell demonstrates without a shadow of a doubt — the New Deal hampered recovery from the contraction, prolonged and added to unemployment, and set the stage for ever more intrusive and costly government." [16]

President Lyndon Johnson, who assumed office after the assassination of President John F. Kennedy in 1963, declared an "all-out war on human poverty and unemployment" in his 1964 State of the Union address and then launched the Great Society domestic programs. In a short period of time, Johnson issued a series of executive orders, established new government agencies, reinforced the welfare state, raised taxes, and dramatically expanded the government's authority.

It is interesting to note the similarities between Johnson's administrative measures and the goals outlined in communist literature at the time. Former CPUSA General Secretary Gus Hall said: "The Communist attitude towards the Great Society can be summarized in an old saying that two men sleeping in the same bed can have different dreams. ... We support these measures because we dream of socialism."

The CPUSA may have supported the Great Society initiative, but its intentions differed from Johnson's; while the Johnson administration aimed to improve the United States under the democratic system, the Communist Party sought to ease the United States into socialism.

The most serious consequences of the Great Society and the War on Poverty were threefold: They increased dependence on welfare, discouraged people from working, and damaged the family structure. Welfare policies favored single-parent families, thus encouraging divorce and out-of-wedlock childbearing. According to statistics, the rate of out-of-wedlock births in 1940 was 3.8 percent; by 1965, this figure had increased to 7.7 percent. In 1990, twenty-five years after the Great Society reform, the figure was at 28 percent and subsequently rose to 40 percent by 2012. [17] These policies disproportionately affected minorities, particularly African Americans.

The weakening of the family had far-reaching consequences, such as generational poverty, soaring crime rates, increased financial burdens for the government, the decline of household education, and a mentality of entitlement, which led to a higher rate of voluntary unemployment.

A quote attributed to Scottish historian and jurist Lord Alexander Fraser Tytler says: "A democracy cannot exist as a permanent form of government. It can only exist until the majority discovers that it can vote themselves largesse from the public treasury. After that, the majority always votes for the candidate promising the most benefits from the public treasury, with the result the democracy collapses because of the loose fiscal policy ensuing, always to be followed by a dictatorship, then a monarchy." [18] A form of this quote is also sometimes attributed to French historian Alexis de Tocqueville.

As the Chinese saying goes, "From thrift to extravagance is easy; from extravagance to thrift is hard." After people develop a dependence on welfare, it becomes nearly impossible for the government to reduce the scale and types of benefits. The Western welfare state has become a political quagmire for which politicians and officials have no solution.

In the 1970s, the extreme left gave up the revolutionary terms that kept the American people on guard and replaced them with the more neutral-sounding "liberalism" and "progressivism." People who have lived in communist countries are no strangers to the latter, as "progress" has long been used by communist parties as a quasi-synonym for "communism." For example, the term "progressive movement" referred to the "communist movement," and "progressive intellectuals" referred to "pro-communist individuals" or underground members of the Communist Party.

Liberalism, meanwhile, is not substantially different from progressivism, as it carries the same connotation of high taxes; expansive welfare; big government; the rejection of religion, morality, and tradition; the use of "social justice" as a political weapon; "political correctness"; and the militant promotion of feminism, homosexuality, sexual perversity, and the like.

We do not intend to point fingers at any individual or political figure, for it is indeed difficult to make correct analyses and judgments in the midst of complex historical developments. It is clear that the specter of communism has been at work in both the East and the West since the beginning of the twentieth century. When violent revolution succeeded in the East, it spread the influence of communism to the governments and societies of the West, shifting them ever leftward.

In the decades since the Great Depression, the United States has adopted increasingly socialist policies, and atheism and materialism have eroded the moral fabric of American society. People have grown distant from the divine and from traditional morality, weakening their resistance to deception.

4. The Cultural Revolution of the West

The 1960s, a watershed moment in modern history, saw an unprecedented counterculture movement sweeping from East to West. In contrast to the CCP's Cultural Revolution, the Western counterculture movement appeared to have multiple points of focus or, rather, a lack of focus.

From the mid-1960s to mid-'70s, the mostly young participants of the counterculture movement were motivated by various pursuits. Some opposed the Vietnam War; some fought for civil rights; some advocated for feminism and denounced patriarchy; some strove for homosexual rights. Topping this off was a dazzling spectacle of movements against tradition and authority that advocated sexual freedom, hedonism, narcotics, and rock 'n' roll music.

The goal of this Western Cultural Revolution was to destroy the upright Christian civilization and its traditional culture. While apparently disordered and chaotic, this international cultural shift stemmed from communism. Many participants of the movement revered "the Three M's" — Marx, Marcuse, and Mao.

Herbert Marcuse was a key member of the Frankfurt School, a group of Marxist intellectuals associated with the Institute for Social Research, first established in 1923 at what was then the University of Frankfurt. Its founders used the concept of "critical theory" to attack Western civilization and apply Marxism to the cultural sphere.

One of the Frankfurt School's founders was Hungarian Marxist György Lukács. He stated the school's purpose was to answer the question "Who shall save us from Western civilization?" [19] Elaborating on this, he deemed the West guilty of genocidal crimes against every civilization and culture it had encountered. American and Western civilization, according to Lukács, are the world's greatest repositories of racism, sexism, nativism, xenophobia, anti-Semitism, fascism, and narcissism. This intellectual narrative paved the road to "political correctness."

In 1935, the Frankfurt School Marxists relocated to the United States and became affiliated with Columbia University in New York. This gave them an opening to disseminate their theories on American soil. With the assistance of other leftist scholars, they corrupted several generations of American youth.

Combining Marxism with Freudian pansexualism, Marcuse's theories catalyzed the sexual liberation movement. Marcuse believed that repression of one's nature in capitalist society hindered liberation and freedom. Therefore, it was necessary to oppose all traditional religions, morality, order, and authority in order to transform society into a utopia of limitless and effortless pleasure.

Marcuse's famous 1955 work *Eros and Civilization: A Philosophical Inquiry Into Freud* occupies an important place among the vast number of works by Frankfurt scholars for two specific reasons: First, the book combines the thought of Marx and Freud, turning Marx's critiques on politics and economy into a critique on culture and psychology. Second, the book builds bridges between Frankfurt theorists and young readers, which enabled the cultural rebellion of the 1960s.

Marcuse said that the counterculture movement could be called "a cultural revolution, since the protest is directed toward the whole cultural establishment, including the morality of existing society." He continued: "There is one thing we can say with complete assurance: the traditional idea of revolution and the traditional strategy of revolution has ended. These ideas are old-fashioned. ... What we must undertake is a type of diffuse and dispersed disintegration of the system." [20]

Few among the rebellious youth could grasp the arcane theories of the Frankfurt School, but Marcuse's ideas were simple: Be anti-tradition, anti-authority, and anti-morality. Indulge in sex, drugs, and rock 'n' roll without restraint. He even coined the phrase "make love, not war." As long as one said no to all authority and societal norms, he or she would be counted as a participant in the "noble" revolutionary cause. It was so simple and easy to become a revolutionary, it's little wonder that so many young people were attracted to the movement at that time.

It must be emphasized that although many rebellious youths acted of their own accord, the most radical student leaders at the forefront of the movement had been trained and manipulated by foreign communists. For instance, the leaders of the US student activist organization Students for a Democratic Society (SDS) were trained by Cuban espionage agents, according to FBI reports.

The anti-war student protests were directly organized and instigated by communist groups. One of these groups was the far-left organization Weather Underground, which stepped in when SDS collapsed in 1969.

In a statement that year, Weather Underground used the following quote: "The contradiction between the revolutionary peoples of Asia, Africa, and Latin America and the imperialists headed by the United States is the principal contradiction in the contemporary world. The development of this contradiction is promoting the struggle of the people of the whole world against US imperialism and its lackeys."

These were the words of Lin Biao, then the second-most powerful leader of communist China, from his series of articles "Long Live the Victory of People's War!" [21]

Just as the Cultural Revolution wrought irreversible damage upon

Chinese traditional culture, the counterculture movement caused a titanic upheaval in Western society. First, it normalized many subcultures that belonged to the lower fringes of society or were deviant variations of mainstream culture. Sexual liberation, drugs, and rock 'n' roll rapidly eroded the moral values of the youth and turned them into a corrosive force that was against God, against tradition, and against society.

Second, the counterculture movement set a precedent for chaotic activism and fostered a wide range of antisocial and anti-American ways of thinking, setting the stage for the street protests and culture war that would follow.

Third, after the youth of the 1960s ended their activist lifestyles, they entered universities and research institutes, completed their master's degrees and doctorates, and moved into the mainstream of American society. They brought the Marxist worldview and its values into education, media, politics, and business, furthering a nonviolent revolution across the country.

Since the 1980s, the Left has largely taken over and established strongholds in the mainstream media, academia, and Hollywood. The presidency of Ronald Reagan briefly reversed this trend, only for it to restart in the 1990s and reach a peak in recent years.

5. The Anti-War and Civil Rights Movements

In George Orwell's novel *Nineteen Eighty-Four*, one of the four main Oceanian ministries is the Ministry of Peace, which oversees the Party's military affairs. The inverted meaning of its name reflects a strategy often employed by communists: When one's strength is inferior to that of the enemy, proclaim one's desire for peace; extending an olive branch is the best way to hide an imminent attack.

The Soviet Union and other communist countries proved adept

practitioners of this strategy, which is employed to infiltrate and disarm the West. Directly after the end of World War II — with the United States still the only country to produce and deploy the atomic bomb — the World Peace Council was formed. Its first chairperson was French physicist Frédéric Joliot-Curie, a member of the French Communist Party.

Having suffered huge losses in the war, the Soviet Union aggressively promoted world peace as a stratagem to stave off pressure from the West. The World Peace Council was directly influenced by the Soviet Committee for the Defense of Peace, an organization affiliated with the Soviet Communist Party. The council ran a worldwide campaign proclaiming that the Soviet Union was a peace-loving nation and condemning the United States as a hegemonic warmonger. The "struggle for peace," a catchphrase promoted by high-ranking Soviet official and ideological leader Mikhail Suslov, became a fixture of Soviet rhetoric.

"The present anti-war movement testifies to the will and readiness of the broadest masses of the people to safeguard peace and to prevent the aggressors from plunging mankind into the abyss of another slaughter," Suslov wrote in a 1950 propaganda tract. "The task now is to turn this will of the masses into active, concrete actions aimed at foiling the plans and measures of the Anglo-American instigators of war." [22]

"World peace" became one of the communist frontlines in the public-opinion war against the free world. The Soviet Union sponsored a multitude of organizations and groups to push communist aims, such as the World Federation of Trade Unions, Women's International Democratic Federation, International Federation of Journalists, World Federation of Democratic Youth, and the World Federation of Scientific Workers.

Vladimir Bukovsky, a prominent Soviet dissident, wrote in 1982: "Members of the older generation can still remember the marches, the rallies, and the petitions of the 1950s. ... It is hardly a secret now that the whole campaign was organized, conducted, and financed from Moscow, through the so-called Peace Fund and the Soviet-dominated World Peace Council." [23]

Hall, the former CPUSA general secretary, said, "It is necessary to widen the struggle for peace, to raise its level, to involve far greater numbers, to make it an issue in every community, every people's organization, every labor union, every church, every house, every street, every point of gathering of our people." [24]

The Soviets pushed the "struggle for peace" movement throughout the Cold War. Stanislav Lunev, a former officer of the Soviet GRU (military intelligence) who defected to the United States in 1992, said that "the GRU and the KGB helped to fund just about every antiwar movement and organization in America and abroad." [25]

Ronald Radosh, a former Marxist and activist during the anti-Vietnam war movement, admitted, "Our intention was never so much to end the war as to use anti-war sentiment to create a new revolutionary socialist movement at home." [26]

The last major anti-war movement pushed by the Soviets took place during the early 1980s, when the United States deployed intermediate-range nuclear missiles in Europe. Anti-war protesters demanded that both the United States and the Soviet Union limit their nuclear arsenals, and in 1987 the Intermediate-Range Nuclear Forces Treaty was created. Given the lack of free speech and political transparency in the Soviet bloc, the treaty's terms could only be effectively guaranteed in the democratic West. Following the Cold War, organizations with communist or radical left-wing ties continued to play a major role in steering the US anti-war movement, particularly after the start of the War on Terror. [27]

Communists also made efforts to hijack the American civil rights movement. As early as the late 1920s, the Communist Workers Party of America believed there to be great potential for revolution among black Americans. [28] A communist propaganda handbook published in 1935, *The Negroes in a Soviet America,* proposed a racial revolution in the South, including the establishment of a Negro Republic, to be combined with the overall proletarian revolution. [29]

In the 1960s, elements of the civil rights movement received support from the Soviet and Chinese communist parties. The extremist Revolutionary Action Movement and the Maoist Black Panther Party were supported or directly influenced by the CCP. In the summer of 1965, several American cities were torn by race riots. After Leonard Patterson withdrew from the CPUSA, he testified that those leading the violent African-American organizations enjoyed the Party's strong support. Both he and Hall had received training in Moscow. [30]

Whether in terms of its organizational structure or ideological program, the Black Panther Party looked up to the CCP as its role model, using slogans such as Mao's "political power grows out of the barrel of a gun" and "all power belongs to the people." Mao's Little Red Book was a must-read for all members. Like the CCP, the Black Panthers advocated violent revolution. One of the party's leaders, Eldridge Cleaver, predicted in 1968 a wave of terror, violence, and guerrilla warfare. At many Black Panther gatherings, participants waved the Little Red Book, mimicking the Red Guards who were doing the same thing in China. [31]

The civil rights movement successfully brought race relations into public discussion and helped Americans heal some of the nation's deepest divides through peaceful means, such as legislation, demonstrations, boycotts, and education. However, left-wing revolutionaries have continued to use racial conflict as a springboard for their radical agendas. [32]

6. The American Marxist

When the youth protest movement of the West was in full swing in the 1960s, one radical activist dismissed their naivety, sincerity, and idealism. "If the real radical finds that having long hair sets up psychological barriers to communication and organization, he cuts his hair," he said. The man was Saul Alinsky, an activist, organizer, and author who became the "para-communist" agitator with the most baneful influence for decades.

Alinsky is best termed a para-communist because, unlike the Old Left (political leftists) of the 1930s and the New Left (cultural leftists) of the 1960s, Alinsky refused to affirmatively describe his political ideals. His overall view was that the world was made up of "the haves," "the have-a-little-want-mores," and "the have-nots." He called upon the "have-nots" to rebel against "the haves" by any means, and to seize wealth and power in order to create a completely "equal" society, destroying the existing social system. He has been called the Lenin and the Sun Tzu of the post-communist Left. [33]

Alinsky not only lavished praise on communist dictators such as Lenin and Fidel Castro, but also declared his allegiance to the devil. In his book *Rules for Radicals*, published in 1971, one of the epigraphs says, "Lest we forget at least an over-the-shoulder acknowledgment to the very first radical: from all our legends, mythology, and history (and who is to know where mythology leaves off and history begins — or which is which), the first radical known to man who rebelled against the establishment and did it so effectively that he at least won his own kingdom — Lucifer."

In *Rules for Radicals,* Alinsky systematically set forth his theory and methods of community organizing, which use unscrupulous means to achieve goals and gain power. These rules include "a tactic that drags on too long becomes a drag"; "keep the pressure on"; "the threat is usually more terrifying than the thing itself"; "ridicule is man's most potent weapon"; and "pick the target, freeze it, personalize it, and polarize it." [34]

The true nature of Alinsky's seemingly dry rules becomes clear when they are applied in the real world. In 1972, during the Vietnam War period, then-US Ambassador to the United Nations George H. W. Bush gave a speech at Tulane University. Anti-war students at the university sought advice from Alinsky, who said that protesting with the usual methods would likely result in their simply being expelled. He thus suggested that they don Ku Klux Klan garb and, whenever Bush defended the war, cheer and stand up with placards that read "The KKK Supports Bush." The students followed his advice, and it became a masterful example of deceptive propaganda. [35]

In 1964, Alinsky concocted a plan to get 2,500 activists to occupy the toilets in Chicago's O'Hare International Airport, one of the busiest in the world, to bring the airport's service operations to a grinding halt. The plan was leaked to Chicago authorities, who were thus forced to negotiate, and the protest never took place. [36]

In order to force Kodak, the major employer in Rochester, New York, to recognize community organization FIGHT as the official representative of the Rochester black community, Alinsky had a similar idea. Seizing on an important cultural tradition in the city — an upcoming performance of the Rochester Philharmonic Orchestra — Alinsky planned to purchase one hundred tickets for his activists and provide them with a pre-show banquet of baked beans so they could ruin the performance with flatulence. This plan also didn't come to fruition, but Alinsky's tactics eventually forced Kodak to comply with his demands.

Alinsky's books and interviews leave the impression of a charismatic but ruthless and calculating individual. His "community organizing" was really a form of gradual revolution. However, he differed from his forerunners in several ways. First, both the Old and the New Left were at least idealistic in their rhetoric, while Alinsky stripped "revolution" of its idealistic veneer and exposed it as a naked power struggle. When he conducted training for "community organizations," he would routinely ask the trainees, "Why organize?" Some would say that it was to help others, but Alinsky would roar back, "You want to organize for power!" The training manual that Alinsky's followers went by read: "We are not virtuous by not wanting power. ... We are really cowards for not wanting power," because "power is good ... [and] powerlessness is evil." [37]

Second, Alinsky didn't think much of the rebellious youth of the '60s who were publicly against the government and society. He stressed that, whenever possible, one should enter the system and bide one's time for opportunities to subvert it from within.

Third, Alinsky's ultimate goal was to subvert and destroy, not to benefit any group. Thus, in implementing his plan, it was necessary to conceal his true purpose with localized or staged goals that were seemingly reasonable or harmless by themselves. When people were accustomed to being mobilized, it was relatively easy to mobilize them to act toward more radical goals.

In *Rules for Radicals,* Alinsky wrote: "Any revolutionary change must be preceded by a passive, affirmative, non-challenging attitude toward change among the mass of our people. ... Remember: once you organize people around something as commonly agreed upon as pollution, then an organized people is on the move. From there it's a short and natural step to political pollution, to Pentagon pollution."

An Alinsky-influenced leader from SDS nailed the essence of radicalizing protests when he said, "The issue is never the issue; the issue is always the revolution." The radical Left after the '60s was deeply influenced by Alinsky, and always spun its responses to social issues into dissatisfaction with the status quo overall, using it to advance the revolutionary cause.

Fourth, Alinsky turned politics into a guerrilla war without restraint. In explaining his strategy for community organizing, he told his followers that they need to hit the enemy's senses: "First the eyes; if you have organized a vast, mass-based people's organization, you can parade it visibly before the enemy and openly show your power. Second the ears; if your organization is small in numbers, then do what Gideon did: conceal the members in the dark but raise a din and clamor that will make the listener believe that your organization numbers many more than it does. Third, the nose; if your organization is too tiny even for noise, stink up the place."

Fifth, Alinsky emphasized using the negative aspects of human nature, including indolence, greed, envy, and hatred. Sometimes participants in his campaigns would win petty gains, but this only made them more cynical and shameless. In order to subvert the political system and social order of free countries, Alinsky was happy to lead his followers to moral bankruptcy. From this, it can be inferred that had he truly gained power, he would have treated his former comrades with the same ruthlessness seen of communist leaders in countries like Russia or China.

Decades later, two prominent figures in American politics who were deeply influenced by Alinsky helped advance the silent revolution underway in the country. At the same time, the no-holds-barred, unrestricted guerrilla warfare-type protests advocated by Alinsky became popular in America from the 1970s on, as seen in the Occupy Wall Street movement, the Antifa movement, and so on.

It is salient to note that it wasn't just in the opening pages of *Rules for Radicals* that Alinsky gave his "acknowledgment to the very first radical," Lucifer. In an interview with *Playboy* magazine shortly before his death, Alinsky also said that when he died, he would "unreservedly choose to go to hell" and begin to organize the "have-nots" there, saying, "They're my kind of people." [38]

7. The Long March Through the Institutions

In the 1930s, prominent Italian communist Antonio Gramsci wrote that in order to subvert Western society from within, socialists needed to fight a "war of position," a concept that later came to be called "the long march through the institutions." He realized that it was difficult to incite a revolution to overthrow a legitimate government when the people still had faith in the divine, and so communists needed to rely on a large number of foot soldiers who shared their dark vision of morality, faith, and traditions. The revolution of the proletariat, then, must begin with the subversion of religion, morality, and civilization.

After the unrest of the 1960s, the rebels who had pushed for revolution began entering academia. They obtained degrees; became scholars, professors, government officials, and journalists; and entered the mainstream of society to carry out the long march through the institutions. They infiltrated and corrupted the organizations that are crucial for the maintenance of the morality of Western society, including the church, the government, the education system, the legislative and judicial bodies, the art world, the media, and NGOs.

There are numerous ostensibly legitimate means by which unscrupulous people or groups can ruin a free society from within. For democracy to be effective, the people must be disposed toward civic virtue and possess a certain moral standard. Since the 1960s, the United States has been like a sick patient who cannot identify the cause of his affliction. Para-Marxist ideas have been deeply planted into American society and are spreading virtually unchecked.

Among the many revolutionary strategies that have been put forward, one of the most well-known is the Cloward-Piven strategy, proposed in 1966 by a Columbia University sociologist couple (who were also members of the Democratic Socialists of America). The core concept of the strategy was to bloat the public welfare system and push states into bankruptcy. The authors claimed that since the number of people eligible for welfare benefits far exceeded the number of people actually receiving them, it was possible to exhaust state coffers by encouraging people to apply for benefits en masse. The state government thus would be forced to step in to "rescue" and reform the system by giving the government even more control and moving toward a socialized system.

The National Welfare Rights Organization, active from 1966 to 1975, sought to implement this strategy after President Lyndon B. Johnson's War on Poverty was underway. From 1965 to 1974, the number of single-parent families receiving benefits surged from 4.3 million to 10.8 million — more than doubling. In 1970, 28 percent of the annual budget of New York City was spent on welfare expenses. From 1960 to 1970, the number of people receiving benefits in New York City rose from 200,000 to 1.1 million. "By the early 1970s, one person was on the welfare rolls in New York City for every two working in the city's private economy," journalist Sol Stern wrote in the City Journal. In 1975, the city effectively went bankrupt. [39]

The Cloward-Piven example in New York can be regarded as another implementation of Alinsky's theories, specifically that radicals should "make the enemy live up to its own book of rules." In the case described, where anyone eligible for welfare was entitled to receive it, the tactic was to hold the "enemy" to their word, with the aim of causing its bankruptcy without any need for hostile action by the radicals.

W. Cleon Skousen wrote in his book *The Naked Communist* that one of the forty-five communist goals is to "capture one or both of the political parties in the United States." The Communist Party saw that this could be achieved using a small number of people and organizing them to create "crises" and "revolutions" that could be used to the Party's advantage. Lenin once said that labor unions are "the transmission belts from the Communist Party to the masses." [40] The communists found that as long as they controlled labor unions, they controlled a large number of votes. As long as they controlled the votes, they could make elected officials and lawmakers do their bidding. Ordinary workers are forced to join the labor unions in order to maintain their basic rights and interests, and thus they become the unions' pawns. An identical principle is at work when paying protection fees to organized crime syndicates.

Loudon, the Florida-based communism expert, explains how communist entities use unions and other groups as conduits to implement their policies and hijack democratic countries.

First, the foreign or local communist entity sets its agenda, e.g., strengthening labor legislation, implementing a more socialist school curriculum, or relaxing trade sanctions on Cuba. Second, the communists and their socialist allies adopt these policies as union policies. The unions then put pressure on the local Labor Party, Socialist Party, or Democratic Party to adopt these union policies as their own. "As labor [unions] effectively control these major parties, the process is often not that difficult," Loudon wrote in 2014. Thus, as communist policies become union policies, they in turn become "mainstream" political party policies. "This process has been carried out countless times all over the world," Loudon wrote. [41]

Communists and those who ignorantly act on their behalf have worked to subvert the political and social systems of free societies in any way they can. After decades of communist planning and operations, the governments and the societies of the United States and other Western countries have been severely eroded.

8. Political Correctness

Communist countries have always exercised strict control over speech and thought. Since the 1980s, another form of such control has appeared in the West, as "thought police" use the banner of "political correctness" to run amok in the media, society, and education system, using slogans and mass criticism to restrain speech and thought. Although many have recognized the inherent wrongness of this control, they have not grasped its ideological origins.

Terms such as "political correctness," together with "progress" and "solidarity," have long been used by communist parties. Their superficial meaning is to avoid using language that is discriminatory toward minorities, women, the disabled, and others. However, the hidden implication behind political correctness is the classification of individuals into groups according to their status as victims. Those who are deemed to be the most oppressed should be accorded the most respect and courtesy. This judgment, rendered solely on one's identity and disregarding individual conduct and character, is the basis of what's called "identity politics." This style of thinking is extremely popular in the United States and other Western countries today.

This type of classification is identical to what occurred in China, where individuals were classified within the "five classes of red" or the "five classes of black" according to their wealth and class status before the revolution. The CCP eliminated and oppressed landowners and capitalists because of their "wrong" class status, attacked intellectuals as the "Stinking Old Ninth," and chanted that "the poor are the smartest; the nobles are the dumbest."

The differences in political and socioeconomic status between various groups stem from complex historical reasons and cannot be simply explained as oppression. But political correctness sets up a flat binary: only those who show sympathy for the designated "victims" and disdain for "oppressors" are to be considered moral, while those who deviate from the narrative are accused of being racist, sexist, homophobic, Islamophobic, and so on.

Political correctness has been pushed by many Western governments and NGOs to further a left-wing agenda. In some countries, the legal definition of "hate speech" has been expanded significantly and punishments for such speech are now enforced throughout schools, the media, and social media. [42] These blanket restrictions on free speech move democratic societies closer toward the thought control exercised by communist states.

These days, the Left abuses political correctness to deprive others of having a legitimate outlet for their voices. This became more pronounced after the 2016 US presidential election, with left-leaning media, organizations, and academics mobilizing to deplatform and silence supporters of President Donald Trump. Protest marches erupted in major cities, and violations of freedom of speech occurred with greater frequency. Universities, which are supposed to be bastions of free thought and expression, have become centers of radical indoctrination. Organizations acting under the banner of opposing hate speech have labeled regular conservative groups as "hate groups," and conservative authors and scholars have been threatened after being invited to speak at or attend various events. [43]

In March 2017, American social scientist Charles Murray was invited to speak at Middlebury College in Vermont. As he attempted to speak, the more than four hundred protesters crowding the room jeered and shouted, preventing him from being heard. Later, as he was leaving the campus, protesters swarmed him and an accompanying professor, pushing and shoving them. The professor was taken to the hospital for a neck injury.

In September 2017, a scheduled appearance by conservative author Ben Shapiro at the University of California–Berkeley's Free Speech Week met with threats of violence by the far-left extremist group Antifa. Dozens of Berkeley police officers stood ready in riot gear as police helicopters hovered overhead; the security measures were estimated to have cost more than $600,000. [44] Ironically, one signature event that marked the start of the student movement in 1964 was a fight for freedom of speech at Berkeley. The next month, when Shapiro was scheduled to speak at the University of Utah, a student group vowed to shut down the event. A reporter pointed out to the young leader of the group that preventing Shapiro from speaking wouldn't agree with the First Amendment. The student replied, "I don't care. I don't think that's a, like, relevant document right now." [45]

In March 2018, tenured professor Amy Wax of the University of Pennsylvania School of Law was relieved of some teaching duties after she voiced a politically incorrect observation during an interview with a professor from Brown University. Wax said black students "rarely" graduate at the top of the class. [46]

The political correctness and restrictions on free speech championed by the Left are not intended to foster healthy debate between differing viewpoints; they are ideological weapons used by those acting in bad faith. Political correctness is the communist specter's "thought police" for suppressing dissent and obscuring the truth.

9. Socialism Across Europe

All of Europe — not just the countries of Eastern Europe — is dominated by communism. Non-communist countries in northern, southern, and Western Europe are all intentionally or unintentionally promoting and hosting communist ideologies and policies. To say Europe is "in enemy hands" is not an exaggeration.

Socialist International is the largest international political organization in the world, consisting of more than 135 political parties and organizations. The organization grew out of the Second International, founded by Engels in 1889. The early socialists included people like Karl Johann Kautsky and Eduard Bernstein, who promoted progressive reform. When the Second International was established, there existed more than one hundred political parties around the world that were founded on Marxism. Of them, sixty-six were ruling parties that adhered to socialism in their respective countries. The name "Socialist International" originated in 1951.

Today, many socialist parties that descended from the Second International exist all over Europe, with many of them ruling their respective countries.

The Party of European Socialists, established in 1992, is active in the European Parliament and is associated with the Socialist International. Its members are the social democratic parties of the EU and surrounding countries, including the United Kingdom. Its members can be found in most leading European organizations, including the European Parliament, the European Commission, and the European Council. The Party of European Socialists currently has thirty-three member parties, as well as twelve associate members and twelve observers, for a total of fifty-seven political parties from across the European Union, the United Kingdom, and Norway. Its main objectives are to "shape progressive European policies" and to develop close cooperation between member parties, parliamentary groups, and the like. Essentially, it works to vigorously promote the socialist cause.

The guiding principles of the United Kingdom's Labour Party are based on Fabian socialism. As previously discussed, Fabian socialism is simply another version of Marxism, one that stresses using gradual methods to effect the transition from socialism to communism. It also advocates high taxes, high welfare benefits, and other socialist ideas. The Labour Party has been the ruling party of the United Kingdom many times in recent decades and has always advocated Fabian socialist ideas.

Britain's communist party and its various iterations also have been very active in trying to influence British politics, even sponsoring its own newspaper, *Daily Worker* (renamed *Morning Star* in 1966). The Party grew from the Communist Party of Great Britain, established in 1920, and during its peak, its members were elected to the House of Commons. At the start of the 2017 general election in the United Kingdom, the Communist Party of Britain suddenly announced that it intended to support the leader of the left-wing Labour Party. This politician, who has headed the Labour Party since September 2015, has spent forty years promoting socialist policies, including the nationalization of assets. When a BBC reporter enquired about his views on Marx, he praised him as a great economist and a "fascinating figure who observed a great deal and from whom we can learn a great deal."

The Swedish Social Democratic Party, the ruling party of Sweden, is a member of the Socialist International. During the several decades under its rule, it has promoted the socialist ideologies of equality and welfare. One of France's Socialist Party leaders was elected president in 2012. The Party also is a member of the Socialist International and the Party of European Socialists. In Italy, veteran communist Gramsci not only founded the Italian Communist Party in 1921, but also served as its general secretary. Up until the 1990s, the Italian Communist Party was very active, for years maintaining its position as the country's second-largest political party. In 1991, the party was renamed the Democratic Party and is now part of the ruling coalition. Other European countries, like Spain and Portugal, have active communist political parties with significant influence. Germany is no exception; it is the birthplace of Marx and Engels, and home to the Frankfurt School.

10. Falling for the Devil's Tricks

Everywhere communism goes, it is accompanied by violence, lies, war, famine, and dictatorship. The question is, why do so many people still wholeheartedly help this devil spread its lies, even becoming its obedient and fanatical tools?

American sociologist Paul Hollander, in his 1981 book *Political Pilgrims: Travels of Western Intellectuals to the Soviet Union, China, and Cuba,* tells the stories of many young intellectuals enamored with communism. These young "pilgrims" were naturally shown none of the horrifying abuses taking place at the same time as their visits. Upon returning to their countries, they enthusiastically sang the praises of the communist system. [47]

In the United States, people have been attracted to or coerced into supporting communism for a variety of reasons. Many of the early leaders and members of the CPUSA were immigrants from Russia and Eastern European countries. Their economic status was low, and it was difficult for them to assimilate. Mainly due to influences from their homelands, they joined the Party.

After the Great Depression, the influence of Marxism in the West dramatically increased, and almost the entire intellectual class in the West began to take a leftward turn. Numerous intellectuals went to visit the Soviet Union and, after returning home, gave speeches and wrote books promoting communist ideology. Those involved included many influential thinkers, writers, artists, and reporters.

The baby boomer generation entered college during the 1960s, after growing up in post-war affluence, yet they were misled by communist-inflected ideologies into taking up other countercultural stances, in the form of anti-war protests, feminism, and the like. The next generation of students was taught left-leaning material right out of their textbooks because their teachers were the "tenured radicals" — thus communism's long march through the institutions had finally succeeded, beginning a cycle intended to reproduce and maintain itself forever.

In the book *Masters of Deceit*, FBI Director J. Edgar Hoover, whose tenure ran thirty-seven years, classified communist supporters into five levels of thought control: open Party members (card-carrying tools of the Party), underground Party members (those who act as covert influencers for the communist agenda), fellow travelers (those who are not Party members, but often choose to supplement Party work), opportunists (those who support the Party out of self-interest), and dupes (innocent victims who don't know they're under communist thought control). [48] In reality, there are very few extremely evil and die-hard communist activists. It's much more the case that the majority of people controlled by communist thought were simply taken in by it.

American journalists John Silas Reed and Edgar Snow played major roles in promoting communist ideology around the world. Reed, author of the book *Ten Days That Shook the World,* is one of three Americans buried in the Kremlin Wall Necropolis, meaning that he himself was a communist activist. His description of the October Revolution was not an objective reporting of the actual events, but rather carefully crafted political propaganda.

Snow, author of the book *Red Star Over China,* was a communist fellow traveler whose glowing portrayal of the CCP leadership left a deep impression on many Americans. In 1936, he traveled to the CCP stronghold of Bao'an, in the northern province of Shaanxi, and conducted interviews with Mao Zedong about the revolutionary cause. Snow was used as a propaganda tool by the CCP to broadcast its narrative to an international audience.

Bezmenov, the former KGB spy, recalled his job of receiving foreign "friends" when he worked as a spy. The visitors' schedule was partially arranged by the Soviet Foreign Intelligence Service; visits to churches, schools, hospitals, kindergartens, and factories were all prearranged. Everyone the visitors met was a communist or a politically trustworthy person who had undergone training to ensure he or she would speak with the voice of the Party. In 1967, the major American magazine *Look* sent journalists to the Soviet Union to cover a story. Talking about the journalists' articles, Bezmenov said, "From the first page to the last page, it was a package of lies: propaganda cliché[s] which were presented to American readers as opinions and deductions of American journalists. Nothing could be [further] from [the] truth." Soviet propaganda was thus distributed to the American public by a US magazine.

Bezmenov said that many journalists, actors, and star athletes could be excused for being blind to reality while visiting the Soviet Union, but the behavior of many Western politicians was unforgivable. These morally corrupt individuals wove lies and sought cooperation with Soviet communists for their own reputation and profit, he said. [49]

In the book *You Can Still Trust the Communists ... to Be Communists*, Schwarz analyzed why young intellectuals became fond of communism. He listed four reasons: disenchantment with capitalism; belief in a materialist philosophy of life; intellectual pride; and an unfulfilled religious need. Intellectual pride refers to the experience of young people, from the ages of about eighteen to twenty, who easily fall prey to communist propaganda due to their partial understanding of history, their arrogance and anti-authoritarian resentment, and their disenchantment with family and national heritage. "An unfulfilled religious need" refers to the fact that everyone has a kind of spiritual impulse inside them, driving them to transcend themselves. However, atheism and the theory of evolution instilled by their education make these young people unable to derive satisfaction from traditional religions. The communist fantasy of liberating mankind takes advantage of this latent human need and serves as their ersatz religion. [50]

Intellectuals tend to be fooled by radical ideologies. Such a phenomenon has drawn the attention of scholars. In the 1955 book *The Opium of the Intellectuals*, French philosopher and sociologist Raymond Aron pointed out that while on one hand, twentieth-century intellectuals severely criticized the traditional political system, on the other, they generously tolerated or even turned a blind eye to the dictatorship and slaughter in communist states. He saw the left-wing intellectuals who turned their ideology into a secular religion as hypocritical, arbitrary, and fanatical. British historian Paul Johnson analyzed the lives and radical political views of Jean-Jacques Rousseau and a dozen intellectuals who followed him, in his book *Intellectuals: From Marx and Tolstoy to Sartre and Chomsky.* He found that they all shared the fatal weaknesses of arrogance and egocentrism. [51]

Since the 1960s, communism has engaged in a large-scale invasion of American education. On top of that, many young people indulge in television, computer games, the internet, and social media. They get turned into "snowflakes," people who lack knowledge, a broad perspective, a sense of responsibility, a sense of history, and the ability to cope with challenges. With communist or communist-derived ideologies instilled in them by their parents' generation, they become indoctrinated and henceforth use a warped framework for evaluating the new facts they see and hear. That is, communist lies have formed a film around them, preventing them from having a clear view of reality.

The communist specter exploits both negative and positive human emotions to lure people into its snares. While the specter's key agents and representatives are driven by traits like selfishness, ambition, and greed, communist ideology appeals to its true followers' heartfelt desire for idealism, altruism, and self-sacrifice.

That so many people can be seduced by the lies of socialism and communism is due to humankind's abandonment of spiritual belief and its now disordered moral standards. Only through righteous faith and moral elevation can humanity safeguard itself against the specter's demonic manipulation.

CHAPTER SIX

The Revolt Against God

THE PEOPLES OF THE WORLD have their own ancient myths and legends about how the divine created man in the image of the divine. These traditional beliefs are the foundation of morality and culture for their people and leave a path of return to Heaven for those who believe. In the East and the West, there are legends about how Nüwa and Jehovah created their people.

The divine calls on man to follow their commandments or else face divine retribution. In times of widespread moral decay, the divine destroys man in order to preserve the purity of the universe. Many races in the world have legends about great floods that destroyed civilizations. The legendary Atlantis was said to have been lost to the sea overnight.

To maintain the morality of human beings, there are times when enlightened beings or prophets are born in the human world to rectify people's hearts and lead civilizations to develop and mature. Such sages include Moses and Jesus of the Near East, Lao Tzu in

China, Shakyamuni in India, and Socrates in ancient Greece.

Human history and culture help people to understand what Buddhas, Taos, and gods are; what it means to believe in God; and how to practice spiritual cultivation. The different schools of practice provide standards for how to distinguish truth from falsehood and good from evil. They teach humanity to await the Creator's return to Earth before the end of the world, so that people may be saved and return to Heaven. Once people sever their connection with the deities that created them, their morality will quickly deteriorate. Moral corruption leads to the destruction of culture and civilization, and ultimately humankind itself.

In the East, especially in the ancient land of China, beliefs are rooted in the hearts of people through traditional culture, handed down through the millennia. Therefore, it is difficult to deceive the Chinese people into accepting atheism with simple lies. In order to uproot China's five thousand years of beliefs and culture, the communist specter used violence on a mass scale to slaughter the elites of society who had kept these traditions alive from generation to generation. The Chinese Communist Party also launched multiple campaigns to destroy traditional Chinese beliefs and heritage, replacing these with its atheistic communist culture.

In the West and other parts of the world, religions and faith are the means of maintaining contact between man and the divine, and are important cornerstones for maintaining moral standards. Although the evil specter has not established communist tyranny in these countries, it has achieved its goal of destroying orthodox religions and corrupting human beings through deception, deviance, and infiltration.

1. In the East: A Violent Revolt Against God

a. The Soviet Union's Violent Destruction of Orthodox Faith

The Communist Manifesto calls for the destruction of the family, the church, and the nation-state. Eliminating and subverting religions is one of the important goals of the Communist Party.

From believing in God to becoming a follower of Satan, Karl Marx clearly knew about the existence of the divine and the devil. He also knew that unvarnished demonic teachings were hard for people — especially religious people — to accept. Therefore, he advocated atheism from the start, declaring that "religion is the opium of the people," "communism begins from the outset with atheism," and so on. [1]

As long as people no longer believe in the divine, the devil can corrupt and occupy the soul, eventually dragging people toward hell. That is why the "Internationale," the communist anthem, insists that there are no supreme saviors — not God, nor human rulers — on which to depend. Marx vilified religion and the divine in his theories, while Vladimir Lenin was able to use the machinery of the state to attack religion after seizing power in 1917. Lenin used violence and other high-pressure tactics to oppress orthodox religions and righteous faith in order to force people to depart from gods.

In 1919, Lenin introduced a new Party program that included the large-scale elimination of religion. Then, in 1922, he passed a secret resolution stipulating that all valuables including precious stones must be removed from churches and religious institutions "with ruthless resolution, leaving nothing in doubt, and in the very shortest time." He declared: "The greater the number of representatives of the reactionary clergy and the reactionary bourgeoisie that we succeed in shooting on this occasion, the better because this 'audience' must precisely now be taught a lesson in such a way that they will not dare to think about any resistance whatsoever for several decades." [2]

In the following years, a large amount of church property was looted, churches and monasteries were closed, and an unknown number of Orthodox and Catholic clergy members were executed.

After Lenin died, Joseph Stalin followed his example and started an extremely cruel cleansing in the 1930s. Stalin ordered that the whole country implement the Five-Year Plan of Atheism. He declared that when he completed the plan, the last church would be closed, the last priest would be executed, and the Soviet Union would become a fertile land for communist atheism — one would not find a trace of religion anywhere. In the 1930s, hundreds of thousands of clergy members were arrested and tortured to death. By 1941, there were just 4,225 Orthodox churches open to the public; there had been more than 46,000 before the Soviets seized power. Ninety-seven percent of Orthodox monasteries were destroyed or closed, leaving just 37. During this period, cultural elites and intellectuals were sent to the gulag or shot.

During World War II, to take advantage of the church's financial resources and manpower in the fight against Nazi Germany, Stalin seemed to pause in his persecution of Orthodoxy and Catholicism, giving the impression that he might rehabilitate these religions. But his actions were motivated by simple opportunism: to exercise strict control over the restored Orthodox and Catholic churches as a tool to undermine religious faith by placing the clergy under the management of the Communist Party. Religion was thus made a tool of the communist specter for deceiving and controlling the public, especially believers whose traditional faith was too strong to be destroyed by overt persecution.

Alexy II, of the former Soviet Union, was promoted to bishop of Tallinn and Estonia in 1961, archbishop in 1964, and metropolitan in 1968. He became patriarch of the Orthodox Church in 1990, before the Soviet Union's disintegration. Following the Soviet collapse, the briefly declassified KGB archives revealed that Alexy II had worked for the intelligence agency.

Later, Alexy II confessed that he had been compromised and had acted as a Soviet agent. He openly repented, in a 1991 interview with the daily newspaper *Izvestia*: "Defending one thing, it was necessary to give somewhere else. Were there any other organizations, or any other people among those who had to carry responsibility not only for themselves but for thousands of other fates, who in those years in the Soviet Union were not compelled to act likewise? Before those people, however, to whom the compromises, silence, forced passivity or expressions of loyalty permitted by the leaders of the church in those years caused pain, before these people, and not only before God, I ask forgiveness, understanding, and prayers." [3]

The Soviet Union did not keep this adulterated religion merely to its own territory, but spread its malignant influence to the rest of the world.

b. The Chinese Communist Party's Destruction of Culture and Religion

The Destruction of Traditional Chinese Culture

China has the world's oldest surviving civilization, with continuous historical records reaching back five thousand years. Known as the "Celestial Empire," its splendid and magnificent traditional culture earned the esteem of many nations. Chinese culture deeply influenced the entire East Asian region and led to the formation of a Chinese civilizational sphere. The opening of the Silk Road and the spread of China's Four Great Inventions (papermaking, the compass, gunpowder, and printing) to the West helped accelerate the development of European civilization.

Although Chinese faith is not characterized by a single predominant religion as is often the case in other countries, the Chinese people have a firm belief in gods and Buddhas, and religious beliefs are the foundation of China's traditional culture. Confucianism, Buddhism, Taoism, and even Western religions have coexisted peacefully in China for thousands of years.

Communism sought to destroy this ancient culture, but it could never achieve this goal by simply deceiving the Chinese people into giving it up. Therefore, upon coming to power, the CCP used all manner of evil tactics over decades of persistent political campaigns, starting with mass slaughter. The CCP persecuted religious practitioners, worked to undermine and distort the orthodox teachings of traditional faiths, and destroyed their material culture, such as temples, cultural relics, antique paintings, and ancient artifacts.

Throughout the history of communist rule in China, incessant political campaigns, persecutions, and mass killings have given the Party an unparalleled understanding of how to use propaganda, terror, economic coercion, and other tactics to bring and keep people under its power. In destroying traditional culture, the CCP established a malicious Communist Party culture that has poisoned generations of Chinese.

Steeped in the evil characteristics of the CCP — deception, perniciousness, and struggle — millions of Chinese have lost all understanding of the universal values built up over millennia of civilization. This was the communist specter's twisted arrangement, made in preparation for the final confrontation in our world between the forces of righteousness and evil.

The landlords and gentry in rural areas and the merchants and scholars in urban areas were the elites carrying China's traditional culture. In the early stages of the CCP's seizure of power in 1949, the Party used a series of campaigns to massacre landlords, gentry in villages, and capitalists in cities, thus plundering social wealth while creating terror. At the same time, the Party subjected scholars to "ideological transformation" — indoctrinating them with materialism, atheism, and the theory of evolution — to systematically brainwash a new generation of students and instill in them hatred and contempt toward traditional culture.

Through the Anti-Rightist Movement in the 1950s, all disobedient intellectuals were exiled and sentenced to re-education through forced labor, casting them to the bottom of society. The Party made scholars the subject of mockery and ridicule. The eradication of the traditional elites ended the process of inheriting and passing on traditional Chinese culture over the generations. Young people at the time were no longer socialized and nurtured in that culture through the family, the schools, the society, or the village — and thus became a generation without traditional culture.

After the Anti-Rightist Movement, few independent voices remained, yet the CCP was still not satisfied. After all, the elderly still preserved the memory of traditional culture, and material objects, such as ancient artifacts and architecture, were everywhere. Moreover, art still carried traditional values.

In 1966, the CCP initiated the Cultural Revolution, a devastating movement aimed at destroying traditional culture on a nationwide scale. Using students who had been brainwashed after the establishment of the People's Republic of China, the Party stirred up adolescent restlessness and rebelliousness and used the campaign of Destroying the Four Olds (old customs, old culture, old habits, and old ideas) to wreak havoc.

The unbridled brutality of the campaign raged across the land of China. Monasteries, temples, cultural sites, and Buddhist statues and paintings were destroyed beyond hope of restoration. Before the Cultural Revolution, every city and town in China was rich with ancient artifacts. Just one foot under the ground lay many items from recent history; down another two, three, or twenty feet, countless artifacts left by preceding dynasties could be found. The campaign not only ruined the sites of religious practice, prayer, and cultivation — ancient places that represented the harmony between man and Heaven — but also went about purging basic principles of ancient wisdom from the hearts of the Chinese people, such as the belief in harmony between man and the cosmos.

Furthermore, to cut off the Chinese people's connection to their ancestors and gods, the CCP took the lead in cursing the ancestors and defiling traditional culture. Countries around the world usually revere their ancestors and kings of the past, and value their traditions. Yet in the CCP's eyes, the great emperors, valiant generals, talented scholars, and famed beauties of ancient China were good for nothing. Making such insults toward one's own ancestors is indeed a rarity throughout history. Led by the CCP, the Chinese people came to oppose the divine, reject their ancestors, and destroy their own culture, putting them on a perilous path.

Persecuting Religions

After the CCP obtained power, it followed the Soviet Union's approach to eradicating religions. On one hand, the CCP promoted atheism and launched ideological attacks against religious beliefs. On the other hand, through a series of political movements, it suppressed and killed religious practitioners. The persecution of those with orthodox faiths became more and more severe, until it reached a peak with the bloody persecution of Falun Gong (also known as Falun Dafa) starting in 1999.

Shortly after seizing power in 1949, the CCP banned religious gatherings and burned numerous copies of the Bible and scriptures from other religions. It demanded that Christians, Catholics, Taoists, and Buddhists register with the government and repent their "mistakes." Those who refused to comply were severely punished. In 1951, the CCP declared that those who continued to attend religious gatherings would be executed or imprisoned for life. Numerous Buddhist monks were chased away from temples or forced to live and labor in secular settings. Catholic and Christian priests were jailed and tortured. Believers were executed or sent to be "reformed" through forced labor. According to incomplete statistics, within the first few years of the CCP's rise to power, nearly three million religious followers and members of religious organizations were arrested or executed.

Like the Communist Party of the Soviet Union (CPSU), the CCP established regulatory agencies for each religious group, such as the Chinese Taoist Association, the Buddhist Association of China, and the like. To control Catholics, the CCP established the Chinese Patriotic Catholic Association. All religious associations were made to follow the will of the Party, which "thought-reformed" members. At the same time, the CCP used these associations to perform deeds that could not be done by the evil specter directly: to sow discord and corrupt orthodox religions from within.

Similarly, after dispatching troops to occupy Tibet in 1950, the CCP began its severe repression of Tibetan Buddhism. The 14th

Dalai Lama escaped Tibet in 1959 to live in exile in India, which the CCP considered a rebellion. In May 1962, the 10th Panchen Lama submitted to the CCP's State Council a petition describing the Party's sabotage of Tibetan culture and Buddhist traditions, carried out by the Chinese army:

As for the eradication of Buddhist statues, Buddhist scriptures and Buddhist stupas, basically speaking, apart from a very small number of monasteries, including the four great monasteries which were protected, in Tibet's other monasteries and in the villages, small towns and towns in the broad agricultural and animal herding areas, some of our Han cadres produced a plan, our Tibetan cadres mobilized, and some people among the activists who did not understand reason played the part of executors of the plan.

They usurped the name of the masses and put on the face of the masses, and stirred up a great flood of waves to eliminate statues of the Buddha, Buddhist scriptures and stupas, threw them into water, threw them onto the ground, broke them and melted them. They recklessly carried out wild and hasty destruction of monasteries, Buddhist halls, "mani" walls and stupas, and stole many ornaments from statues of the Buddha and precious things from the Buddhist stupas.

Because the government purchasing bodies were not careful in making distinctions when purchasing non-ferrous metals, they purchased many statues of the Buddha, stupas, and offering vessels made from non-ferrous metals, and showed an attitude of encouraging the destruction of these things. As a result, some villages and monasteries looked as if they were not the result of man's deliberate actions, but rather they looked as if they had been accidentally destroyed by bombardment, and a war had just ended, and they were unbearable to look at.

Furthermore, they unscrupulously insulted religion, using the "Tripitaka" as material for fertilizer, in particular using pictures of the Buddha and Buddhist sutras to make shoes. This was totally unreasonable. Because they did many things that even lunatics would hardly do, people of all strata were thoroughly shocked, their emotions were extremely confused and they were very discouraged and disheartened. They cried out, with tears flowing from their eyes: "Our area has been turned into a dark area," and other such piteous cries. [4]

After the start of the Cultural Revolution in 1966, many lamas were forced to turn secular, and numerous precious scriptures were burned. By 1976, out of the 2,700 monasteries originally in Tibet, only 8 were left. Jokhang Temple, built more than 1,300 years ago and the most important temple in Tibet, was ransacked. [5]

In China, the cultivation of Taoism has an ancient history. More than 2,500 years ago, Lao Tzu left behind the Tao Te Ching, which contains in five thousand Chinese characters the essence of Taoist cultivation. Taoism's influence was not limited to China or the East; the Tao Te Ching has been translated into dozens of languages and provided spiritual inspiration for many people around the world. Yet during the Cultural Revolution, Lao Tzu was criticized as hypocritical and the Tao Te Ching was deemed "feudal superstition."

The core beliefs of Confucianism are benevolence, righteousness, the moral disposition to do good, proper conduct, wisdom, and trust. Confucius set the moral standards for generations. During the Cultural Revolution, the rebels in Beijing led the Red Guards to Qufu, Confucius's hometown, where they desecrated and burned ancient books, and smashed thousands of historical tombstones, including that of the great teacher himself. In 1974, the CCP started another movement to "Criticize Lin Biao, Criticize Confucius." The CCP considered the traditional thinking of Confucianism — how one should live and the moral standards to uphold — to be worthless.

However, the most brutal and tragic of the CCP's campaigns against Chinese faith is the ongoing persecution of Falun Gong.

In 1999, an estimated one hundred million people were practicing Falun Gong, which teaches the principles of truthfulness, compassion, and tolerance. Then-CCP leader Jiang Zemin saw the spiritual practice as an existential threat to communism; that July, he mobilized the PRC's well-developed security forces and propaganda machine against Falun Gong, beginning a campaign of a scale and intensity not seen since the Cultural Revolution.

The persecution of Falun Gong boosted Jiang's political authority and allowed him to place his allies in positions of power and profit. Jiang's brutal policies against Falun Gong, and the corruption he encouraged, laid the foundations for the CCP's modern resurrection of totalitarianism and threw China into an unprecedented moral freefall.

Furthermore, to this day, the Party has carried out a crime that has never before existed on the planet — the harvesting of organs from living Falun Gong practitioners.

In only a few decades, the CCP devastated thousands of years' worth of China's traditional culture, moral values, and beliefs in self-cultivation. As a result, people no longer believe in gods, turn away from the divine, and experience the pain of spiritual emptiness as moral corruption takes hold.

2. In the West: Infiltrating and Weakening the Church

The communist specter has made systematic arrangements for

attacking religious believers in noncommunist countries. Through the CPSU and the CCP, it used money and spies to infiltrate the religious institutions of other countries under the pretext of "religious exchange," in order to warp righteous beliefs or directly attack them and introduce socialist and communist ideologies into religion. Believers continued to worship and practice in religions that had been irrevocably altered by communist ideology.

a. Infiltrating Religion

In the United States, Marxists infiltrated Christian churches and entered the seminaries, miseducating class after class of priests and pastors, who then went on to influence religion on a broader scale throughout the country.

In testimony given before the Committee on Un-American Activities in July 1953, high-level Communist Party member Manning Johnson said:

> *Once the tactic of infiltrating religious organizations was set by the Kremlin, the actual mechanics of implementing the "new line" was a question of following the general experiences of the living church movement in Russia, where the Communists discovered that the destruction of religion could proceed much faster through infiltration of the church by Communist agents operating within the church itself. ...*
>
> *In general, the idea was to divert the emphasis of clerical thinking from the spiritual to the material and political — by political, of course, is meant politics based on the Communist doctrine of conquest of power. Instead of emphasis towards the spiritual and matters of the soul, the new and heavy emphasis was to deal with those matters which, in the main, led toward the Commu-*

nist program of "immediate demands." These social demands, of course, were of such a nature that to fight for them would tend to weaken our present society and prepare it for final conquest by Communist forces. [6]

Bulgarian historian Momchil Metodiev, after extensive research into the Cold War-era archives of the Bulgarian Communist Party, exposed the fact that the Eastern European communist intelligence network closely collaborated with Party religious committees to influence and infiltrate international religious organizations. [7]

On a global scale, one organization that was infiltrated by communism in Eastern Europe was the World Council of Churches (WCC). Established in 1948, the WCC is a worldwide interchurch Christian organization. Its members include churches of various mainline forms of Christianity, representing around 590 million people from 150 different countries. The WCC is thus a major force in world religious circles. It also was the first international religious organization to accept communist countries as members during the Cold War and to accept financial support from them.

Based on a released KGB file from 1969, Cambridge University professor and historian Christopher Andrew wrote that during the Cold War, five KGB agents held seats on the WCC Central Committee, exerting covert influence on the committee's policies and operations. A released KGB file from 1989 shows that these KGB-controlled agents ensured that the committee issued public communications that aligned with socialist aims. [8]

In 1975, Russian Orthodox bishop Nikodim (birth name Boris Georgievich Rotov), metropolitan of Leningrad, was elected as one of the WCC's six presidents. A veteran KGB agent, Nikodim served three years in the position, until his death in 1978. [9]

Another victory was the election of Bulgarian communist spy Todor Sabev as deputy general secretary of the WCC in 1979. Sabev served until 1993.

Knowing how the Eastern European communists infiltrated and manipulated the churches, it is not difficult to understand why the WCC insisted on giving grants to the Zimbabwe African National Union-Patriotic Front (ZANU-PF) in January 1980, despite the opposition of its members. The ZANU-PF, a communist terror group in what was then Rhodesia, was notorious for murdering missionaries and shooting down commercial aircraft.

The WCC also was infiltrated by the CCP through the China Christian Council. Due to monetary and other influences, the WCC has for years gone along with the CCP's interests. The general secretary of the WCC officially visited China in early 2018 and met with several Party-controlled Christian organizations, including the China Christian Council, the National Committee of Three-Self Patriotic Movement of the Protestant Churches in China, and the State Administration for Religious Affairs. In China, the membership of non-official Christian groups (known as house or underground churches) far exceeds that of official groups, yet WCC delegates didn't arrange to meet with any non-official Christian groups, in order to avoid friction with Beijing.

b. Restricting Religion

Communist infiltration is omnipresent in the West, and religions have been buffeted by ideologies and behaviors that vilify God. Ideas like "separation of church and state" and leftist "political correctness" have been used to marginalize and sabotage righteous, orthodox religions.

The United States was built as one nation under God. All US presidents, when sworn in, put one hand on the Bible and ask God to bless America. Nowadays, when religious people criticize behaviors, ideas, and policies that depart from the divine, or when they speak out against abortion or homosexuality, communists in the United States or the militant Left go on the offensive. They use "separation of church and state" to say that religion should have nothing to do with politics, and so seek to restrict divine will and the traditional moral standards laid out for humankind.

For thousands of years, divine beings have made themselves known to those who have faith. People with righteous beliefs accounted for the majority of society in the past and had a tremendously positive influence on social morality. Today, people can only talk about God's will in church. Outside of church, they are largely prevented from criticizing or resisting the broad societal trend against religious teachings and wisdom. Religion has almost lost its function in maintaining the morality of society, and as a result, morality in the United States has collapsed like a landslide.

In recent years, political correctness has been promoted to new heights, to the point where people are hesitant to say "Merry Christmas" in a country that was founded on Christianity, because some claim that it's politically incorrect and hurts the feelings of non-Christians. Similarly, when people openly speak of their belief in God or pray to God, some claim it is discriminatory against people with other beliefs, including nonbelievers. The fact is, all people should be allowed to express their beliefs, including respect for their gods, in their own ways, and this has nothing to do with discrimination.

In schools now, classes that involve righteous beliefs and traditional values are not allowed to be taught. Teachers are not to speak of Creation, since science has yet to prove the existence of the divine.

Science also has yet to prove atheism and evolution — but these ideas are taught in schools as truth or near-truth.

The communist specter's infiltration of society, and its restraints against and manipulation of religion, culture, education, the arts, and the law, is an exceedingly complex and systemic issue.

3. Communism's Twisted Theology

In the past century, various distorted theologies gained currency as communist thought swept through the religious world, subverting clergy and infiltrating and subtly corrupting orthodox religions. Clergy shamelessly interpreted the scriptures according to their whims, distorting the righteous teachings left by enlightened beings. Especially in the 1960s, "revolutionary theology," "theology of hope," "political theology," and other distorted theologies saturated in Marxist thought sowed chaos in the religious world.

Many Latin American priests in the past century were educated in European seminaries and were deeply influenced by the new theological theories that had been altered by communist trends. "Liberation theology" was prevalent in Latin America during the 1960s to 1980s. Its main representative was the Peruvian priest Gustavo Gutiérrez.

This school of thought introduced class warfare and Marxian thought directly into religion, and it interpreted God's compassion for humanity to mean that the poor should be liberated — and, thus, that religious believers should take part in class warfare in order for the poor to attain equal status. It used the Lord's instruction for Moses to lead the Jews out of Egypt as the theoretical basis for the belief that Christianity should liberate the poor.

Liberation theology was greatly praised by Fidel Castro, the leader of the Cuban communist regime. Although the traditional Catholic

Church has resisted the proliferation of these so-called emerging theologies, the new pope, appointed in 2013, invited Gutiérrez to attend a press conference in the Vatican on May 12, 2015, as the main guest, thus showing the present-day Catholic Church's tacit acquiescence and support of liberation theology.

In various parts of the world, many emerging theologies similar to liberation theology have appeared, such as "black liberation theology," "feminist theology," "liberal theology," "queer theology," and even "Death of God theology." These distorted theologies have greatly disrupted Catholic, Christian, and other orthodox beliefs around the world.

In the United States in the 1970s, Jim Jones, the leader of the infamous Peoples Temple of the Disciples of Christ, who called himself the reincarnation of Lenin, set the original teachings of Marxism-Leninism and Mao Zedong Thought as his cult's doctrine. He claimed that he was proselytizing in the United States in order to achieve his communist ideals. After killing American congressman Leo Ryan, who was investigating allegations against the cult, Jones knew that it would be difficult for him to escape, so he cruelly forced his followers to commit mass suicide. He even killed those who were unwilling to commit suicide with him. In the end, more than nine hundred people died. The cult tarnished the reputation of religious groups and adversely affected the righteous faith people had in orthodox religions. Thus, it had a serious negative impact on the American people in general.

4. Religious Chaos

The book *The Naked Communist*, published in 1958, lists forty-five goals for communists in their mission to destroy the United States. Astonishingly, most of the goals have already been achieved. Number twenty-seven in the list states: "Infiltrate the churches and replace revealed religion with 'social' religion. Discredit the Bible. ..." [10]

For thousands of years, religion has been an important cornerstone of the Western world, yet in recent generations, the communist specter has twisted this sacred institution beyond recognition. The three orthodox religions in particular — Christianity, Catholicism, and Judaism (together referred to as the revealed religions) — have been altered and controlled by the communist specter, and they have lost the functions they had in their original forms. New denominations, established or demonically altered with communist principles and concepts, have become even more direct promulgations of communist ideology.

In today's churches, many bishops and priests preach deviated theology while corrupting and consorting with their followers in a nonstop series of scandals. Many believers go to church for habit's sake, or even as a form of entertainment or socializing, rather than out of genuine commitment to cultivating their character or coming closer to God.

Religions have been corrupted from within. The result is that people lose their confidence in religions and their righteous belief in the divine, and end up abandoning them. If man does not believe, then the divine will not protect him and, ultimately, humankind will be destroyed.

In 2002, *The Boston Globe* carried a series of reports on the sexual molestation of children committed by Catholic priests. The investigation revealed that over several decades, close to 250 Boston priests had molested children, and that the church, in an attempt to cover it up, had shifted these clergy members around from one area to another, rather than informing the police. The priests continued to molest children in their new locations, thus creating more victims.

Similar revelations quickly spread across the United States and extended to priests in other countries with a Catholic presence, including Ireland, Australia, and so on. Other religious groups began to publicly denounce the corruption of the Roman Catholic Church.

Eventually, public pressure compelled Saint John Paul II to gather the cardinals for a conference in the Vatican to address the scandals. Following the meeting, he stated that the administrative structure of the church would be reformed and that it would expel priests who had committed sexual offenses. To date, the church has paid more than $2 billion in settlements for such abuses.

Religious corruption is rife in other Christian denominations and in other faiths around the world. In China, official religious groups are prone to the same malfeasance found throughout the Party-state. Monks and Taoist priests have turned religion into a business, rampantly embezzling money from believers by taking advantage of their faith in Buddhas and traditional Chinese deities. Fees for religious ceremonies and incense burnings can run into the tens of thousands of dollars. Temples in China have turned into commercialized tourist sites, where monks earn salaries and Buddhist and Taoist abbots preside as CEOs.

More churches and temples have been built, looking all the more splendid on the surface, while righteous belief in gods diminished. Disciples who genuinely cultivate are harder and harder to find. Many temples and churches have become gathering places for evil spirits and ghosts.

The five Party-sanctioned religions in China have been converted into organizations to distort the original faiths and serve the Party's atheist ideology. Buddhism in China has lost its character as a community for spiritual cultivation. It is full of politician-monks who praise the CCP and take it as their deity.

The deputy chairman of China's Buddhist Association, referring to the report of the Chinese Communist Party's Nineteenth Congress, said, "The Nineteenth Congress Report is the contemporary Buddhist scripture, and I have hand-copied it three times." He also stated, "The Chinese Communist Party is today's Buddha and Bodhisattva, and the Nineteenth Congress report is contemporary Buddhist scripture in China, and it shines with the glowing rays of the Communist Party's belief." Other monks called upon Buddhist believers to follow the deputy chairman's example and apply the method of hand-copying scriptures to copy the Nineteenth Congress report with a "devout heart" so that they could experience enlightenment. [11]

For more than a thousand years, bishops around the world were directly appointed or recognized by the Vatican. The thirty or so bishops previously recognized by the Vatican in the Chinese region have not been acknowledged by the CCP. Likewise, the Vatican and the Catholics loyal to it in China (particularly the underground believers) have not acknowledged the Communist Party-appointed bishops. However, following a long period of coercion and enticement by the CCP, in 2018, the pope recognized seven CCP-appointed bishops, who previously had been excommunicated by the Vatican. Critics believed that the move to share the church's authority with a totalitarian regime would set a dangerous precedent that could affect the rest of the world. The church is a faith community whose purpose is to enable believers to uplift their morality, come closer to God, and ultimately return to Heaven. When deals are done in the human world with an evil specter in revolt against God, where the CCP is allowed to arrange and appoint bishops and thus take charge of matters concerning the belief of tens of millions of Catholics in China, how would God look at the matter? What will the future hold for the tens of millions of Catholics there?

In China, the specter of communism created a political abomination that destroyed traditional culture and crushed faith through mass murder and terror. The CCP's atheistic persecutions and destruction of tradition aim to forcibly sever human connections to the divine, and they have brought about China's moral collapse.

In the West and other parts of the world, deception and infiltration have led to the corruption and demonization of upright religions, confusing and misleading people into giving up their orthodox beliefs. In its rebellion against the divine, the specter of communism acts as the devil ruling our world. If humanity continues to lose its knowledge of and connections to the divine, man will fall further under the specter's control until there is no longer hope for salvation.

CHAPTER SEVEN

The Destruction of the Family

THE FAMILY IS THE BUILDING BLOCK of human society, allowing people not only to raise children in a stable and nurturing environment, but also to pass the knowledge of one generation to the next. Marriage is a sacred institution arranged by the divine for humanity to form families, preserving traditional heritage and morality.

Today, the traditional family is being slowly destroyed. The writings of Karl Marx and other communists describe the family as a form of private ownership to be abolished. In addition to persecuting religion and spiritual faith, communist regimes place love for the Communist Party above love for even one's own parents, spouse, or children, encouraging people to struggle against their own kin.

Since the 1960s, a variety of anti-traditional movements, including modern feminism, "sexual liberation," and gay rights, have risen to prominence in the West. The institution of the family has been

hit the hardest. Under the banners of equality and emancipation —
implicitly and explicitly backed by modern laws, school curricula,
academic theory, and economic policies — these movements are
twisting the traditional bonds between the sexes, corrupting children, and dragging human behavior to previously unimaginable
lows. This trend, which surfaced at the beginning of the nineteenth
century, is deeply infused with communist ideological factors. Friedrich Engels ultimately hoped for widespread "unconstrained sexual
intercourse," with the aim of dissolving traditional marriage and
ultimately eliminating the family institution. [1]

Communism excels at continuous mutation and deception, which
has led to constant confusion about what exactly people are supporting when they endorse its policies and ideologies. Over time, they
come to accept communism's underlying ideas. The tragic situation today — the degradation of the traditional family and people's
confusion about the true nature of this trend — is the result of
meticulous planning and the gradual implementation of communism over the past two hundred years.

Laws passed in the United States and other countries have opened
the floodgates to divorce and broken families. In the 1950s, about
11 percent of American children born in a married family saw their
parents divorce; by 1970, that number had soared to 50 percent. [2]
In 1956, less than 5 percent of newborn infants in the United States
were born out of wedlock, according to the US Centers for Disease
Control and Prevention (CDC). By 2016, the figure was close to 40
percent. [3][4]

In traditional societies in both the East and the West, chastity
in relations between men and women was considered a virtue.
Today, it's thought to be outmoded and oppressive. Premarital sex
and homosexuality, which were regarded as shameful and aber-

rant for thousands of years in traditional societies, are not only increasingly normalized, but are sometimes explicitly promoted by today's educators and the public school system. Children are being hypersexualized and exposed to deviant sexual concepts and pornography at ever earlier ages. As things stand, communism's goal to destroy the family will become reality long before it fulfills its elusive promise of a classless society. The destruction of the family, a basic unit of social stability, also means the destruction of traditional morality established by the divine and of the role the family plays in nurturing the next generation within a framework of traditional culture.

1. Communism's Aim to Abolish the Traditional Family

In the traditional cultures of the East and the West, marriage was established by the divine and was considered to be arranged by heaven. Once formed, the bond of marriage could not be broken. Both men and women were created by the divine, in its image and equal before it. At the same time, the divine also made men and women different and established different roles for them in the family and in society.

In Eastern traditional culture, men are associated with the yang of the yin-yang relationship and thus are symbolically connected to the sun and the sky. It is a man's natural duty to continuously strive to make progress and shoulder the responsibility of taking care of the family. Women belong to the yin principle, which is symbolically connected to the earth, meaning they bear and nurture everything with great virtue. They should be yielding and considerate of others, and they have the duty to support their husbands and educate their children. Only when men and women work well in their respective roles can the yin and the yang be harmonized and children grow and develop in a healthy manner.

In Western religious belief, women are the bone of men's bones and flesh of their flesh. [5] A man must love his wife as though she were part of his own body, and if necessary, sacrifice himself to protect her. In turn, a woman should cooperate with and help her husband, making the couple an integral whole. Men are responsible for working hard and making a living to support the family, while women suffer in childbirth. All this stems from the different original sins people carry.

None of this is meant to imply that men are superior to women in ability or intelligence, as men's and women's talents manifest in different competencies. Attempts to eliminate differences between the sexes run counter to common sense and prevent both men and women from fulfilling their potential.

Families play the role of transmitting beliefs and morality, thus maintaining a stable and healthy society. Parents are the first teachers in children's lives. If children can learn traditional virtues such as selflessness, humility, gratitude, endurance, and more from their parents' words and deeds, they will benefit for the rest of their lives.

Traditional married life helps men and women grow together in their moral conduct, as it requires husbands and wives to temper their emotions and desires, and to treat each other with consideration and tolerance. Marriage is fundamentally different from casual romantic love. Human emotions are fickle; a relationship that can be formed and broken up at will is hardly distinguishable from a common acquaintanceship.

According to communism, however, the family unit is an obstacle to human liberation. Classical communism regards economic factors as key in determining the formation of familial relationships, and it requires the private family unit to be revolutionized into a form of public ownership.

The "liberation of mankind" is the fantastic delusion sitting at the heart of communist ideology. Communist thought holds that oppression is not merely economic or social, but ingrained in the very culture of a society. For communists, "liberation" thus means the destruction of cultural norms "imposed" by traditional social morality. In their view, the patriarchy of the traditional family structure oppresses women, and traditional sexual morality represses human nature.

Contemporary Marxism-derived theories, mixed with Freudian concepts, place sexual desire at the center of questions associated with the family. The common characteristic of these two ideologies is their denial of basic human morality and their worship of materialism and desire.

2. Communism's Promotion of Promiscuity

One of Marx's ideological forerunners was the Welsh socialist Robert Owen, known for his 1825 attempt to implement his vision of a "utopian" society in New Harmony, Indiana. In 1826, Owen said:

> *I now declare, to you and to the world, that Man, up to this hour, has been, in all parts of the earth, a slave to a Trinity of the most monstrous evils that could be combined to inflict mental and physical evil upon his whole race. I refer to private, or individual property — absurd and irrational systems of religion — and marriage, founded on individual property combined with some one of these irrational systems of religion.* [6]

Owen's time in New Harmony was short-lived; he left in 1828, abandoning his socialist experiment. But his ideas had lasting influence.

Another influential utopian socialist, French philosopher Charles Fourier, provided much inspiration for Marx and his followers. The influence of Fourier's writings could be seen in the revolutions of 1848 and the 1871 Paris Commune, and his ideas later spread to the United States. Significantly, Fourier is the first philosopher known to have used the term "feminism" ("féminisme" in French).

In Fourier's ideal communist society (known as phalanges, or phalanxes), the traditional family was rejected, and bacchanals and orgies were praised as fully liberating human inner passions. He also declared that a fair society should take care of those who are sexually rejected (such as the elderly or unprepossessing) to ensure that everyone has the "right" to sexual gratification. He believed that any form of sexual gratification, including sadomasochism and even incest and bestiality, should be allowed as long as it was consensual.

The influence of Owen and Fourier sparked dozens of communist utopian communes in the United States in the nineteenth century, most of which were short-lived and ended in failure. The longest-running was the Oneida Commune, which was established on the basis of Fourier's theory and lasted thirty-three years. The commune eschewed traditional monogamous marriage and advocated polygamy, group sex, and selective breeding. In the end, the founder, John Humphrey Noyes, fled to Canada to avoid legal action. Though the commune was forced to abandon wife-sharing, Noyes later wrote several books, one of which, "Bible Communism," started an ideology in its own right.

Communism's theoretical underpinnings go hand in hand with promiscuity. From the very beginning, communism has encouraged people to abandon divine teachings and reject tradition, over-throwing moral restraints and indulging in base urges, for the sake of revolution and liberation. By communist logic, social problems originally caused by the degeneration of human morality can be attributed to private ownership. Communism leads people to believe that if private property becomes public, people will not fight over it. However, even if all property were shared, people might still have conflicts over each other's spouses. Therefore, utopian social-ists openly advocate promiscuity and "free love" as the answer to sexual desire.

These communist "paradises" either directly challenged the traditional family or advocated a system of common wives, which led local communities, churches, and governments to see them as a challenge to traditional morality and ethics and to take action to suppress them.

The failure of utopian communes taught Marx and Engels a lesson: It was not yet the time to openly advocate the so-called "community of women" (that is, sexual relationships unrestricted by marriage) mentioned in *The Communist Manifesto*. Although their goal of eliminating the family had not changed, they adopted a more covert approach: attacking marriage as an instrument of oppression.

After Marx's death, Engels wrote *The Origin of the Family, Private Property, and the State, in the Light of the Researches of Lewis H. Morgan* to complete Marx's theory on the family and further expound the Marxian view of marriage. In it, he claimed: "[The emergence of monogamy] is based on the supremacy of the man, the express purpose being to produce children of undisputed pater-nity; such paternity is demanded because these children are later to come into their father's property as his natural heirs. It is distinguished from pairing marriage by the much greater strength of the marriage tie, which can no longer be dissolved at either partner's wish. As a rule, it is now only the man who can dissolve it, and put away his wife." [7]

Engels argued that monogamy was based around private property, and that once all property was shared, there would be a brand new model of marriage based purely on "sexual love." He boasted that in a communist society, private property would become public, housework would become professionalized, and there would be no need to worry about looking after children since childcare and education would be the responsibility of the state. He wrote: "This removes all the anxiety about the 'consequences,' which today is the most essential social — moral as well as economic — factor that prevents a girl from giving herself completely to the man she loves. Will not that suffice to bring about the gradual growth of unconstrained sexual intercourse and with it a more tolerant public opinion in regard to a maiden's honor and a woman's shame?" [8]

As with their economic theories, Marx and Engels's social ideology may appear cogent, but fails upon practical implementation. Feelings are unreliable; a person can love someone today and another person tomorrow. Without traditional norms of courtship and marriage, the inevitable result is sexual promiscuity and the breakdown of social order. Adding to the utopian communes mentioned above, the Soviet and Chinese communist regimes' initial attempts to apply Marxist doctrine in family policy ended in utter failure and were quickly reversed.

Relationships between husbands and wives aren't always smooth sailing. The vow "till death do us part" during a traditional wedding is a vow to God. It also represents the idea that both parties are prepared to face and overcome hardships together. What maintains a marriage is not merely emotion or feelings, but also a sense of moral and social responsibility. The need to treat one's other half well, as well as care for children and extended family, transforms husbands into mature men and wives into mature women.

What Marx and Engels promoted, despite buttressing it with phrases like "freedom," "liberation," and "love," was in fact nothing more than the abandonment of personal moral responsibility and the giving of oneself to desire.

Most people were still religious during the eras of Fourier and Marx and therefore wary of open attempts to promote sexual immorality. However, during the twentieth century and beyond, Marx himself could hardly have imagined the rationalizations that people would come up with to embrace the sexual chaos of Marxian thought and push forward the destruction of family and marriage.

3. Early Attempts at Sexual Liberation Under Communism

Today, authoritarian socialist regimes are often associated with strict social conservatism, including gender roles and marital laws that seem out of touch with Western liberal progressivism. However, such policies are not borne of a desire to preserve traditional culture or morality, but exist solely based on the communist regime's desire to turn love and familial relations into instruments of state power. In fact, at the beginning of communist rule in countries like Russia and China, Party leaders tried to implement the entire Marxist program at once, including disastrous experiments with sexual liberation.

As expounded previously, sexual chaos is an innate feature of communist ideology. Marx is believed to have raped his maid; he had Engels raise the resulting child. Engels cohabitated with a pair of sisters. Lenin carried out extramarital affairs for years and contracted syphilis from prostitutes. Stalin is known to have taken advantage of married women.

After the Bolsheviks seized power in Russia, they instituted the practice of wife-sharing. The Soviet Union at the time can be viewed as the pioneer of sexual liberation. In 1990, one year before the fall of the Soviet Union, state-run Russian magazine *Rodina* published an article outlining the phenomenon of wife-sharing during early Soviet rule. The piece described the private lives of Soviet leaders Leon Trotsky, Nikolai Bukharin, Alexandra Kollontai, and others, saying that they were "as casual as dogs" in their sexual activities. As early as 1904, Lenin wrote disparagingly of the situation, "Lust can emancipate the energy of the spirit; not for pseudo-family values, but for the victory of socialism must this blood-clot be done away with." [9]

At a meeting of the Russian Social Democratic Labor Party, Trotsky proposed that once the Bolsheviks seized power, new fundamental principles of sexual relations would be drafted. After the destruction of the family, communist theory demands there be a period of unconstrained satisfaction of sexual desires. Trotsky also said that the responsibility to educate children should reside solely with the state.

In a letter to Lenin in 1911, Trotsky wrote: "Undoubtedly, sexual oppression is the main means of enslaving a person. While such oppression exists, there can be no question of real freedom. The family, like a bourgeois institution, has completely outlived itself. It is necessary to speak more about this to the workers."

Lenin replied: "And not only the family. All prohibitions relating to sexuality must be abolished. ... We have something to learn from the suffragettes: Even the ban on same-sex love should be lifted." [10]

a. The Soviet 'Glass of Water' Theory

After the Bolsheviks seized power, Lenin rolled out a series of regulations effectively abolishing marriage and decriminalizing homosexuality. At that time, there was also the slogan "Down with shame!" This was part of the Bolshevik attempt to create the "New Man" of socialist ideology. Sometimes followers even roamed the streets naked, screaming slogans like "Shame is in the bourgeois past of the Soviet people." [11]

In the early 1920s, former People's Commissar for Social Welfare Alexandra Kollontai popularized the "glass of water" theory about sexuality. Kollontai was a revolutionary from a traditional family who fought her way into the Bolshevik faction in search of "women's liberation." "Glass of water" is an allusion to sexual indulgence; the theory held that in a communist society, quenching one's sexual desire should be as normal and easy as drinking a glass of water. The concept became widespread among factory workers and especially teenage students.

"The current morality of our youth is summarized as follows," the well-known communist Madame Smidovich wrote in the Communist Party newspaper *Pravda* in March 1925. "Every member, even a minor, of the Communist Youth League and every student of the Rabfak [Communist Party training school] has the right to satisfy his sexual desire. This concept has become an axiom, and abstinence is considered a bourgeois notion. If a man lusts after a young girl, whether she is a student, a worker, or even a school-age girl, then the girl must obey his lust; otherwise, she will be considered a bourgeois daughter, unworthy to be called a true communist." [12]

Divorce also became normalized and widespread. "The divorce rate skyrocketed to levels unseen in human history. In short order, it seemed as though everyone in Moscow had a divorce," professor

Paul Kengor noted in his 2015 book *Takedown: From Communists to Progressives, How the Left Has Sabotaged Family and Marriage.* [13] In 1926, the American magazine *The Atlantic* published an article about the astonishing situation in the USSR, with the headline "The Russian Effort to Abolish Marriage."

The phenomenon of "Swedish families" — which has nothing to do with Sweden, but instead refers to a large group of men and women living together and engaging in casual sex — also appeared during this period of sexual liberation. This opened the doors to promiscuity, rape, broken families, sexually transmitted diseases, and other symptoms of moral collapse. [14]

Following the expansion of socialist communes, these "Swedish families" spread across the Soviet Union. This was known as the "nationalization" or "socialization" of women. The socialist women in Yekaterinburg of 1918 are a sad example: After the Bolsheviks seized the city, they issued an ordinance that young women between the ages of sixteen and twenty-five must be "socialized." An unknown number of women were thus delivered to Red Army soldiers and civil officials to be "socialized." [15]

During a conversation with feminist activist Clara Zetkin in 1921, Lenin deplored the "glass of water" theory, calling it anti-Marxist and anti-social. [16] The reason for this was that sexual liberation brought about an undesirable byproduct: an influx of unwanted babies, many of whom were abandoned, as there were no means to care for them. The Bolsheviks tightened their policies on sex at the end of the 1920s.

The years following Lenin's death thus saw the Communist Party of the Soviet Union crack down on the sexual permissiveness which it had previously encouraged and sometimes made mandatory. Along with countless other idealistic believers in the revolutionary program, many communists who had championed free love and homosexuality ended up in Stalin's gulags. Soviet women were exhorted to resume their traditional roles as mothers, produce more children, and raise them to serve the Communist Party.

b. Sexual Liberation in the Chinese 'Soviet Regions'

The circumstances during the Chinese Communist Party's (CCP) early years were similar to those in the Soviet Union; communist parties are all varieties of poisonous fruit from the same tree. Chen Duxiu, an early communist leader, was known for his debauched personal life. According to the memoirs of Trotskyist cadres Zheng Chaolin and Chen Bilan, communists such as Qu Qiubai, Cai Hesen, Zhang Tailei, Xiang Jingyu, and Peng Shuzhi all had somewhat confused sexual histories, and their attitudes toward sex were similar to the "glass-of-waterism" of the early Soviet revolutionaries.

Sexual liberation was embraced not only by the Party's intellectual leaders, but also by ordinary people living in the CCP's early "Soviet regions," which were revolutionary enclaves set up in the provinces of Hubei, Henan, and Anhui during the time of rebellion against the Nationalist Party prior to Japan's invasion in World War II. Due to the promotion of equality of women and of absolute freedom to marry and divorce, revolutionary work was often disrupted in order to satisfy sexual desire.

Young people in the Soviet regions frequently indulged in promiscuous relations in the name of "connecting with the masses." It wasn't unusual for young women to have six or seven sexual partners. According to the *Collection of Revolutionary Historical Documents in the Hubei-Henan-Anhui Soviet Districts*, among local party chiefs in places like Hong'an, Huangma, Huangqi, Guangshan, and elsewhere, "about three-quarters of them had sexual relations with dozens or hundreds of women."

In the late spring of 1931, when CCP military commander and founding member Zhang Guotao took charge of a Soviet region, he noted that syphilis was so widespread that he had to make a request to Party Central for doctors who specialized in treating the disease. Many years later, in his memoirs, he vividly recalled stories of women in the enclaves being sexually harassed, including some of the senior generals' mistresses. [17]

During the 1930s, sexual freedom came to be perceived as a threat to the Chinese communist movement. The same problem of social disintegration found in Soviet Russia repeated itself: CCP Red Army conscripts began worrying that their wives would have extramarital affairs or divorce them once they joined the revolution. This impaired the combat effectiveness of the troops. Moreover, the sudden explosion of promiscuity created strong popular backlash against the idea of "common wives" and similar notions. The enclaves began implementing policies such as protecting military marriages and limiting the number of divorces.

4. How Communism Destroys Families in the West

Communism's ideological trends originated in the nineteenth century. After more than a century of transformation and evolution in the West, they came to the fore in the United States and other free countries in the 1960s.

During that decade, deviant social and cultural movements appeared, influenced and encouraged by neo-Marxism and various other radical ideologies. These included the hippie counterculture, the radical New Left, the feminist movement, and the sexual revolution. These turbulent social movements were part of a fierce attack on America's political system, traditional values system, and social fabric. They quickly spread to Europe, rapidly altering mainstream thought about society, the family, sex, and cultural values. This led to the weakening of traditional Western family values and the decline of the institution of the family and its centrality in social life. The resulting social turmoil brought a host of issues, including the proliferation of pornography, the spread of drug abuse, the collapse of sexual morality, the rise of the juvenile crime rate, and the expansion of groups dependent on social welfare.

a. Promoting Sexual Liberation

Sexual liberation (also known as the sexual revolution) saw explosive growth in the United States during the 1960s. The free love movement, which violates traditional sexual morality, paved the way for the gradual erosion and disintegration of traditional family values. The concept of "free love" posits that sexual activity of all forms should be completely unrestrained. In this view, marriage, abortion, and adultery should not be restricted by the government or by law, nor subject to social regulation.

Followers of Fourier and John Humphrey Noyes were the first to coin the term "free love." In recent times, almost all the main promoters of free love ideas have been socialists or people deeply influenced by socialist thought. For example, socialist philosopher Edward Carpenter was among those pioneering the free love movement in Britain and was an early activist for gay rights. The main forerunner of the free love movement in France was Émile Armand, an anarcho-communist in his early days who later built on Fourier's utopian communism, founded French individualist anarchism (which falls under the broader category of socialism), and advocated promiscuity, homosexuality, and bisexuality. The pioneer of the free love movement in Australia was John "Chummy"

Fleming, a unionist and a proponent of anarchism (another offshoot of socialism).

The free love movement in America bore fruit with the 1953 launch of erotic magazine *Playboy*. The magazine made use of glossy paper to create the impression that it was artistic and not seedy. It also used expensive color printing, with the result being that pornographic content — typically regarded as low-class and vulgar — swiftly entered the mainstream, and *Playboy* became a "high-class" leisure magazine.

In the middle of the twentieth century, with hippie culture increasing in popularity and free love gaining widespread acceptance, the sexual revolution made its official debut. The term "sexual revolution" was coined by Wilhelm Reich, the Austrian founder of communist psychoanalysis. He combined Marxism with Freudian psychoanalysis, believing that the former liberated people from "economic oppression," while the latter liberated people from "sexual repression."

Another founder of sexual liberation theory was Herbert Marcuse of the Frankfurt School. During the Western counterculture movement of the 1960s, his slogan "Make love, not war" embedded the notion of sexual liberation deep within people's hearts.

The notion of sexual liberation swept through the West with the best-selling Kinsey Reports — two books titled *Sexual Behavior in the Human Male* and *Sexual Behavior in the Human Female* — as well as the widespread availability of oral contraception. It is worth mentioning that contemporary scholars have discovered distorted statistical data in Alfred Kinsey's work, as well as exaggeration, oversimplification, and other fallacies driven by his political and ideological commitments. Kinsey set out to show that extramarital sex, homosexual sex, sexual desire in children as young as infants, and so on were common, and thus to direct society to accept the normalization of these phenomena, a task at which he was largely successful. He worked with pedophiles in his research and sexual experiments on infants and children. [18]

All at once, being "sexually liberated" became fashionable. Among young people, promiscuity was considered normal. Teens who admitted to being virgins were ridiculed by their peers. Data show that of those who turned fifteen between 1954 and 1963 (the '60s generation), 82 percent had premarital sex by the age of thirty. [19] By the 2010s, only 5 percent of new American brides were virgins, while 18 percent already had had ten or more sexual partners. [20] The cultural mainstream has become saturated with sex, as seen in advertising, literature, film, and television.

b. Promoting Feminism and Rejecting the Traditional Family

The Communist Ideology Behind the Feminist Movement

The feminist movement is another tool communism has used to destroy the family. When it began in Europe in the eighteenth century, the feminist movement (also known as first-wave feminism) advocated that women should be accorded the same treatment as men in education, employment, and politics. In the mid-nineteenth century, the center of the feminist movement shifted from Europe to the United States.

The arrangements made by communists during the first wave introduced a variety of radical ideas that paved the way for the anti-tradition, anti-marriage, and anti-family second- and third-wave feminism of the twentieth century.

When first-wave feminism began, the notion of the traditional family still had a strong foundation in society, and the feminist movement did not advocate challenging it directly. The influential feminists at that time, such as Mary Wollstonecraft of eighteenth-century England, Margaret Fuller of nineteenth-century America, and John Stuart Mill of nineteenth-century England, all believed that, in general, married women should prioritize the family, that the potential of women should be developed within the domain of the family, and that they should enrich themselves (for example, via education) for the betterment of the family. These early feminists advocated the relaxation of strict social norms so that women of particular talent would be free to develop their skills in environments where participation was mostly male.

First-wave feminism died down with the promulgation of women's suffrage in many countries, as the goal of making men and women equal before the law had been achieved. In the following years, with the impact of the Great Depression and World War II, the feminist movement was effectively put on hold.

But the specter of communism had begun far in advance to sow the seeds of destruction for traditional marriage and sexual ethics. The early utopian socialists in the nineteenth century laid the foundation for modern radical feminist movements. Fourier, called "the father of feminism," declared that marriage turned women into private property. Owen cursed marriage as evil. The ideas of these utopian socialists were inherited and developed by later feminists, including Frances Wright, who took on Fourier's ideas and advocated for women's sexual freedom in the nineteenth century. British feminist activist Anna Wheeler inherited Owen's ideas and fiercely condemned marriage for supposedly turning women into slaves. Socialist feminist activists were also an important part of the feminist movement in the nineteenth century. At that time, among the most influential feminist publications in France were *La Voix des*

Femmes, La Femme Libre (later renamed *La Tribune des Femmes*), and *La Politique des Femmes*. The founders of these publications were either followers of Fourier or of Henri de Saint-Simon, an advocate of modern industrial socialism.

The second wave of feminist movements began in the United States in the late 1960s, then spread to Western and Northern Europe, and quickly expanded to the entire Western world. American society in the late 1960s went through a period of turmoil, with the civil rights movement, anti-Vietnam War movement, and various radical social trends. Amid this unique set of circumstances, a more radical strain of feminism emerged and became popular.

The cornerstones of the second wave were the book *The Feminine Mystique* by Betty Friedan, published in 1963, and the National Organization for Women (NOW), which Friedan co-founded. Friedan fiercely criticized the traditional familial roles of women and argued that the classic image of a content and joyful housewife was a myth forged by a patriarchal society. She argued that the middle-class suburban home was "a comfortable concentration camp" for American women, and that modern educated women should reject the sense of accomplishment attained through supporting their husbands and educating their children, and instead realize their worth outside the family. [21]

A few years later, even more radical feminists dominated NOW, inheriting and developing Friedan's ideas. They said that women had been oppressed by patriarchy since ancient times, and attributed the root cause of women's oppression to the family. In response, they came to advocate the complete transformation of the social system and traditional culture as well as struggle in all areas of human affairs — the economy, education, culture, and the home — to achieve female equality. [22]

Classifying the members of a society into "the oppressors" and "the oppressed," in order to advocate for struggle, liberation, and equality, is exactly what communism does. Traditional Marxism classifies groups according to their economic statuses, while neo-feminist movements divide people based on gender.

Friedan was not, as her book described, an average middle-class suburban housewife bored with housework. In fact, Friedan, under her maiden name Betty Goldstein, had been a radical socialist activist from her college years up to the 1950s. While at the University of California–Berkeley, Friedan was a member of the Young Communist League and even requested, twice, to join the Communist Party USA (CPUSA). Friedan's authorized biographer, Judith Hennessee, also indicates that Friedan was a Marxist. At different times, she was a professional journalist — or, more accurately, a propagandist — for several radical labor unions in the orbit of the CPUSA. [23] [24]

American scholar Kate Weigand described in her book *Red Feminism: American Communism and the Making of Women's Liberation* how feminism in the United States gained strength between the early twentieth century and the 1960s. During that period, a large group of feminist writers with communist backgrounds paved the way for the subsequent second-wave feminist movement, including Susan B. Anthony, Betty Millard, and Eleanor Flexner. As early as 1946, Anthony applied the Marxist analytical method to draw an analogy between whites oppressing blacks and males oppressing females. McCarthyism during that period made such writers hide their communist backgrounds. [25]

In Europe, French writer Simone de Beauvoir's iconic 1949 work *The Second Sex* ushered in a craze for the second wave of feminism. De Beauvoir was a socialist, and in 1941, together with communist philosopher Jean-Paul Sartre and other writers, she founded the

French underground socialist organization Socialisme et Liberté. With the rise of her reputation for promoting feminism in the 1960s, de Beauvoir declared that she no longer believed in socialism and claimed that she was only a feminist.

De Beauvoir held that "one is not born, but rather becomes, a woman." She argued that while sex is determined by physiological characteristics, gender is a self-perceived psychological concept formed under the influence of human sociality. She believed that obedience, submissiveness, affection, and maternity are all derived from the "myth" carefully designed by the patriarchy for its oppression of women, and advocated that women break through traditional notions and realize their unrestrained selves.

Since then, various feminist thoughts have emerged in a constant stream, all looking at the world through the lens of women being oppressed by a patriarchy within the institution of the traditional family — ultimately making the family an obstacle to the realization of female equality. [26]

Many contemporary radical feminists hold that women are restrained by their husbands due to marriage, and even call the institution a form of prostitution. Like the early communist utopians who spoke of "shared wives" or the "community of women," they advocate "open relationships" and uninhibited sexual activity.

Results of the Feminist Movement

Feminism is now prevalent in all sectors of society. One major assertion of contemporary feminism is that apart from the physiological differences in male and female reproductive organs, all other physical and psychological differences between men and women are social and cultural constructs. By this logic, men and women should be completely equal in all aspects of life and society, and all manifestations of "inequality" between men and women are the result of a culture and society that is oppressive and sexist.

For example, the number of men working as executives in large companies, high-level academics in elite universities, or senior government officials far outstrips the number of women in similar positions. Many feminists believe this is primarily caused by sexism, when in fact a fair comparison between the sexes can be made only when considering factors such as ability, working hours, work ethic, life goals, and the like. Success in high-level positions often requires long-term, high-intensity overtime work — the sacrifice of weekends and evenings, attendance at sudden emergency meetings, frequent business travel, and so on.

Having children tends to interrupt a woman's career, and women are inclined to reserve time to be with their families and children instead of dedicating themselves completely to their work. In addition, people with the aptitude to fill high-level positions tend to possess strong and forceful personalities, whereas women tend to be more agreeable. However, feminists regard women's tendencies to be gentle and to orient themselves around family and children as traits imposed upon them by a sexist society. According to feminists, publicly funded services such as daycare and other forms of welfare should compensate for these differences.

Contemporary feminism cannot tolerate any explanation of the differences between men and women that is based on natural physiological or psychological qualities. According to this ideology, all blame must be laid at the feet of social conditioning and traditional values.

At a 2005 academic conference, Lawrence Summers, then-president of Harvard University, outlined why women are less likely than men to teach in the scientific and mathematics fields at top universities. In addition to highlighting the eighty-some hours per week and unpredictable work schedules required for these positions (which would cut into time most women reserve for family), Summers proposed that men and women may simply differ in their competence in advanced science and math, and that discrimination is no longer a barrier. [27] Summers supported his arguments with relevant studies but still became the target of protests by major feminist organization NOW. The group accused him of sexism and demanded his removal. Summers was roundly criticized in the media and forced to issue a public apology for his statements. He then announced that Harvard would dedicate $50 million to increasing the diversity of its faculty. [28]

In 1980, *Science* magazine published a study showing that male and female middle school students had substantial differences in their mathematical reasoning abilities, with boys outperforming girls. [29] A subsequent study that compared SAT math test scores found that male examinees were four times more likely than females to achieve a score higher than 600. This gap became even more extreme at the 700-point threshold, with thirteen times more male test-takers reaching such scores than females. [30]

The same research team conducted another study in 2000 and found that test takers who demonstrated mathematical genius in their SAT scores tended to obtain advanced degrees in science and math-related fields and were satisfied with their achievements, regardless of their gender. [31]

Some reports noted that Summers's treatment following his 2005 speech mirrors the re-education policies used by communist regimes to suppress dissidents. Even as the causes of inequality were yet to be determined, equality of outcome was enforced by encouraging "diversity" — that is, ensuring there was a larger number of female instructors in math and science subjects.

The links between feminism and socialism are readily apparent. Alexis de Tocqueville said in 1848: "Democracy and socialism have nothing in common but one word: equality. But notice the difference: While democracy seeks equality in liberty, socialism seeks equality in restraint and servitude." [32]

While the reasons for psychological and intellectual disparities between men and women may not be obvious, denying their physical and reproductive differences flies in the face of fact. In both Eastern and Western traditional views, men are protective figures. It's normal that firefighters, for example, are overwhelmingly male. However, feminists, believing in absolute equality between men and women, demand that women take on traditionally male duties, often with unexpected results.

In 2015, the New York Fire Department allowed a woman to become a firefighter without passing the physical test, which includes completing tasks while wearing an oxygen tank and other equipment weighing 50 pounds. The department hired the woman in part to avoid a lawsuit, as feminist groups had long blamed its high physical standards for the low proportion of women entering the firefighting force. Other firefighters, including women who had passed the test, expressed concerns about colleagues who couldn't meet the physical standards. They said such individuals would inevitably be a burden on, and a danger to, the team and the public. [33]

In Australia, fire departments implemented gender quotas in 2017. For each male hired, a woman must also be hired. To meet this requirement, vastly reduced physical standards have been set for women, despite that the dangerous, high-stress job is the same for both sexes. [34]

This illogical campaign for equality of outcome didn't stop there. The quotas created friction between male and female firefighters, who reported that their male coworkers blamed them for being unqualified and incompetent. Feminist groups latched onto this as "bullying" and "psychological pressure." The situation created yet another battle for feminists to fight in their ostensible crusade for equality.

But this absurdity is a deliberate step taken by the communist specter: By challenging the supposed patriarchy — that is, the traditional social order — feminism undermines the traditional family in the same way that class struggle is used to undermine the capitalist system.

In traditional culture, it is taken for granted that men are masculine and women are feminine. Men shoulder responsibility for their families and communities by protecting women and children — the very patriarchal structure that feminism challenges on the grounds that it confers unfair advantages to men while restraining women. Feminism has no place for the traditional spirit of chivalry or gentlemanly behavior. In a feminist world, the men aboard the sinking Titanic would not have sacrificed their places in the lifeboats so that the female passengers could have a better chance at survival.

Feminism's crusade against patriarchy has had a strong impact on education. A 1975 court ruling on a lawsuit against the Pennsylvania Intercollegiate Athletic Association ordered schools to allow female students "to practice and compete with boys" in sports teams and other physical activities, including wrestling and American football. Girls could no longer be excluded from a male team on the basis of gender alone. [35]

In the 2013 book *The War Against Boys: How Misguided Feminism Is Harming Our Young Men,* American scholar Christina Hoff Sommers demonstrates how masculinity is under attack by showcasing the example of Aviation High School in Queens, New

York, which primarily accepts students from low-income families. The school, which specializes in teaching its students about the structure and function of aircraft via hands-on projects, raises its students to high standards of academic achievement, and is ranked highly by *US News & World Report*. The class body is overwhelmingly male. Girls, while making up a smaller percentage of students, also perform remarkably and earn the respect of their peers and instructors.

Nevertheless, Aviation High School has faced a barrage of criticism and threats of lawsuits from feminist organizations demanding that more female students be admitted. Speaking at a roundtable discussion at the White House in 2009, the founder of the National Women's Law Center took specific aim at Aviation High School as an "egregious example of continuing segregation in vocational-technical schools." The chair of the White House Council on Women and Girls concluded the discussion by saying, "We are hardly going to rest on our laurels until we have absolute equality, and we are not there yet." [36]

For feminists, raising boys to pursue masculine traits of independence and adventure, and encouraging girls to be gentle, considerate, and family-oriented, amounts to nothing more than oppression and sexist inequality. Modern feminism is forcing society into a "gender-free" future by attacking the psychological characteristics of men and women that characterize their respective sex. This has particularly severe implications for children and young people who are in their formative years.

In some European countries, more and more children report feeling that they were born in the wrong body. In 2009, the Gender Identity Development Service, based at the Tavistock and Portman NHS Foundation Trust in London, received 97 referrals for sex transitioning. In 2017, the service received more than 2,500 such referrals. [37]

Traditional societies regard childbirth and the education of children as sacred duties of women, ordained by the divine. In the annals of both the East and the West, behind every hero was a great mother. Feminism discards this tradition as patriarchal oppression, and holds that expecting women to be responsible for raising their children is a key example of this oppression. Contemporary feminist literature is replete with denunciations of motherhood and married life as being monotonous, boring, and unfulfilling. The bias of this dim view is apparent when considering the personal lives of leading feminists, the majority of whom suffered from broken relationships or failed marriages, or were childless.

Radical feminist views insist that "the personal is political" and see domestic conflicts as gender wars. Some consider men parasites who enslave women's bodies and minds. Others describe children as a hindrance to women looking to reach their full potential and claim that the roots of oppression are in the family structure. Modern feminism openly proclaims that its aim is to destroy the traditional family. Typical statements include the following: "Being a housewife is an illegitimate profession. ... The choice to serve and be protected and plan towards being a family-maker is a choice that shouldn't be. The heart of radical feminism is to change that," [38] and, "We can't destroy the inequities between men and women until we destroy marriage." [39]

Feminist movements resolved supposed social problems by promoting moral degeneracy and destroying human relations in the name of "liberation." According to Sylvia Ann Hewlett, an American economist and gender specialist, modern feminism is the major contributing factor to the proliferation of single-mother households, while no-fault divorce actually provides a convenient means for men to abandon their responsibilities. Ironically, feminism's assault on the existing family structure works to destroy the haven that ensures the happiness and security of most women.

Easy divorce did not emancipate women. A 2009 study at the London School of Economics found that 27 percent of separated women were living below the poverty line, whereas a man's income tended to rise more than 30 percent post-separation. [40] Communism cares not at all about women's rights; feminism is merely a tool to corrupt humankind.

c. Promoting Homosexuality to Undermine the Family

Man and woman were created in divine likeness, and the divine laid out the conditions for human existence. Everyone deserves kindness and respect, and true compassion means upholding divinely established moral codes.

In recent decades, same-sex marriage and other lesbian, gay, bisexual, and transgender (LGBT) causes have been aggressively promoted throughout Western society. The LGBT movement has been closely associated with communism ever since the first utopians began touting the practice of homosexuality as a human right. Since the communist movement claims to emancipate people from the bondage of traditional morality, its ideology naturally calls for LGBT rights as part of its program of sexual liberation. Many proponents of sexual liberation who staunchly support homosexuality are communists or leftists. By tying together LGBT rights and sexual liberation, and thereby normalizing promiscuity in general, communists have undermined the sanctity of marriage.

Communism isn't genuinely interested in the rights of the LGBT community. It uses the vehicle of advocating for LGBT rights as a means to its own end — to destroy the family structure.

The world's first major gay rights organization was established in 1897 by members of Germany's Social Democratic Party (SPD), including Magnus Hirschfeld, the co-founder of the Scientific-Humanitarian Committee, known in German as the Wissenschaftlich-humanitäres Komitee (WhK). Hirschfeld publicly campaigned for the decriminalization of homosexuality.

One of the most radical examples of sexual liberation in that era followed the Bolsheviks' October Revolution in 1917. Soviet sexual policies, which were discussed earlier in this chapter, abolished legal prohibitions on homosexual relationships, making the Soviet Union the most liberal country on earth by leftist standards.

In 1924, inspired by Hirschfeld's WhK, Henry Gerber founded the first American gay rights organization, The Society for Human Rights. The organization disbanded the following year after several of its members were arrested. In 1950, American communist and Marxist teacher Harry Hay founded the Mattachine Society in his Los Angeles residence. The organization was the first influential gay rights group in the United States. It released its own publications and expanded to other cities. Hay also advocated for pedophilia.

In the 1960s, accompanying the wave of sexual liberation and the hippie movement, the homosexual cause went mainstream. In 1971, NOW adopted a resolution recognizing that "lesbian rights are 'a legitimate concern of feminism.'"

In 1997, the African National Congress (ANC) of South Africa passed the world's first constitution that recognized homosexuality as a human right. The ANC, a member of the Socialist International (formerly a branch of the now-defunct Second International), has consistently supported homosexuality.

Communism's advocacy for homosexuality has contributed to the growth of a number of unhealthy states in that community. A study by researchers at the CDC found that the estimated rate of diagnoses of HIV among homosexuals in 2008 was between 59 to 75 times that of other men; the syphilis diagnosis rate was 63 to 79 times higher than that of the heterosexual population. [41] Before breakthroughs in AIDS treatment were made in the 1990s, the average lifespan of 20-year-old homosexuals was eight to twenty-one years shorter than that of the average population. [42]

d. Promoting Divorce and Abortion

Before 1969, when states started to legalize no-fault divorce, state laws across the United States were based on traditional religious values. In order for a divorce to be considered, it required a legitimate claim of fault from one or both of the spouses. Western religions teach that marriage is established by God. A stable family is beneficial to the husband, wife, children, and society overall. For this reason, the church and US state laws all stressed the importance of preserving marriages, except in extenuating circumstances.

But in the 1960s, the ideology of the Frankfurt School had radiated out to the wider society. Traditional marriage came under attack, and the most damage was done by liberalism and feminism. Liberalism rejects the divine nature of marriage by reducing its definition to a social contract between two people, while feminism views the traditional family as a patriarchal instrument in the suppression of women. Divorce was promoted as a woman's liberation from the oppression of an unhappy marriage, or her path to a thrilling life of adventure. This mindset led to the legalization of no-fault divorce, allowing either spouse to disband a marriage as irreconcilable for any reason.

The US divorce rate grew rapidly in the 1970s and peaked in 1981. For the first time in American history, more marriages were being ended not by death but by disagreements. Advocates of sexual liberation believe that sex should not be limited to the confines of marriage, but unwanted pregnancy presents a natural obstacle to this sort of lifestyle. Contraceptives may fail, so the promoters of unrestricted sex took up the cause of legalizing abortion. The official report from the 1994 UN International Conference on Population and Development in Cairo stipulates that reproductive health "implies that people are able to have a satisfying and safe sex life and that they have the capability to reproduce and the freedom to decide if, when and how often to do so." [43]

At the same time, feminists introduced the slogan "My body, my rights" to argue that women have the right to choose whether to give birth to or kill their unborn children. The debate expanded from allowing abortion under special circumstances to giving women the power to end human life due to personal inconvenience.

By accepting abortion, people have been led to permit the murder of babies and, at the same time, abandon the traditional understanding that sex is for procreation.

e. Using the Welfare System to Encourage Single-Parent Families

In the early 1960s, relatively few children were born out of wedlock. At the time, it was taken for granted that children grew up knowing their biological fathers.

Just half a century later, unwed mothers accounted for more than a third of births. [44] From 1965 to 2012, the number of single-parent families in America shot up from 3.3 million to 13.2 million. [45] Though some fathers stayed involved, through cohabitation or later marriage, the majority of children born to these single mothers grew up without their fathers.

Fathers serve as role models to their sons, teaching them how to be men, and show their daughters what it feels like to be respected in the way women deserve. Children suffer greatly from the absence of a father; research shows that those who grow up without fathers often suffer from low self-esteem. They are more likely to drop out of school, abuse drugs, join gangs, commit crimes, and commit suicide. The majority of jailed youths come from fatherless homes. Early sexual experience, teen pregnancy, and promiscuity are also common. People who grow up without their fathers are 40 times more likely to commit sexual offenses compared with the rest of the population. [46]

The Brookings Institution offers three key pieces of advice for young people looking to escape poverty: graduate from high school, get a full-time job, and wait until age twenty-one to marry and have children. According to statistics, only 2 percent of Americans who meet these conditions live in poverty, and 75 percent are considered middle class. [47] In other words, that is the most reliable path toward becoming a responsible adult living a healthy, productive life.

Most single mothers rely on government aid. A report published by The Heritage Foundation used detailed statistical data to show that the welfare policy so strongly advocated by feminists actually encourages the creation of single-mother households, even to the point of penalizing couples who marry, as they are eligible for fewer benefits. [48] In many cases, the government has effectively replaced the father with welfare.

Welfare policies have not helped families living in poverty. Instead, they have simply supported an ever-increasing number of single-parent families. With the children of such households themselves prone to poverty, the result is a vicious cycle of expanding reliance on state aid. This is exactly what communism aims to achieve: control over every aspect of the individual's life.

f. Promoting Degenerate Culture

In 2000, 55 percent of Americans between the ages of twenty-five and thirty-four were married, and 34 percent had never been married. By 2015, these figures had flipped, with 40 percent married and 53 percent never married. Researchers studying this trend at the University of Texas–Austin found that young people in the United States were avoiding marriage because, in today's culture, sex has been largely separated from marriage. [49]

In this degenerate environment, the trend is toward casual, no-strings-attached hookups, in which sex has nothing to do with affection, let alone commitment and responsibility. Even more absurd is the profusion of new sexual orientations, which are now thrown around like fashion statements. Facebook's user-profile options in the United Kingdom, for example, at one point included more than seventy different genders. If young people can't even tell whether they are male or female, how will they view marriage? Communism has used the law and society to completely rework these divinely given concepts.

"Adultery" used to be a negative term referring to immoral sexual conduct. Today, it has been watered down to "extramarital sexual relations" or "cohabitation." In the classic 1850 novel *The Scarlet Letter* by Nathaniel Hawthorne, the protagonist, Hester Prynne, committed adultery and struggled to remake herself through repentance. But in today's society, repentance is not necessary: Adulterers can proudly enjoy life, holding their heads high. Chastity used to be a virtue in both Eastern and Western cultures; today, it is treated as an anachronistic joke. Passing judgment on homosexuality and sexual morality is forbidden under today's political correctness. The only acceptable stance is to respect others' "free choice." This is true not only in everyday life, but throughout academia, in which morality is divorced from practical reality. Deviated and degenerated behaviors have been normalized. Those who indulge in their desires feel no pressure or guilt.

Western people under the age of fifty can barely remember the culture that used to exist in society, in which almost all children grew up with the presence of their biological fathers. "Gay" meant "happy." White wedding gowns represented chastity. Pornographic content was banned from television and radio. All that has been undone in just sixty years.

5. How the Chinese Communist Party Destroys Families

a. Breaking Up Families in the Name of Equality

Mao Zedong's slogan "Women hold up half the sky" has now made its way to the West as a trendy feminist catchphrase. The ideology that men and women are the same, as promoted by the Chinese Communist Party, is essentially no different from Western feminism. In the West, "gender discrimination" is used as a weapon to maintain a state of "political correctness." In China, the label "male chauvinism" is used to similar destructive effect, though the specifics of its use differ.

The gender equality advocated by Western feminism demands equality of outcome between men and women through measures such as gender quotas, financial compensation, and lowered standards. Under the CCP's slogan that women hold up half the sky, women are expected to show the same ability in the same work as their male counterparts. Those who attempted to perform tasks for which they were hardly qualified were lauded as heroines and awarded titles such as March 8th Red Banner Holder, which is given to contemporary women who "vigorously promote socialist core values."

CCP propaganda posters in the 1960s and '70s typically portrayed women as physically robust and powerful, while Mao enthusiastically called on women to turn their love for makeup toward military uniforms. Mining, lumbering, steelmaking, fighting in the battlefield — every type of job or role was opened up to women.

On October 1, 1966, the People's Daily ran a story titled "Girls Can Slaughter Pigs, Too." It described an eighteen-year-old woman who became a local celebrity by working as a slaughterhouse apprentice. Studying Mao Zedong Thought helped her to work up the courage to slaughter pigs. She said, "If you can't even kill a pig, how can you expect to kill the enemy?" [50]

Although Chinese women "hold up half the sky," feminists in the West still find China's gender equality lacking in many areas. The CCP's Politburo Standing Committee, which currently has seven members, has never included a woman. For the CCP, to include a woman in its top decision-making body could encourage social activism demanding more political rights, thus posing a fatal threat to the Party's totalitarian rule.

Out of similar concerns, the Party also refrains from publicly supporting homosexuality and takes a relatively neutral stance on the issue. However, the Party has at times quietly encouraged homosexuality in China by using the influence of media and popular culture. For example, the media discreetly substituted the colloquialism "gay" with "comrade," a term with more positive connotations. In 2001, the Chinese Society of Psychiatry removed homosexuality from its list of mental disorders. In 2009, the CCP approved the first Shanghai Pride Week.

The approaches may vary, but the communist specter pursues the same goal everywhere: to abolish the traditional ideal of a good wife and loving mother, to force women to abandon their gentle character, and to destroy the harmony between men and women that is needed to create a balanced family and bring up well-adjusted children.

b. Turning Husbands and Wives Against Each Other

Traditional Chinese values are based on family morality. The devil knows that the most effective way to undermine traditional values is to start by sabotaging human relations. In the continuous political struggles launched by the CCP, family members reported each other to the authorities in a mad competition for a better political status. By betraying those closest to them, they could demonstrate a firmer, more loyal stance in favor of Party orthodoxy.

In December 1966, Mao's secretary Hu Qiaomu was dragged to the Beijing Iron and Steel Institute, where his own daughter took to the stage and shouted, "Smash Hu Qiaomu's dog head!" Although she did not take part, others did injure him. Around the same time, the Red Guards found a "capitalist" family in the Dongsi subdistrict of Beijing and proceeded to beat the parents to near-death, then force the middle-school-age son to smash in his father's skull with dumbbells. The boy went insane afterward. [51]

Often, those condemned by the Party as "class enemies" disowned their families so as to spare them from implication. Even "class enemies" who committed suicide would first have to break off family ties, lest the CCP hound their relatives afterward. For example, when the literary theorist Ye Yiqun was persecuted and driven to suicide in the Cultural Revolution, his parting letter to his family read, "Going forward, the only thing that is required of you is to resolutely listen to the Party's words, stand firm on the Party's position, gradually recognize my sins, stir up hatred against me, and unwaveringly break off our familial ties." [52]

In the modern era, the persecution of the spiritual practice Falun Gong is the largest political campaign launched by the CCP. A common strategy the authorities use against Falun Gong practitioners is to coerce their family members into aiding the persecution. The CCP imposes administrative harassment, financial penalties, and other forms of intimidation and leverage upon family members to get them to pressure practitioners into giving up their faith. The CCP blames the victims of persecution for the harassment their families endure, saying it only continues because the practitioners refuse to compromise their beliefs. Many Falun Gong practitioners have been divorced or disowned by their loved ones due to this form of persecution. Countless families have been torn apart by the Party's campaign.

c. Using Forced Abortion for Population Control

Shortly after Western feminists succeeded in the battle to legalize abortion, women in the People's Republic of China had mandatory abortions imposed upon them by the CCP's family-planning policies. The mass killing of the unborn has resulted in a humanitarian and social disaster on an unprecedented scale.

The CCP follows Marxist materialism and believes that childbirth is a form of productive action no different from steelmaking or agriculture. It thus follows that the philosophy of economic planning should be extended to the family. Mao said: "Mankind must control itself and implement planned growth. It may sometimes increase a bit, and it may come to a halt at times." [53]

In the 1980s, the Chinese regime began to enforce the one-child policy with extreme and brutal measures, as exhibited by slogans unfurled across the country: "If one person violates the law, the whole village will be sterilized"; "Birth the first, tie your tubes after the second, scrape out the third and fourth!" (A variation of this slogan was simply "Kill, kill, kill the third and fourth."); "We would rather see a stream of blood than a birth too many"; and "Ten more graves is better than one extra life." Such bloodthirsty lines were ubiquitous throughout China.

The National Health and Family Planning Commission used heavy fines, plunder, demolition of residences, assault, detention, and other such punishments to deal with violations of the one-child policy. In some places, family-planning officials drowned babies by throwing them into paddy fields. Even expecting mothers just days away from giving birth were forced to have abortions.

In 2013, the regime's health ministry published figures revealing that at least 336 million abortions had been performed in China since 1971. The one-child policy began in 1979, meaning that for the more than thirty years of its existence, at least several million unborn children were murdered by the CCP every year.

One of the most serious consequences of the one-child policy is the disproportionate number of female infants aborted or abandoned, leading to a serious imbalance in the male-to-female ratio of Chinese under the age of forty. Due to the shortage of females, it was estimated that by 2020, some thirty million young men would be unable to marry a woman of childbearing age.

China's man-made sex imbalance has triggered serious social problems, such as an increase in sexual abuse and prostitution, commercialized marriage, and the trafficking of women.

6. The Consequences of Communism's Assault on the Family

Marx and other communists played up phenomena like adultery, prostitution, and illegitimate children in order to lend credence to their anti-marriage and anti-family theories — as though the existence of such vices meant that the prevailing social norms were hypocritical and corrupt.

The gradual degeneration of morality that began in the Victorian era eroded the sacred institution of marriage and led people further away from divine teachings. Communists urged women to violate their marital oaths for the sake of their supposed personal happiness, but the result was just the opposite.

Communism's "solution" for oppression and inequality amounts to nothing more than dragging down the standards of human morality to hellish depths. It turns behavior once universally condemned as ugly and unforgivable into the new norm. In the "equality" of communism, all are marching toward the same fate — destruction.

The specter of communism created the mistaken belief that sin is not caused by the degeneration of morality, but by social oppression. It led people to look for a way out through turning their backs on tradition and moving away from the divine. It used the beautiful rhetoric of freedom and liberation to advocate feminism, homosexuality, and sexual perversion. Women have been stripped of their dignity, men have been robbed of their responsibility, and the sanctity of the family has been trampled upon, turning the children of today into the devil's playthings.

How Communism
Sows Chaos in Politics

COMMUNIST IDEOLOGY DID NOT FADE into history at the end of the Cold War; before and after the fall of the communist regimes in Eastern Europe, subversion has spread Marxist ideas throughout the free world, and left-wing movements have taken hold in many democratically elected governments. Superficially, the free world appears to understand the damage wrought by communism. Yet in the 170 years since the publication of *The Communist Manifesto*, governments around the globe have been openly or covertly influenced by Marxist theory.

Most people associate communist politics only with countries under the rule of communist parties, or where Marxist economic doctrines are openly followed. But in reality, Western leftism follows the same underlying philosophy of struggle embodied by the "traditional" communist regimes of the East. In some respects, the free world has even surpassed the self-avowed communist states when it comes to putting leftist causes into practice.

Even as America faced off with the Soviet threat during the Cold War, forms of communism found their way into almost every aspect of Western society under the guises of liberalism, progressivism, and socialism. The left wing has a strong foothold in the US political landscape and is dominant in many European countries. Thus, without bringing the Western world under its overt political control through war or violent revolution, the communist specter has co-opted the governance of Western nations by feeding social unrest, undermining traditional morality, and pushing socialist policies. Its aim is to set the West on a demonic path, bringing about the destruction of mankind.

The United States has been and remains a strong bastion of freedom and anti-communism. Given the vital role America plays on the world stage, it is crucial that we pay particular attention to communism's influence in US politics and government.

1. Communism: The Politics of Humanity's Destruction

For thousands of years, the main institution of political power was the monarchy, which received its authority from the divine. Heaven endowed the ruler with the divine right of kings. Emperors and kings performed a sacred role as intermediaries between man and the divine.

Today, many nations are run by democracies. In practice, democracy isn't direct rule by the people, but rather the rule of representatives *chosen by* the people. The election of a president is a democratic procedure. Once in office, the president has broad powers over politics, economics, the military, foreign relations, and so on.

Since the Declaration of Independence in 1776 and the drafting of the US Constitution during the following decade, democracy has been linked with freedom, prosperity, and individual rights. But the fundamental cornerstone of social stability and harmony, as well as human rights and freedom, is a society's moral values. Democracy alone cannot guarantee that good people will be elected. As the overall moral standard of society sinks, the winning candidates may well be those who specialize in empty or inflammatory rhetoric or are prone to cronyism. The damage to a democratic society is huge when it does not make provisions for maintaining the moral standards set by the divine. The advantages of electoral representation disappear and are subsumed into mob politics that throw society into chaos and fragmentation.

a. The Convergence of Politics and Religion in Communist Regimes

Communist ideology functions like that of a cult. It forces its followers to accept its malign philosophy of struggle, submit to its political programs, and betray their conscience in carrying out the directives of the revolutionary movement or party. Communist regimes persecute religion and spirituality with the cruelest means, so as to destroy the divine and replace traditional faith with communism's own atheistic religion.

The communist regimes of the East, especially that of the Chinese Communist Party, are often mistakenly described as a modern form of ancient despotism. Many see the CCP as having continued the imperial system. However, traditional Chinese monarchs did not claim to define moral values. Instead, they saw themselves as acting with restraint under moral standards set by gods or Heaven. The CCP, on the other hand, monopolized the very concept of morality.

No matter how many evils it commits, the CCP still insists that it is "great, glorious, and correct."

Universal standards of good and evil stem from divine commandment, not the ideological pretension of some political party. Monopolizing the right to define morality inevitably leads to the mixing of church and state, which, as in the case of the CCP and other communist parties, manifests as the typical features of a cult.

Communist parties enshrine Marx as their spiritual "Lord" and take Marxism as universal truth. Communism's promise of a heaven on earth lures its followers to lay down their lives for it. Its cult-like features include, but are not limited to, the following: inventing doctrine, crushing opposition, worshipping the leader, regarding itself as the sole source of righteousness, brainwashing and using mind control, running a tight organization that one can join but never leave, promoting violence and bloodlust, and encouraging martyrdom for the religious cause.

Communist leaders such as Vladimir Lenin, Joseph Stalin, Mao Zedong, and Kim Il Sung all had their own cults of personality. They were the "popes" of the communist cult in their respective countries, with unquestioned authority to determine right and wrong. Whether or not they killed and lied, they were always correct, which was justified by explanations that they were motivated by a higher purpose or that they were playing the long game. The citizens of these countries were made to abandon their own understandings of moral good. Being forced to lie or do evil under the Party's command brought people psychological and spiritual trauma.

Traditional orthodox religions teach people to be good, but the cult of communism, being built on hatred, takes the exact opposite stance. Though the Party also speaks of love, the "love" it advocates is predicated on hate. For example, proletarians are capable of class friendliness because they face a common hated enemy: the capitalists. In modern China, the way to show patriotism (literally "love of country" in Chinese) is to hate America, hate France, hate Japan, hate Korea, hate Taiwan, and hate overseas Chinese who criticize the CCP.

b. The Religious Character of Liberalism and Progressivism

Liberalism and progressivism have now become the standard of "political correctness" in the West. In fact, they have developed to the point of becoming a secular religion. Western leftists have used different labels throughout history, sometimes calling themselves "liberal" and sometimes calling themselves "progressive." Proponents of liberalism and progressivism advocate "progress" as absolute moral good and attack any dissenting opinion as heresy. Similar to communism, atheism, evolution, and scientism, liberalism and progressivism replace the belief in God with humanist reason, effectively trying to overthrow the divine. They have the same enemies as communism and blame social problems on perceived injustices or defects in the capitalist system, which they intend to subvert or overthrow. The methods of radical liberals and progressives are similar to those of communist revolutionaries. They think their cause is so important that no means are off-limits.

The quasi-religious characteristics of liberalism and progressivism are inseparable from the theories that gave rise to them. Rapid scientific progress since the eighteenth century greatly strengthened humankind's confidence in its own ability and fueled the progressive intellectual trend. French philosopher Marquis de Condorcet, a pioneer of progressive thinking, stated in his work *Sketch for a Historical Picture of the Progress of the Human Mind* that reason leads people to the path of happiness and morality or goodness. Following this, progressivism became more aggressive and began pushing reason onto the altar of worship.

Progressive thinking allows one to view reason, conscience, and the Creator as separate, fostering the idea that humans do not need the Creator's salvation and can use their own rationality and conscience to sweep away the evils of greed, fear, jealousy, and the like. In this view, humans can do away with the divine and establish a paradise on earth. The arrogance of progressivism is exhibited in a statement by nineteenth-century French politician and art critic Jules-Antoine Castagnary: "Beside the divine garden from which I have been expelled, I will erect a new Eden. ... At its entrance, I will set up Progress ... and I will give a flaming sword into his hand and he will say to God, 'Thou shalt not enter here.'" [1]

Filled with this kind of thought, people entertain an illusion of controlling humanity's destiny and manipulating its future — that is, playing God — to create a utopia. This is the essential idea of communism. The struggle to achieve this so-called paradise has caused a deluge of blood and misery.

c. Contemporary Liberalism and Progressivism: Variants of Communism

The Betrayal of Classical Liberalism

Classical liberalism, working from the philosophy of natural individual rights, advocated constitutional restrictions on the power of royalty or government so as to protect personal freedom. Individual rights and dignity are divinely bestowed, while a government is built by its citizens and has the express duty of protecting its people. Separation of church and state was established to prevent the government from infringing upon the thoughts and beliefs of the citizenry.

Contemporary liberalism is nothing other than the betrayal of classical liberalism in the name of "freedom," and it is the direct result of communist infiltration. On one hand, it emphasizes absolute individualism — that is, extreme indulgence in desires and disregard for morality. On the other hand, it emphasizes equality of outcome instead of equality of opportunity.

For instance, when discussing the distribution of wealth, modern liberals focus only on the needs of the recipients instead of the rights of taxpayers. When it comes to policies designed to address discrimination, they focus only on those who were historically wronged and ignore the people who become victims under these policies. In law, they obstruct the need to punish criminals for the ostensible purposes of protecting the innocent from unjust sentencing or of protecting the underprivileged, who are presumably victims of oppression. In education, they ignore the potential of talented students with the pretext of supporting and helping low achievers and those from underprivileged families. They use the excuse of free speech to lift restrictions on publishing obscene or pornographic material.

The focus of contemporary liberalism has silently evolved from advocating freedom to promoting equality. Yet it is unwilling to be termed "egalitarianism," as this would instantly brand it as a form of communism.

John Locke, known as the father of liberalism, stated his views on religious tolerance and the separation of church and state in his "A Letter Concerning Toleration." The main aspect of toleration as Locke envisioned it is that the state, which holds coercive power, must respect and tolerate the personal beliefs of the individual.

Whether one's belief in the path to Heaven is right or wrong is a matter to be left to divine judgment. One's soul should be under one's own control; the state should not use its power to impose belief or disbelief.

The tolerance that classical liberalism advocates is indeed a virtue deserving of promotion, but communism has appropriated "tolerance" as an avenue to moral corruption. Contemporary liberalism neglects the real purpose of toleration, transforming it into the absence of judgment. It developed the political concept of being "value-free," which in truth means losing one's moral bearings and confusing good with bad and virtue with evil. It uses an attractive phrase to open the floodgates to an onslaught of demonic concepts, pushing anti-morality and anti-tradition under the guise of freedom.

For example, now tolerance is often taken to mean the disproportionate defense of the LGBT movement, a typical manifestation of the value-free concept. Anyone who speaks out against the promotion of LGBT lifestyles risks being attacked under the pretext of safeguarding individual freedom and equality and of fighting discrimination against a minority group.

The Essence of Progressivism: Moral Relativism

Under the guidance of humanity's traditional values, it is normal to use our intelligence to improve our living conditions, increase wealth, and reach new heights of culture. In the "progressive era" of American history, from the late nineteenth century to the early twentieth century, governmental reforms corrected various corrupt practices that arose in the process of economic and societal development. But after communists infiltrated the United States, they hijacked terms such as "progress" and "progressivism" and infused them with their deleterious ideology. It was only logical for communism to hijack progressivism, though this was unbeknownst to most people. Modern-day progressivism is the direct application of Darwin's theories of evolution in social science, with the result being continuous deviation and perversion of traditional morality in the name of "progress." Even today, communism continues its open deception under the progressive banner.

During this progressive revolution, atheists viewed traditional morality as a hindrance to progress and demanded a reevaluation of all moral standards. They denied the existence of absolute moral standards and used society, culture, history, and the special conditions of the time to establish their system of relative morality.

Moral relativism is a core aspect of Marxist ideology. It holds that whatever conforms to the interests of the proletariat (the Marxist ruling class, in essence) is moral, while whatever does not conform is immoral. Morality is used not to regulate the actions of the proletariat, but as a weapon for the dictatorship of the proletariat to use against its enemies. In tandem with the progressive movement, this moral relativism has gained influence in politics, education, culture, and other aspects of Western society.

It is not wrong for people to seek happiness and progress, but when certain "-isms" begin to supplant traditional moral values and beliefs, they act as the tools with which the communist specter leads people toward degeneracy and destruction.

2. Bringing Government Under Leftist Control

In *The Communist Manifesto*, Marx and Engels list ten measures by which to destroy fair exchange and the rights of the individual, which they call capitalism. Many of these measures have already been implemented to move the United States and other countries progressively to the left and eventually establish communist political control, such as the creation of "a heavy progressive or graduated income tax" and the "centralization of credit in the hands of the state, by means of a national bank with state capital and an exclusive monopoly." On the surface, communists seem to advocate some positive things, such as the end of child factory labor and the creation of a free public education system. However, their goal isn't to ensure a nation's welfare, but rather to seize and maintain political power. Marx and Engels wrote:

> *The first step in the revolution by the working class is to raise the proletariat to the position of ruling class to win the battle of democracy.*
>
> *The proletariat will use its political supremacy to wrest, by degree, all capital from the bourgeoisie, to centralize all instruments of production in the hands of the State, i.e., of the proletariat organized as the ruling class; and to increase the total productive forces as rapidly as possible.*
>
> *Of course, in the beginning, this cannot be effected except by means of despotic inroads on the rights of property, and on the conditions of bourgeois production; by means of measures, therefore, which appear economically insufficient and untenable, but which, in the course of the movement, outstrip themselves, necessitate further inroads upon the old social order, and are unavoidable as a means of entirely revolutionizing the mode of production.* [2]

In America, the Left has spent decades fighting Marx's "battle of democracy" in order to control the levers of power and introduce socialism. Thus, while overt communist influences in the United States were relatively few during the twentieth century, the situation has since changed drastically.

In the 2016 and 2020 US elections, an openly socialist candidate came within reach of the presidency. Socialism, which, in communist vocabulary, is the "primary stage" of communism, was once viewed with scorn by most Americans. The candidate himself said he thinks there are a lot of people who get very nervous when they hear the word "socialist."

However, surveys conducted throughout the 2010s showed that roughly half of those born in the millennial generation (between 1980 and 1996) held a positive view of socialism. A 2018 Gallup poll showed that 57 percent of Democrats said they had a positive opinion of socialism. [3] This continues a trend seen in a 2011 poll by the Pew Research Center that showed 49 percent of US adults under the age of thirty viewed socialism positively, while 46 percent had a positive view of capitalism. [4]

The illusions that many in the West today hold about socialism mirror those of countless impressionable young people in the past century who once embraced communism in the Soviet Union, China, and elsewhere. Those belonging to the younger generation lack a deep understanding of their own history, culture, and traditions. Their resistance to socialism, which to them looks mild and humane, is nonexistent. The great communist deception of the twentieth century is repeating itself in the twenty-first.

Marx's axiom "From each according to his ability, to each according to his need" is quite effective for deceiving the young, who fantasize about a life of generous socialist welfare as seen in various parts of Europe. However, these countries' welfare systems have caused many social problems. Government-established welfare states are riddled with inherent weaknesses; there is no such thing as a free lunch. High levels of welfare are based on high taxation, which causes all manner of social ills. The Nordic model of socialist welfare was once considered a positive example of socialist prosperity to be imitated by the West, yet in Northern Europe, the tax rate-to-GDP ratio is among the highest in the world, with some countries' tax rates hovering at around 50 percent.

High-welfare socialism promotes the continuous expansion of government and leads people to vote away their freedoms. This is an important step in the specter's plans for enslaving humanity. When all or most countries make the transition to socialism, it takes but a few simple steps to replace democracy with totalitarianism. Once the socialist primary stage is completed, political leaders will immediately implement communism. Private property and the democratic process will be abolished. The welfare state will metamorphose into a yoke of tyranny. As American economist Milton Friedman said: "A society that puts equality — in the sense of equality of outcome — ahead of freedom will end up with neither equality nor freedom. ... On the other hand, a society that puts freedom first will, as a happy by-product, end up with both greater freedom and greater equality." [5]

The extent to which communism has subverted US politics is quite severe. To enter the political mainstream in the United States, communists must infiltrate one or both of the two major parties and use them to take control of congressional votes. Meanwhile, communist candidates must take up key positions in the government and the courts. A billionaire with a history of supporting left-wing movements has heavily funded leftist candidates to run for president of the United States and other important positions across the country. Key among these have been secretaries of state, who, in many states, are responsible for electoral affairs and play a critical role in resolving disputes. [6] In order to secure a stable voting block, US leftist parties have magnified the animosity between low-

and high-income groups, while attracting an increasing number from "vulnerable" groups such as immigrants, the LGBT community, women, minorities, and so on.

In addition, left-wing parties fight for voting rights for illegal immigrants, and leftist authorities turn a blind eye when illegal immigrants commit crimes on US soil, even going so far as to implement sanctuary policies to protect convicted criminals from immigration law enforcement. Of course, the motive isn't necessarily to benefit the illegal immigrants or the general population, but rather to bolster the Left's voter base. On September 12, 2017, a city near the District of Columbia passed a bill to grant noncitizens the right to vote in local elections, including green card holders, temporary residents on student and work visas, and even those with no documentation of legal immigration status. It attracted widespread media attention for its potential effects on the electoral system in other parts of the country. [7]

The administration of the 44th US president was heavily infiltrated by communists and socialists. Many groups that supported the president had clear links to socialist organizations. The president himself granted amnesty to almost one million illegal immigrants via an executive order, after legislation to do so failed to pass Congress. This former president is a follower of the para-Marxist Saul Alinsky. Following his election, he appointed advisers from far-left think tanks and brought in a universal health care system that fined those who refused to enroll in it. He furthered leftist aims by ceasing the enforcement of federal laws against marijuana, supporting the legalization of gay marriage, allowing transsexuals to join the army, and so on. In 2016, his administration issued a directive to public schools to allow students who identified as transgender to enter the bathrooms of their chosen gender, regardless of their physical sex — in other words, boys and men could enter girls' bathrooms simply by identifying as female, and vice versa. Schools were told that if they refused to implement the bill, they would lose federal funding. In response, a coalition of thirteen states sued the federal government, arguing that the directive was unconstitutional.

3. Hatred and Struggle: The Invariable Course of Communist Politics

Struggle and hatred lie at the core of communist politics. Turning people against each other by sowing hatred and division is the primary means by which communism corrupts society, overturns its morality, and usurps political power to establish its dictatorship.

In 1926, Mao wrote in his article "Analysis of Classes in Chinese Society": "Who are our enemies? Who are our friends? This is a question of the first importance for the revolution." Mao was talking about the dialectic, a "magical weapon" that Marxist groups use in their rise to power. [8] Communist parties arbitrarily create concepts of class where none previously existed and then incite these arbitrarily divided groups to struggle against each other. To promote their cause, the revolutionaries select and exaggerate certain issues that stem from the decline of a society's moral values. Then it claims that the root cause of these issues is not moral weakness, but rather the structure of society. It singles out particular classes as the "oppressors" and promotes popular struggle against these classes as being the solution to society's ills.

The hatred and struggle of communist politics are not limited to the antagonism between workers and capitalists. Cuban communist leader Fidel Castro said that the enemy of the Cuban people was the corruption of former President Fulgencio Batista and his supporters and that supposed oppression by large plantation owners was the source of inequality and injustice. Communism promises that by overthrowing the so-called oppressors, an egalitarian utopia can be created. Castro and his fellow revolutionaries used this promise to take over Cuba.

In China, Mao's innovation was to promise the peasants ownership of the land they worked on; the workers, ownership of their factories; and the intellectuals, freedom, peace, and democracy. This turned peasants against landlords, workers against capitalists, and intellectuals against the government, allowing the Chinese Communist Party to seize power.

In Algeria, communist leader Ahmed Ben Bella stirred up hatred between different religions and ethnic groups: Muslims against Christians, and the Arabs against the French. This became Ben Bella's springboard to secure communist rule.

The Founding Fathers of the United States built the country on the principles outlined in the Constitution. Family, church, and community formed strong bonds across American society, which became ever more prosperous throughout the nineteenth and twentieth centuries. The success of the American Dream de-emphasized concepts of social class and made it difficult to concoct class struggle in the United States.

But communism uses any opportunity it can to promote division. Using labor unions, it magnifies conflicts between employees and employers. It uses racial divides to foment struggle between different groups. It promotes the women's rights movement to foment struggle against the traditional social structure. It creates divisions around sexual orientation, using the LGBT movement. It divides the believers of different religions and uses "cultural diversity" to challenge traditional Western culture and heritage. It divides people of different nationalities by pushing for the "rights" of illegal immigrants and creating conflicts between foreigners and citizens. It pits illegal immigrants and the general public against law enforcement officers.

As society becomes increasingly atomized, a single misstep can trigger a struggle — the seeds of hatred already have been planted in the hearts of the masses. This is precisely the sinister aim of communism. Lenin is widely quoted as saying, "We can and must write in a language which sows among the masses hate, revulsion, scorn and the like toward those who disagree with us." [9] The political tactics used in the West employ all sorts of "social justice" issues to incite hatred and intensify social conflict.

In the 1931 Scottsboro Boys case, nine black boys were accused of raping two white women, triggering severe racial discord across the country. The Communist Party USA (CPUSA) sprang into action, using the incident to attract many new followers, including Frank Marshall Davis, future mentor to the 44th US president. The goal of the American communists in the Scottsboro Boys case was not merely to boost Party membership among the black population and progressive "social justice" activists, but to vilify America, casting it as a country rife with inequality and racial discrimination. Claiming that these were the prevailing conditions throughout the entire country, they promoted communism and leftist ideology as the only means of liberating Americans from this supposedly pathological and evil system.

In 1935, riots broke out in black communities in New York's Harlem neighborhood following rumors that a black teen had been beaten to death after he was caught shoplifting. (In reality, the Puerto Rican teen had bitten a shop assistant and was himself unscathed.) The CPUSA jumped at the chance to organize protests, according to Leonard Patterson, a former Party member who had played a role in the incident. Patterson described how communists were specifically trained in Leninist tactics for instigating and inflaming conflicts, such as transforming protests into violent riots and street fighting, as well as deliberately fabricating conflict where there was none to be found. [10]

In contemporary America, communist groups have been involved in every large-scale social conflict or riot. In 1991, footage widely broadcast by the media showed Rodney King, a black resident of Los Angeles, being beaten by white police officers after a high-speed chase. The widely viewed clip cut out the first 15 seconds of footage, which showed King, a paroled felon, resisting arrest and behaving belligerently, though his vehicle companions had cooperated with police. The four officers involved in the incident were ultimately acquitted of criminal charges. After the verdict, a crowd of protesters outside the Los Angeles Police Department's headquarters was about to disperse when something suddenly spurred them to riot. Someone hit the back of a passing car with a metal sign, and the protest swiftly descended into violence, with burning, smashing, and looting. [11]

When asked about the participation of communists in the incident, Los Angeles County Sheriff Sherman Block said there was no question that the Revolutionary Communist Party (RCP) was involved in the rioting, looting, and arson. During the events, fliers circulated by various communist groups, like the RCP, the Socialist Workers Party, the Progressive Labor Party (PLP), and the CPUSA, could be found all over the streets and on college campuses. One of the fliers distributed by the PLP read: "Avenge the King verdict! ... All the racist cops must pay! ... Turn the guns around! Soldiers unite with the workers!" According to a police officer in the Los

Angeles Police Department, people were already handing out such fliers before the verdict was even announced. [12]

Whatever the profusion of organizations that incite riots and violence in Western society today may call themselves, be it "Indivisible," "Anti-Fascist," "Stop Patriarchy," "Black Lives Matter," or "Refuse Fascism," they are all communist groups or proponents of communist ideas. The violent Antifa group consists of people of various communist leanings, such as anarchists, socialists, liberals, social democrats, and the like. Refuse Fascism is a radical group founded by leftists including those from the RCP. The group was behind many large-scale protests aiming to overturn the result of the 2016 US presidential election.

Under the guise of exercising free speech, these groups work tirelessly to provoke conflicts in Western society. To understand their real objective, one need only look at a 1943 directive by the CPUSA to its members:

> When certain obstructionists (to Communism) become too irritating, label them, after suitable buildups, as fascist or Nazi or anti-Semitic and use the prestige of antifascist and tolerance organizations to discredit them. In the public mind, constantly associate those who oppose us with those names which already have a bad smell. The association will, after enough repetition, become 'fact' in the public mind. Members and front organizations must continually embarrass, discredit and degrade our critics. [13]

4. Politics Through Violence and Lies

In communist doctrine, no means are considered too excessive. Communist parties publicly proclaim that violence and lies are their tools for conquering and ruling the world. From the first appearance of the communist regime in the Soviet Union to today, within only a century, communism has caused the deaths of at least one hundred million people. Communist Party members have abducted, tortured, murdered, destroyed, and lied.

The lies told by communists vary in size, both in communist countries and in the West. They range from relatively small lies, such as a hoax, fake news, or the framing of a political opponent, to a series of systematic lies of considerable scale through major propaganda operations. For instance, the CCP staged a self-immolation incident in Tiananmen Square and blamed members of the spiritual practice Falun Gong — all to incite public hatred against the practice.

Big lies, or great deceptions, are also used, and this is the hardest to manage, because the big lies are almost equivalent to the entirety of communist ideology. Their scale is so enormous, their operations so multifaceted, their duration so long, and the people they touch so numerous — including some who are sincerely dedicated to the cause — that the truth of the situation is lost. The communist specter fabricated the lie that a "great unity" was the goal of communism. Because this claim cannot be disproven in the short term, it was the deception on which the entire communist project was based. Communists claim that they are establishing a heaven on earth, but this is precisely their greatest lie, and the only fruit borne in the pursuit of this lie is a hell on earth.

The previous chapter analyzed how communism usurped the notion of progressivism through yet another great deception. In the past few decades, communism has hijacked a number of social movements and brought people to turmoil and revolution, which will be discussed in later chapters.

a. How Communism Uses Violence and Lies

Communist parties encourage class conflict — and this conflict is a struggle to the death. As *The Communist Manifesto* states: "The Communists disdain to conceal their views and aims. They openly declare that their ends can be attained only by the forcible overthrow of all existing social conditions." [14] Lenin wrote in *The State and Revolution*: "We have already said above, and shall show more fully later, that the theory of Marx and Engels of the inevitability of a violent revolution refers to the bourgeois state. The latter cannot be superseded by the proletarian state (the dictatorship of the proletariat) through the process of 'withering away,' but as a general rule, only through a violent revolution." [15]

During the process of seizing power — as seen during the Paris Commune, the Russian Revolution, or the CCP's rise — communist parties use extremely violent and bloody methods. Regardless of whether their enemies are young or old, healthy or weak, communist parties burn, rob, and murder them; they exhibit a wickedness that shocks the soul. So numerous are the crimes that have been committed under violent communist regimes that they are impossible to count.

Communist parties are willing to promise anything, but never consider making good on their promises. To satisfy their needs, they change their stories as much as they like, with no moral baseline and no sense of shame. Leaders including Mao, Ben Bella, and Castro all claimed they would never establish totalitarian regimes. But once in power, they immediately took steps to concentrate all authority in their own hands, carrying out purges within the party as well as persecution campaigns against dissidents and the ordinary public.

Additionally, language manipulation is one of the main methods the communist cult uses to deceive people — that is, altering the meanings of words and even turning them on their heads. As the altered language is repeatedly used, its distorted meanings become deeply rooted in people's minds. For example, "God" is equated with "superstition"; "tradition" is equated with "backwardness," "foolishness," and "feudalism"; "Western society" is equated with "hostile" or "anti-China forces"; and the "proletariat" becomes "the masters of state-owned assets." Though the people have no power under communism, the communists say that "all power belongs to the people." Pointing out injustices is labeled as "inciting subversion of state power." Therefore, when talking to those who have been deeply poisoned by the communist cult, people tend to find that the two sides often lack a shared basis for communication because they cannot even agree on the meanings of words.

The cult of communism not only tells lies itself, but also creates an environment to make the entire population join it in lying — including through forced political study, mandatory statements of one's political stance, and political vetting. This is meant to force people to say things they don't believe and thus demoralize them and degrade their sense of right and wrong. After people become aware of communist fabrications, they respond with their own lies. The communist cult knows that people are lying to it, but this is acceptable because lying itself is part of the game. What's dangerous for communists is when people start telling the truth.

The enforcement of a culture of falsehood is a means of moral degeneration engineered by communists. This book has noted repeatedly that the CCP regime desires not only to kill the physical body, but also to engender extreme moral corruption. In this regard, the communist specter has partially achieved its goal.

b. Instigating Violence in the West

The communist specter is composed of the elemental force of hatred, and its theories are infused with hate. It promotes class struggle and attributes the root of every problem to traditional social structures. It talks about the rich exploiting the poor in order to incite grudges and hatred against the rich and incite revolution and violence. With the expansion of communist movements, its manipulation, violence, and lies have become commonplace in the West and have filled society with rancor.

A society with a greater tendency toward violence will become less stable and more divided. In American society, some politicians and political operatives attack their enemies by unscrupulous means, such as deception, personal attacks, and the like. These days, the irreconcilable differences between the two major parties make them appear as incompatible as fire and water.

Left-leaning parties and politicians claim that they'll protect the rights of the people and follow the regulations of a democratic society. But when they come to power, under the influence of the communist specter, they use all methods to suppress dissent and arbitrarily deprive others of their rights.

Not everyone wants conflict, but it only takes a few core communist activists to stir things up. After the 2016 presidential election, Antifa extremists locked onto their target — conservatives — and went after them at rallies and elsewhere. They stopped supporters of the president and conservative thinkers from speaking at events and, in some cases, even physically attacked them. In June 2017, Steve Scalise, the House of Representatives majority whip, was shot and wounded by a supporter of another party while attending a baseball practice session. One leftist official from Nebraska even said he was "glad" that Scalise was shot and wished that he had died. That official was soon removed from his post as a committee chairman at the state level of his party.

c. Confusing the West With Lies

Communism has a negative reputation in the West, so lying is its only means of expanding its influence. Some politicians promote policies that are basically communist but come packaged under another name, using slogans like "freedom," "progress," and "the public interest." For instance, the establishment of a socialized health care system isn't called socialist, but instead "Medicare for all" and "universal health care," or it's justified as being supported by public opinion. When leftist politicians want to force employers to pay a minimum wage, they call it a "living wage." They make empty promises to get elected, similar to what communist parties do to gain power.

Specifically, politicians use warped and redistributionist fiscal and tax policies — such as giving tax incentives to trade unions, government programs, and minority enterprises — while increasing taxes on other enterprises and the wealthy. The result is that the beneficiaries of those policies (including the poor, trade unions, and so on) become reliant on the politicians who favor them, and thus support them in elections. Such politicians then have a stable, long-term hold on that area, and can build their political machine. At the same time, businesses are squeezed financially and thus shrink, go out of business, or move, resulting in a constant decrease in tax revenue and job opportunities in the city, eventually causing the city to go bankrupt.

In the past, people believed that the United States was a truly free society and the last bastion against communism. But today, people see clearly that high taxation, a highly developed welfare state, collectivism, big government, social democracy, "social equality," and the like — all derived in one way or another from socialist and Marxist-Leninist ideological DNA — are enshrined in policies and put into practice. In particular, the younger generation simply isn't aware of the history of brutality in communist countries. They yearn for and pursue an illusory ideal, and are deceived by the new guise that communism has taken on. The result is that they unknowingly walk on the road to ruin.

5. The Road to Totalitarianism

The totalitarian control exercised by communist regimes over the lives of their subjects is well-documented. But communism's ideological offshoots in democratic countries are stealthily working toward the same goal through advocating laws that aggressively expand government power and increase regulation over society and the economy. More frightening is the fact that today's authoritarians have science and technology at their disposal, giving them powers of surveillance and social control on a scale the tyrannies of the past could scarcely have imagined.

a. Suppressing Free Will and Moral Agency

When human beings follow the traditional values established by the divine, the development of their culture will follow an orthodox path, allowing them an important channel to connect with the divine. The different social and political systems seen across humanity are likewise derived from their respective cultures.

People are endowed by the Creator with free will and the ability to manage their own affairs. They must manage themselves through self-discipline, moral conduct, and responsibility for themselves and their families. After studying American politics in the nineteenth century, the French political philosopher Alexis de Tocqueville came to greatly appreciate American society. He was impressed with Americans' ability for introspection, their understanding of evil, their willingness to solve problems with patience, and their general ability to avoid violence when faced with political problems. He thought that the greatness of the United States lay in its ability to correct its own mistakes.

What the communist specter wants, on the other hand, is to instigate people to oppose tradition and morality, and to block the path for them to incline toward goodness and toward the divine. Subjects of communist regimes are transformed from being God's people to becoming subjects of the devil, all without their noticing. In communist countries, the government monopolizes social resources so that everything must be carried out by following the instructions of communist party leaders, who themselves must exhibit sufficient "party nature" if they are to survive the vicious factional struggles that characterize communist regimes. Ordinary citizens or the rank-and-file cadres who try to follow their conscience and act morally almost invariably end up violating the party's ideological line, and are either demoted or labeled enemies of the state. They then become the underclass, forced to struggle at the bottom of society.

In free societies, governments are also moving toward authoritarianism, with "big government" coming to control almost everything. One of the key features of authoritarian politics is a strong central government that plans and directs the economy. At present, Western governments have tremendous power to intervene in and control the economy to achieve government plans; they use the instruments of state revenue and expenditures, taxation, and debt financing.

Expansion of the central administrative power, local governmental control over the lives of citizens, and numerous laws and court rulings have resulted in an all-round expansion of governmental power and unprecedented societal control. "Political correctness" is an excuse to deprive people of their freedom of speech. Those who openly denounce sinister policies are dismissed as engaging in "hate speech." Those who dare to oppose political correctness are marginalized, isolated, in some cases fired, and in extreme instances threatened or attacked.

Deviated political standards have replaced upright moral standards. These standards are then enforced with the power of the law, regulation, and public attacks, thus creating an atmosphere of social terror and pressure. This social terror can then suppress people's free will and their freedom to pursue kindness. This is the essence of totalitarian politics.

b. Totalitarianism via Welfare, Technology, and Excessive Regulation

Contemporary Western society is now rife with laws and regulations governing the minutia of nearly every aspect of society, from workplace practices to childrearing. State welfare is increasingly seen as a default necessity, rather than as a form of emergency aid for the truly disadvantaged. Advances in technology have enabled governments to enforce their red tape on a scale never before seen. Encouraging and accelerating this process are leftist groups and politicians, who market it as progress. In fact, the expansion of government oversight and state welfare poses a grave threat to liberty and morality.

In the nineteenth century, Tocqueville observed that "if despotism were to be established amongst the democratic nations of our days, it might assume a different character; it would be more extensive and mild; it would degrade men without tormenting them." [16] From the federal level down to the state, county, and municipal levels, thousands of new laws are passed every year. The US tax code is tens of thousands of pages long, while the recent health insurance law amounts to over twenty thousand pages. Even judges and lawyers cannot comprehend all the laws, not to mention an average citizen. A person can break a law without even realizing it.

Furthermore, no matter how perfect the law may be, it is only an external form of restraint and cannot govern the human heart. As Lao Tzu said, "The more laws are promulgated, the more thieves and bandits there will be." People ignore the fact that social problems are caused by unleashing the evil side of man. As they create more and more laws, ignoring the crux of the matter, a vicious cycle is formed, and society begins its step-by-step march toward totalitarianism.

Socialized Health Care

Throughout history, charities existed organically in local communities and religious organizations. Meanwhile, competent governments maintained the ability to allocate resources to the poor, such as during times of famine, drought, or flooding. The British jurist A. V. Dicey observed that in the twentieth century, however, governments began to see the welfare of individuals as something to be regulated and provided for by taxation:

> *Now before 1908 the question whether a man, rich or poor, should insure his health, was a matter left entirely to the free discretion or indiscretion of each individual. His conduct no more concerned the State than the question whether he should wear a black coat*

or a brown coat. But the National Insurance Act will, in the long run, bring upon the State, that is, upon the taxpayers, a far heavier responsibility than is anticipated by English electors. ... [Unemployment insurance] is in fact the admission by the State of its duty to insure a man against the evil ensuing from his having no work. ... The National Insurance Act is in accordance with the doctrines of socialism. ... [17]

Analysts have pointed out several fatal problems with socialist medical welfare. It is unsustainable, as people want to benefit from free services more than they pay into them. There are no rewards or penalties for performance, and medical industry practitioners don't need to assume any legal responsibility for what they do. The government sustains huge losses as people steal through loopholes, abuse the system, and engage in underground trade. The government decides matters of life and death through the medical system, and it's plagued by bureaucracy. [18]

In 2010, a 32-year-old man in northern Sweden had to suture his own bleeding wound after waiting hours for medical care. After accidentally cutting himself while renovating his home, he first went to an outpatient clinic, which was closed, then went to the emergency room. There, he waited for an hour for assistance as his wound continued to bleed. Finally, noticing a needle and thread that the nurses had left out, he attempted to treat himself. The hospital staff later reported him for violating the law by using hospital equipment without authorization. [19] This is just one example of how a socialized welfare scheme can lead to ridiculous outcomes. Because everyone wants free medical care, resources are abused. The clash between limitations on resources and the demand that things be free causes imbalances in the supply and demand equation. The lack of supply means long wait times and inadequate care. Those who really need care are thus harmed by socialized medicine.

In addition, while cradle-to-grave welfare appears desirable to many, the population's dependence on the government lays the foundation for an autocratic regime. Greater involvement by the authorities in the regulation of society or in the lives of individual citizens requires larger systems of state control. Meanwhile, the hiring of personnel and drafting of regulations require money, which is generated from taxation. With the expansion of the state also comes the creation of powerful political cliques that have a vested interest in keeping and enlarging the scope of their authority.

Mass Surveillance

Technology makes it even more convenient for governments to control their populations. The Chinese Communist Party is the most obvious representative of this issue, but the same dangers are present in Western countries, particularly in Europe, where socialist programs are already ubiquitous.

Today's China has the largest surveillance system in the world. In public places and on the roads, surveillance cameras are everywhere. In just minutes, faces on a blacklist can be found among a sea of 1.4 billion people. The surveillance software embedded in the smartphone application WeChat enables open surveillance, and privacy is completely absent for anyone with a cellphone. There is simply nowhere to hide.

As technology becomes more and more advanced and governments become bigger and bigger, a continuation on the path of socialism in the West would result in a similarly horrifying fate — one of being constantly monitored, pressured, and managed. This ultimate scenario is by no means an exaggeration. In addition to physical surveillance and censorship, the government can also utilize big data and financial information to have targeted citizens fired from their jobs. Banks can be made to cancel their mortgages. A government with these technological means can revoke the licenses of disobedient citizens and cut off their access to the welfare that, because of other economic policies, is their only means of maintaining their livelihood.

6. Communism's Threat to Basic Values

Communist ideologies have wreaked havoc in the political sphere for centuries. In the East, communist regimes mobilized the forces of the state to crush political opponents, destroy traditional culture, and kill tens of millions of people. In the West, left-wing movements have steadily taken over the democratic process. While eschewing overt violence and dictatorship, the policies they advocate follow the same philosophy of struggle. Lust for power, wealth, and fame have existed as long as humanity itself, as everyone harbors the capacity for evil as well as good. Taking advantage of the moral weaknesses inherent to human nature, the specter of communism has cultivated networks of "agents" around the world.

Due to communist infiltration, today's Western societies are divided to an unprecedented degree, with the Left using all its power to obstruct and thwart those who hold traditional views in politics. It is no exaggeration to say that the West is now in a war over its own values.

Leftist political influence has proven extremely resistant to the attempts taken to weaken or reverse it. Politicians and activists under communism's sway collude with the media to discredit the opposition and spread misleading information to confuse the public. Left-wing officials ignore or obstruct government decrees, divert public resources to support their ideological agendas, and enact policies that exacerbate social division and conflict.

In 2018, according to a poll conducted by The Associated Press-NORC Center for Public Affairs Research, more than 80 percent of respondents said they believed that Americans were heavily divided on important values and that the country was more deeply divided on politics than in the past. [20]

The state is unmatched in its ability to marshal human and economic resources. Wielded properly, political power can bring great benefit to the entire nation, as well as improve the international community. But as seen throughout history, and in the history of the communist movement, abuse of that power leads to monstrous crimes.

Former US President Reagan said in his first inaugural address: "From time to time, we have been tempted to believe that society has become too complex to be managed by self-rule, that government by an elite group is superior to government for, by, and of the people. But if no one among us is capable of governing himself, then who among us has the capacity to govern someone else?" [21] President Donald Trump said that in the United States, "we don't worship government — we worship God." [22]

The unity of a country requires a common set of values and a shared culture. Although doctrines differ among religions, the standards for good and evil are similar. In the United States, this makes it possible for people of different ethnic and cultural backgrounds to live side by side in harmony. However, when the people are divided over questions of basic morality, the very survival of the country is at stake.

CHAPTER NINE

The Communist Economic Trap

COMMUNISM'S INFLUENCE IS PRESENT in every sector of our present economic system. With the trend of ever-expanding government being the norm, virtually every country on earth is moving away from classic free-market principles and gravitating toward communist or socialist economics.

Looking at the countries that abandoned communism or the socialist economic model after the fall of the Soviet bloc, one would think that the communist specter had failed in its goals. But the reality isn't so simple. The specter's methods do not follow a rigid pattern. For the sake of a greater objective, it may abandon certain forms while adopting others to suit the historical or social situation. Nowhere is this truer than in the economic sphere.

More than 150 years ago, Karl Marx advocated the abolition of private property and ascendance of state ownership, in his book *Das Kapital*. Totalitarian communist states tried to achieve this objective directly, using terror, violence, and mass murder. But as overt communist doctrine lost its appeal, leftists in democratic countries devised nonviolent forms. The multitudinous strains of socialism and communism they have introduced over the years defy easy classification.

In addition to curtailing basic rights to private property and enterprise, communist economic policy fosters corruption and contributes to the erosion of traditional culture. To preserve their moral foundations, way of life, and prosperity, nations around the world must awaken to communist subversion in the economic realm, and take measures to counter it.

1. State Ownership and Planned Economies: Systems of Slavery

Heaven created man, endowed him with wisdom and strength, and decreed that in his life he would reap rewards for his labor — and thus be able to obtain enough to secure his life. The Declaration of Independence states, "We hold these truths to be self-evident, that all men are created equal, that they are endowed by their Creator with certain unalienable Rights, that among these are Life, Liberty and the pursuit of Happiness." [1] Naturally, these rights include the right to own and manage property.

In contrast, Marx and Engels stated in *The Communist Manifesto*, "The theory of the Communists may be summed up in the single sentence: Abolition of private property." [2] This is a reference to state ownership, which, under a planned economy, is mandatory. In communist planned economies, the means of production are directly controlled by the state. The essence of this system violates heavenly principles, runs contrary to human nature, and, ultimately, is a form of slavery.

a. State Ownership: A Totalitarian Yoke

Fred Schwarz, an Australian expert on communist ideology, told the following joke in his book *You Can Trust the Communists ... to Be Communists,* about an interviewer who visits a Soviet automobile plant:

"Who owns this factory?"
"We do," they replied.
"Who owns the land on which it is built?"
"We do."
"Who owns the products of the factory when they are made?"
"We do."
Outside in a corner of a large park were three battered jalopies. The visitor asked, "Who owns those cars out there?"
They replied, "We own them, but one of them is used by the factory manager, one is used by the political commissar, and the other is used by the secret police."
The same investigator came to a factory in America, and said to the workers, "Who owns this factory?"
"Henry Ford," they replied.
"Who owns the land on which it is built?"
"Henry Ford."
"Who owns the products of the factory when they are made?"
"Henry Ford."
Outside the factory was a vast park filled with every make and variety of modern American automobile. He said, "Who owns all those cars out there?"
They replied, "Oh, we do." [3]

This story demonstrates the contrast between systems of private and state ownership. Under the latter, resources and the gains from labor are nationalized. Gone are the mechanisms that motivate individual enthusiasm, ambition, and innovation, along with the sense of responsibility that comes with owning one's own property. In theory, state ownership means that the wealth of a country is shared by all citizens, but in practice, it means that the privileged class monopolizes economic resources, and uses authoritarian political power to keep the rest of the population in line.

The ultimate factor in economic growth is people. State ownership chokes people's vitality and motivation to be productive. It undermines morale, promotes inefficiency, and creates oversupply or gross shortages. From Soviet collective farms to the people's communes in China to failed collectivization in Cambodia and North Korea, the system of state ownership brings starvation wherever it goes.

Both evil and kindness exist in mankind. Private property ownership allows man to develop integrity and encourages labor and thrift. Collective property ownership feeds negative traits in human nature, such as jealousy and laziness.

Austrian economist and philosopher Friedrich Hayek wrote that the growth of civilization relies on social traditions that respect private property. Such traditions allowed for the development of the modern commercial system and the economic growth it created. This is an organic, self-generating order that does not require a government to function. Yet communist and socialist movements seek to shape the world according to their wishes — what Hayek called a "fatal conceit." [4]

If private ownership and freedom are inseparable, then the same principle applies to state ownership, which is wed to dictatorship and oppression. By nationalizing wealth and resources, state ownership stymies economic productivity and turns the people into serfs who must obey the commands of the central authorities. A state that controls the economy also has the power to suppress voices inconsistent with the regime, while the people have few means of resistance.

The elimination of private ownership thus inevitably results in a totalitarian order, which imposes collectivism on its subjects like a yoke affixed to the necks of livestock. When wealth becomes public, power becomes private. Freedom is stolen — including the freedom to be moral — as the regime becomes the sole arbitrator of morality.

b. Economic Planning: Destined to Fail

Under a planned economy, an entire society's production, allocation of resources, and distribution of products are based on a plan established by the state. This is completely different from supply and demand economics in a free market.

Planned economies come with natural and obvious flaws. First, they require the collection of a huge amount of data in order to make reasonable arrangements for production. For any country, especially a modern state with a large population, the amount of required information is unimaginably large and impossible to process. For instance, the former Soviet Union's commodity pricing bureau had to set prices for twenty-four million different kinds of goods. [5] The complexity and variability of society and people cannot be solved through a unified planned economy. Even with the use of modern big data and artificial intelligence, human thoughts cannot possibly be inputted as variables, and so the system will always be incomplete.

Austrian economist Ludwig von Mises discussed the relationship between socialism and the market in his article "Economic

Calculation in the Socialist Commonwealth." [6] He notes that without a real market, a socialist society isn't able to make reasonable economic calculations. Thus, the distribution of resources cannot be rationalized, and the planned economy fails.

As described previously, economic planning requires coercive state control of resources. This ultimately requires absolute power, quotas, and commands. When the requirements of the real world fail to conform to state planning, state power tramples on natural economic trends, thus causing the mass misallocation of capital and all its attendant problems. The planned economy uses the limited power and "wisdom" of government in a doomed attempt to play God.

Moreover, an economics of power is first of all beholden to politics, rather than to the actual needs of the people. Economic planning and authoritarian politics are inseparable. Because national plans are inevitably flawed, when problems arise, the plans will be challenged both inside and outside government. Those in power then feel that their authority is being challenged and will fight back with political pressure and purges. Mao Zedong, for instance, ignored the laws of economics and forced through the Great Leap Forward, resulting in a three-year famine that caused tens of millions of deaths. This led to serious challenges to his leadership position in the Communist Party, which is a key reason he later launched the Cultural Revolution.

Chinese state-owned enterprises (SOES) put the disastrous effects of the planned economy and collective ownership on full display. In recent years, a large number of Chinese SOES have stopped or slowed production, have suffered losses year after year, or have become insolvent. They rely on government subsidies and rolling bank credit to maintain operations. They've essentially become parasites on the national economy, and many are widely known as "zombie enterprises." [7] Among the 150,000 state-owned enterprises in China, with the exception of state monopolies in the lucrative sectors of petroleum and telecommunications, other SOEs report lackluster profits and serious losses. By the end of 2015, their total assets accounted for 176 percent of GDP, their debt accounted for 127 percent, and their earnings accounted for only 3.4 percent. [8] Many economists argue that China's economy has been effectively hijacked by these zombie enterprises; the country's apparent success has for many years remained dependent on cheap manufacturing, which is made possible only by the extreme exploitation of low-wage workers and a complete disregard for the environment.

Meanwhile, economic planning deprives people of their freedom and forces the state to look after them. All aspects of people's lives come under the control of the state, which locks people in an invisible prison, seeks to abolish free will, and tampers with the natural way of life arranged for humans by the divine. The essence of the project is about turning people into slaves and machines. This is yet another manifestation of the communist revolt against tradition and morality.

2. Western Countries: Practicing Communism by Another Name

For individuals, Marxism's "abolition of private property" entails the "abolition of bourgeois individuality, bourgeois independence, and bourgeois freedom." For society, it means that "the proletariat will use its political supremacy to wrest, by degree, all capital from the bourgeoisie, to centralise all instruments of production in the hands of the State, i.e., of the proletariat organised as the ruling class." [9]

Many economic policies or structures may not appear socialist on the surface, yet they play the role of restricting, weakening, or depriving people of the right to private property. Others weaken the mechanics of free enterprise, expand government power, and lead society further down the road toward socialism. The methods used include high taxation, generous social welfare, and aggressive state interventionism.

a. High Taxes and Welfare

High taxation is a covert way to gradually phase out the system of private ownership. The end result of high taxation is the same as the state ownership and "egalitarianism" imposed by communist regimes, with the only difference being whether nationalization is effected before or after production.

In the West, production is controlled privately, but the revenue is converted into state assets via taxes and redistribution schemes. This wealth-taking is achieved legally through democracy and legislation rather than through killing and violence.

An important feature of the communist or socialist economics seen in Western countries is robust social welfare, which is used to gradually erode moral wisdom and freedom. While some government aid is reasonable — such as social security for victims of disasters or accidents — it is easy for welfare to become a convenient instrument of deception. Its positive aspects become the excuse for increasing taxes and government control. In this regard, generous welfare has already achieved the same destructive consequences for people, society, and moral values as do overtly communist economics, without a need for violent revolution.

Social welfare in developed Western countries consumes a large portion of revenue, which comes from taxes transferred from private wealth. All socialized benefits must ultimately be paid for by the people, via taxes or national debt. There is no other method to maintain this level of government largesse. In the United States, more than half of the tax revenue is spent on Social Security and medical care. More than 80 percent of this money comes from personal income taxes and Social Security taxes; 11 percent is from corporate tax. [10] This kind of massive government spending only began in the past century.

In 1895, the US Supreme Court declared income taxes unconstitutional. The decision stood until the 1913 ratification of the 16th Amendment. Data from fifteen countries in the year 1900 show that only seven imposed an income tax, with Italy leading at a rate of 10 percent. Australia, Japan, and New Zealand had income tax rates of about 5 percent.

By 2016, according to data on thirty-five market economies published by the Organization for Economic Cooperation and Development (OECD), twenty-seven countries had an income tax rate higher than 30 percent. The countries with the highest income taxes, at 54 and 49.4 percent, are both in Europe. [11] On top of this, eating or shopping in Europe usually adds more than 20 percent in sales tax. Corporate and other taxes further add to the overall tax burden.

High taxation burdens not only the wealthy, but also those at the bottom of the tax scale. While the rich often have various legal means of shielding themselves from taxes, the poor's welfare benefits disappear as their income increases beyond a certain threshold. After taxes, this income is often less than what they received on welfare. People are effectively penalized for working harder and thus encouraged to stay on welfare.

Expansive Welfare

In modern society, vast welfare systems have been expanded to cover unemployment, medical care, pensions, occupational injury, housing, education, child care, and more, far beyond traditional concepts of aid for those in immediate need.

A report from The Heritage Foundation shows that in 2013, more than one hundred million people in the United States, or about a third of the population, received welfare benefits (excluding Social Security and Medicare) worth an average of $9,000 per recipient. [12] According to US Census Bureau data from that year, 14.8 percent of the population were classified as living below the poverty line — basically the same rate as in 1967, a few years after President Lyndon B. Johnson declared an "unconditional war on poverty in America." This suggests that greatly expanding welfare benefits — as was done under Johnson's administration — hasn't achieved the goal of reducing the percentage of people living below the poverty line.

As of 2014, in the fifty years since Johnson launched his War on Poverty, American taxpayers spent $2.2 trillion on welfare. Yet, as statistics from the Census Bureau show, the poverty rate has remained steady for the past forty years. [13]

Moreover, poverty is calculated by income and doesn't factor in the various benefits afforded to welfare recipients, such as food stamps, housing subsidies, and education benefits. Over a century ago, French thinker Alexis de Tocqueville said that when aid is allocated only by using poverty thresholds, it is impossible to know whether eligible individuals are actually suffering from circumstances beyond their control or if their misfortune is of their own making. [14]

The deliberate categorization of large numbers of people into the "impoverished" demographic provides ample excuse for the expansion of welfare. Living standards in poverty today are far superior to those in the 1960s. According to a government survey conducted in 1999, 96 percent of parents in impoverished households said that their children had never gone hungry due to inability to buy food. Almost 50 percent of impoverished households lived in detached houses, and 40 percent lived in townhouses. Just 9 percent lived in mobile homes. Eighty percent had air conditioning and two-fifths owned widescreen LCD TVs. Three-quarters of impoverished households owned cars. [15]

Even still, the benefits provided by the US government are below average compared with those of other members of the OECD. Most people living in Nordic countries and other Western European nations enjoy far greater welfare than Americans. In Denmark, for example, even the wealthiest citizens enjoy a cradle-to-grave social safety net that includes free medical care, university education, and other generous benefits. Swedes are entitled to 480 days of paid parental leave when a child is born or adopted. Greeks, prior to their country's economic collapse, enjoyed an annual fourteen-month salary and retirement at the age of fifty-seven. Greece spent 17.5 percent of its GDP on pension payments.

The expansion of welfare from its traditional role of emergency aid to long-term benefits for entire populations is, in fact, part of the goal of imposing a communist economy.

Social Benefits, Corruption, and Class Conflicts

From an economic point of view, the essence of welfare is to take money from some people and transfer its value to others. Because it is the government that is responsible for distributing the wealth, usually without requiring anything in return, welfare de-emphasizes the principle that one must work in order to gain. The loss of this wisdom is particularly evident in Northern Europe.

Swedish scholar Nima Sanandaji demonstrated this point using data from the World Value Survey. In the early 1980s, 82 percent of Swedes agreed with the statement that "it is wrong to receive government benefits that you do not deserve." In the 2010–2014 survey, only 55 percent of Swedes agreed with this statement. [16]

Under a generous welfare system, those who work hard receive fewer returns, and those who are less industrious are rewarded with benefits. Over time, this wears down the quality of the people, as those who grew up with high government welfare lose the industriousness, independence, responsibility, and diligence of their forefathers. They take the system for granted and consider welfare to be a human right. They form a habit of relying on the government and even holding it hostage for continuous aid. Thus, social values are changed almost irreversibly.

Expansive government welfare also squeezes out the role of traditional charities, depriving the donors of the opportunity to do good works and the beneficiaries of the chance to feel gratitude. In traditional society, charity was given by choice, either by giving aid directly to the less fortunate or by donating to charitable organizations such as churches. There were clear donors and recipients, and being able to receive assistance was a privilege, not a right. Recipients felt gratitude for the donors' kindness and would be motivated to use the charity to supplement their own efforts to improve their lot. Those who received charity and turned their lives around would be likely to return the favor when others confronted the same challenges they once faced.

Tocqueville noted that charity combined the virtues of generosity and gratitude, which interact mutually to improve society and exert a positive moral influence. Meanwhile, the relationship between givers and receivers functioned to ease conflicts and antagonism between the rich and the poor, as charitable behavior on the part of individuals connected members of different economic classes. [17]

The bloated system of modern welfare interrupts the relationship between donors and recipients by bureaucratizing the process of charity. The "donors" of today are taxpayers who are forced to give up their wealth, rather than sharing it voluntarily. Meanwhile, recipients of welfare have no connection to their benefactors and feel no gratitude for their sacrifice.

Tocqueville believed that social welfare exacerbated conflicts between the rich and the poor. Having part of their wealth forcibly confiscated, the wealthy would come to resent welfare recipients. Tocqueville said that the poor, too, would feel discontent if they took their economic relief for granted: "One class still views the world with fear and loathing while the other regards its misfortune with despair and envy." [18]

Bloated welfare also becomes a way for the communist specter to exacerbate jealousy and political conflict. This has been observed in the Greek economic crisis: Among the upper class, tax evasion became a "national sport," according to Greek officials cited by *The Economist*. [19] With reduced tax revenue, the Greek government attempted to cut back on social welfare, only to meet with staunch resistance. So as to not upset its constituents, the government relied on taking out loans to offset diminishing tax revenue, while maintaining the same level of welfare found in other European countries. Greece eventually raised taxes on middle- to high-income earners, farmers, and businesses.

In 2009, an empirical study by Martin Halla, Mario Lackner, and Friedrich G. Schneider showed that social welfare disincentivizes hard work in the long term. The three economists concluded that the dynamics of the welfare state are inimical to the health of a nation's economic base. [20]

The Culture of Poverty

Welfare should be an emergency measure to assist those in genuine need, in special circumstances such as occupational accidents, epidemics, natural disasters, and so on. It shouldn't become the default form of subsistence, as it is incapable of resolving the root causes of poverty.

Expanding the criteria that determines who is entitled to welfare creates an atmosphere of negative reinforcement that encourages the misuse of these benefits. For example, the term "disability" is being continually redefined to extend eligibility to more individuals. The result is economic malaise, which causes a regression in social morality.

In 2012, *The New York Times* ran an opinion article titled "Profiting From a Child's Illiteracy," which discusses the impact of welfare policy on low-income families living in the Appalachian Mountain region in the eastern United States. The article describes how impoverished families stopped sending their children to literacy classes in order to qualify for aid. "Moms and dads fear that if kids learn to read, they are less likely to qualify for a monthly check for having an intellectual disability," the article states. "Many people in hillside mobile homes here are poor and desperate, and a $698 monthly check per child from the Supplemental Security Income program goes a long way — and those checks continue until the child turns 18." [21]

The program began about forty years ago with the goal of helping families whose severely physically or mentally challenged children made it difficult for parents to work — about one percent of poor children. By 2012, more than 55 percent of qualifying children were categorized as mentally challenged, but did not have a defined diagnosis. Across the United States, there are now a total of around 1.2 million "mentally challenged" children for whom taxpayers provide $9 billion annually. [22]

Here, welfare and the flaws of human nature feed each other in a downward spiral. While those who advocate and devise welfare policy may do so with good intentions, the effects of these policies are often detrimental, both to individuals and society as a whole.

Welfare abuse doesn't just tie down public finances; it also affects the futures of children who grow up inside its system. Research conducted in 2009 found that two-thirds of people who received welfare as children continued to receive it into adulthood. [23]

According to American economist William A. Niskanen, the welfare system has spawned a culture of poverty, which in turn has fed a vicious cycle of dependence on government aid, children born out of wedlock, violent crime, unemployment, and abortion.

Niskanen analyzed state data for 1992 and estimated the potential effects of increasing Aid to Families with Dependent Children benefits by 1 percent of the average personal income. He determined that the number of recipients would increase by about 3 percent; the number in poverty would increase by about 0.8 percent; births to single mothers would increase by about 2.1 percent; and unemployment would increase by about 0.5 percent. Abortions and violent crime would both increase by just more than 1 percent each. [24] Niskanen's findings suggest that a robust welfare system fosters dependence on the system and discourages personal responsibility.

The disintegration of families is a chief ingredient in the culture of poverty. In a study of historical and contemporary poverty among blacks in New York City, economist Walter E. Williams found that in 1925, 85 percent of black families were two-parent. By 2015, black single-parent households had reached nearly 75 percent. The welfare system incentivizes this phenomenon, as it provides considerably more benefits to single mothers than to married parents. By purposely remaining single, a parent can access more government subsidies, including welfare payments, housing subsidies, food stamps, and medical care. Welfare has played a significant role in pushing single parenthood, which has proven to cause more poverty. Alternatively, Williams found that the poverty rate among black married couples had remained in the single digits since 1994. [25]

The Left's Use of Welfare Policy to Gain Votes

While welfare has been ever-expanding over the last few decades, the gap between rich and poor has also continuously increased. The average wage, adjusted for inflation, has increased at a snail's pace, while wealth flows to the most wealthy, resulting in a larger class of working poor. The Left weaponizes these societal issues to push for a bigger government, higher taxation, and more welfare to combat poverty, exacerbating the problems even further.

Leftwing politicians use a variety of election slogans to convince voters of their noble intent, portraying themselves as possessing the moral high ground, despite that they are draining taxpayer money to fund their programs. Their method is to seize the wealth of the upper and middle classes and distribute it among the poor. This system of forced charity conceals the relationship between the donors (taxpayers) and the recipients. Politicians present themselves as the benevolent givers and receive the recipients' gratitude in the form of votes, while telling the recipients that they should resent the rich — the actual donors.

b. Aggressive Economic Interventionism in Western Countries

In Western countries, the state, which traditionally only passed and enforced laws, has now become a leading participant in the economic arena. Like a referee joining a soccer match, the state has become responsible for controlling and regulating capital in what used to be a mostly self-regulating economy.

At present, governments in the free world are already practicing interventionism in their national economic systems. One driver of this trend came out of the Great Depression in the 1930s. Following the crisis, Western society was deeply influenced by the economic theory developed by British economist John Maynard Keynes. Keynesian economics advocates active state intervention and regulation of the economy through finance. In his seminal book, *The General Theory of Employment, Interest and Money*, Keynes opposes free market self-regulation and instead favors increased government spending and interventions such as bailouts to stabilize the market.

In a healthy society, the government's role is limited. Only in exceptional situations should the state interfere in the economy, such as during natural disasters or other crises. But today, Keynesian theory has taken root around the world. Governments of virtually all countries are racing to exercise greater control over their respective economies.

When governments play an active role in the economy, each action creates a massive ripple effect in the markets. New policies and laws can make or break entire industries, forcing many businesses and investors to become overly beholden to government decisions.

Active financial control combined with high-welfare policies has caused many governments to incur huge debts. According to data from the OECD, more than one-third of its member states have government debts higher than 100 percent of GDP. One country's debt has exceeded 237 percent of its economic output. [26] This presents a major vulnerability for the social and economic futures of many countries.

Nobel Prize-winning economist Ronald Coase wrote multiple research papers on the impact of government intervention. In his work, Coase found that interventionist policy almost always produces negative results. The most probable explanation, he said, is that "the government now operates on such a massive scale that it [has] reached the stage of what economists call negative marginal returns. Anything additional it does, it messes up." [27]

The Consequences and Reality of Interventionism

There are at least two major consequences of extensive government intervention. First, the power of the state expands in terms of its role and scale. Government officials develop increasing hubris about their ability to interfere with the economy and have the state play the role of savior. After handling a crisis, the government is wont to retain its expanded powers and functions.

Second, interventionism creates more reliance on the government. When the populace encounters challenges, or when the free market cannot provide the desired benefits, the people will lobby in favor of more government intervention to satisfy their demands.

As the power of the state increases, private enterprise weakens and the free market has less space in which to function. People who have benefited from and grown dependent on politicians will increasingly demand that the government take responsibility for allocating wealth, and enact laws to enforce this.

In the West, there is a strong political current pushing society toward the Left. This encompasses followers of the original left wing, including socialists and communists, as well as those not traditionally associated with the Left but who have been co-opted by it. This emboldens leftist politicians to take greater measures to intervene in the economy and interfere with the functioning of private enterprises. This erosion of normal economic activity appears to be caused by various social movements, but in fact, it is the specter of communism that pulls the strings.

Western governments wield their authority under the banner of equality and other political excuses to increase intervention while enacting laws to give themselves more permanent power. There is no doubt that this behavior deprives market economies of their principal arbiters — the free will of the people.

The state is essentially expanding its authority over the free market to turn it into a command economy. The long-term implications are that all aspects of the economy and popular livelihood will come under state control. Economic means will be used to consolidate political power, enslaving society and its citizens.

c. How Socialist Economics Moves the West Toward Authoritarianism

High taxes, high welfare, and widespread state intervention are manifestations of socialism within Western economic systems. As things stand, the only true difference between the planned economies of communist countries and heavy state interventionism in the West is that rule of law and other basic aspects of the system protect human rights from being lost under total government control.

Hayek, the economist and philosopher, cautioned against state-controlled planning and wealth redistribution, saying that it would inevitably tamper with the market and lead to the rise of totalitarianism, regardless of whether the system was democratic or not. Hayek believed that although the socialism practiced in Europe and North America was different from state ownership and planned economies, it would result in the same outcome — people would still lose their freedom and livelihood, just in a slower and more indirect fashion. [28]

As has been discussed earlier in this book, Marx, Engels, and Lenin all saw communism as the final goal, with socialism a mandatory step on the journey. A train's destination will not be affected by its stopping at a station along the way — in fact, it might pick up more passengers. Likewise, the specter of communism is the driving force behind a country's move toward socialism. Once humanity forsakes tradition, whether in the economic sphere or in other areas, and accepts communist ideology, the pace of the development toward communism is irrelevant.

The destination at the end of this path is not heaven on earth, but the destruction of humanity. The specter is not concerned with whether "heaven" is realized or not — this promise is merely bait to lure people into the trap and to their eventual demise.

3. The Dystopian Socialism of the Chinese Communist Party

In 1978, after planned economics and political campaigns had reduced China to a poverty-stricken disaster, the Chinese Communist Party was compelled to introduce economic reforms to keep its hold on power. Embarking on a process of "reform and opening up," the CCP introduced elements of a free market. This led many to imagine that the Party had become capitalist.

a. The Chinese Economy:
No Relaxation of Communist Control

Out of expedience, the CCP liberalized some aspects of the Chinese economy, such as allowing private business. But the communist cadres have not loosened their grip. Although private enterprises exist, the CCP has never promised the people any fundamental right to private property. By law, resources and land remain ultimately at the Party's disposal.

At the same time, the CCP imposes strict controls on economic matters, including large-scale national planning. The market is only a means used by the state to stimulate production; it is not truly independent, and neither are there institutions in place to support a free market.

The Chinese communist model is a monstrous combination of socialism, statism, and market economics. There is no independent rule of law or clear system of property rights. The exchange rate is not allowed to adjust itself naturally. The flow of wealth in and out of the country is controlled, and international firms operating in the country are tightly restricted. The CCP uses government subsidies and export tax rebates to boost exports with the aim of defeating competitors in a price war. This has disrupted the normal order of world trade. It is precisely for these reasons that the World Trade Organization has long refused to acknowledge China as a market economy.

Many in Western governments harbored the naive hope that economic development would bring political liberalization and democracy to China. Instead, with greater financial means, the CCP subjected its people to more brutal and sophisticated forms of repression. For example, in order to carry out the persecution of Falun Gong, the CCP greatly expanded and empowered its security forces, pouring funds into advanced surveillance systems and promoting those responsible for "successful" persecution to high-ranking positions.

Inevitably, the instruments used to persecute Falun Gong were repurposed to repress other faiths and the general population. Since 2009, the CCP has spent far in excess of 500 billion yuan (US$75 billion) annually to cover the costs of "maintaining stability," that is, policing the Chinese population.

b. The Truth Behind China's Economic Rise

Because of China's rapid GDP growth over the past forty years, many have come to believe in the superiority of socialist economics. It has made many Westerners, including elites in political and academic circles, marvel at the efficiency of the totalitarian system.

In fact, the economic model the CCP has built can hardly be replicated elsewhere. On the one hand, despite its economic rise, the socialist system has great internal instability. On the other hand, the Party's model enshrouds an abundance of corruption created by its unscrupulous political system. China's economic growth has been based in large part on the following factors.

First, the relaxation of the state-owned economy and central planning, and the revitalization of the private sector, gave the Chinese economy a powerful productive drive. The Chinese people, who had had their industrious potential stifled for decades, showed their desire to rise out of poverty and their drive to do business. Moreover, China's vast population of more than one billion provided an almost inexhaustible pool of cheap labor.

A second factor was the massive influx of Western capital and technology into China during the reform era. Under the command economy, China's vast expanses of underutilized land, labor, and markets were like gold for which prices were not yet determined. The combination of capital investment and undeveloped resources ignited the blaze of China's economic growth. Had it not been for the Party's totalitarian rule, this fire could have started decades earlier and in a much more controllable and sustainable fashion.

The scale of Western investment in China is immense. According to published figures, American annual direct investment in China reached almost $117 billion in 2018, up from $11 billion in 2000. [29] The total value of foreign capital entering China from 1979 to 2015 amounted to about $1.64 trillion, according to China's Ministry of Commerce. [30]

Western countries gave the People's Republic of China preferential trade status along with broad market access. In May 2000, the US government granted Beijing "permanent normal trade relations." On December 11, 2001, China formally entered the World Trade Organization and joined the international market. Consequently, a huge amount of Western wealth and production was transferred to China, making it the "world's factory."

However, it cannot be forgotten that the PRC's economic power was fed on unethical practices: the extreme exploitation of workers, the use of sweatshops and of forced labor in prison camps across the country, the demolition of housing and forced relocation of the occupants, and the like. For the sake of short-term growth, the CCP welcomed environmental destruction and ignored public health hazards in order to squeeze every last drop of profit from its land, people, and resources. The Communist Party took advantage of Western capital, technology, and markets; its favorable trading status; and cheap domestic production costs in order to make vast sums in foreign reserves. The trade deficit between the United States and China rose from about $83 billion in 2000 to more than $345 billion in 2019.

Eventually, the CCP overturned the conventions of international trade and took full advantage of the opportunities available to it, regardless of whether they were legitimate. It adopted a national strategy of plagiarizing intellectual property in attempts to overtake other countries in industry and technology. This constitutes the biggest case of theft in history. A 2017 report by the Commission on the Theft of American Intellectual Property stated that the PRC's fake goods, pirated software, and stolen trade secrets caused the United States a loss of between $225 billion and $600 billion every year, a figure that did not include losses due to the theft of intellectual property. The report states that over the three preceding years, the United States lost $1.2 trillion due to intellectual theft, the majority of which was perpetrated by Chinese actors. [31] A report by the Office of the Director of National Intelligence stated that 90 percent of cyber attacks on US businesses originated from the PRC and that these had inflicted an estimated $400 billion in total economic damage every year. [32]

The CCP's economic model utilizes state authority to induce rapid economic development while employing underhanded tactics to increase its competitiveness. It also has encouraged other countries to adopt heavier state intervention. These countries have made the grave mistake of looking to the Party's model as an example of success while ignoring the human and moral tragedies it created.

c. Consequences of the CCP's Economic Model

The CCP's economic model goes hand in hand with the communist specter's relentless erosion of human morality.

Today's China is inundated with fake goods, poisonous food, pornography, drugs, gambling, and gangs. Corruption and debauchery have become achievements to take pride in, while social trust is virtually nonexistent. The widening gap between rich and poor is accompanied by social strife and abuse of justice. In the PRC's economy of power, Party officials use their authority to amass wealth. The severity of the corruption increases with rank. The misappropriation of billions is a normal occurrence. There is simply no government as corrupt or morally degenerate as the Chinese communist regime.

Within this environment of corruption, citizens turn a blind eye to the suffering of their compatriots. In October 2011, the world was shocked by the death of Yueyue, a two-year-old girl in Guangdong Province who was hit by a truck. Instead of getting out to help, the driver rode over Yueyue again as he left the scene. Minutes later, another vehicle ran over her legs. Eighteen people walked by without helping Yueyue, until a scrap collector finally moved the crying toddler to safety. She later died in the hospital. International media wondered if China had lost its soul. It might be understandable that people are reluctant to come to the aid of others when there is danger involved, such as in an armed robbery, yet Yueyue did not pose any conceivable threat to anyone as she lay dying in the street.

The communist movement leads to enormous destruction of traditional values and culture, and in communist China, moral standards have already dropped far beyond what one can easily imagine. The harvesting of organs from living people, good people who practice spiritual cultivation and strive for self-improvement, has become a state-sanctioned industrial operation. An unknown number of prisoners of conscience have been killed on operating tables as their organs were plundered for profit. Communists have turned medical personnel, who are supposed to help people, into murderers. The CCP's evil has reached across the world; through economic incentives, the Party entices countries that are supposed to be upholding human rights to turn a blind eye to its crimes.

Economic growth without morality is chaotic, unsustainable, and disastrous. Under the inhumane policies of the CCP, social conflicts abound, and the environment is on the verge of collapse. The consequences of moral decay are fatal. China calls itself a strong country, but its strength is an illusion. Its superficial prosperity, built upon the reckless pursuit of wealth, is doomed to collapse.

There is no good future in store for China if it cannot escape the snare of the CCP. The specter of communism has no intention of implementing healthy and sustainable growth, as its true goal is to destroy China along with the rest of the world.

4. The Ravages of Socialism in the Developing World

a. Eastern Europe: Haunted by Socialism

Nearly thirty years after the fall of the Soviet Union, communism continues to haunt Eastern Europe, as there has never been a full reckoning of the crimes committed by former communist regimes.

The lingering presence of communism can be seen in various facets of Eastern European politics and economics. Russia and Belarus, for example, retain powerful state-owned enterprises, high welfare, and aggressively interventionist policies. During the transitional period from communism, Eastern European countries experienced crises of slow economic growth and high unemployment. All this encouraged the relapse of communism and socialism in new forms. Left-wing parties were animated with renewed vigor, feeding off a sense of nostalgia for the "good old days" under socialism. [33] The ghost of communism has not been banished.

b. How Socialist Economics Failed Developing Nations

In the developing nations of Asia, Latin America, and Africa, many newly independent countries had declared their allegiance to socialism by the 1960s, with disastrous results. In the early 2000s, Venezuela's economy collapsed as a direct result of its socialist policies. Once the richest in Latin America, the country is now rife with poverty, crime, and starvation. Zimbabwe was once one of the wealthiest nations in Africa; today, it has sunk into a state of economic catastrophe, with inflation spiralling beyond imagination.

Venezuela: How Socialism Bankrupted a Prosperous Country

Venezuela is blessed with considerable oil reserves. In the 1970s, it was the fastest-growing economy in Latin America, enjoying the lowest level of income inequality and the highest per capita GDP in the region. [34] Venezuela's relatively free economy attracted skilled immigrants from Italy, Portugal, and Spain. Together with the protection of property rights, these factors enabled the nation's economy to grow rapidly from the 1940s to the 1970s. [35]

In 1999, when the new president took office, he embarked on an ill-fated program of nationalization that eventually threw the Venezuelan economy into chaos. The president publicly declared: "We must transcend capitalism. But we cannot resort to state capitalism, which would be the same perversion of the Soviet Union. We must reclaim socialism as a thesis, a project, and a path, a new type of socialism, a humanist one, which puts humans and not machines or the state ahead of everything." [36]

To build socialism, the Venezuelan government requisitioned or nationalized many private companies across industries including oil, agriculture, finance, heavy industry, steel, telecommunications, energy, transportation, and tourist enterprises. This process was ramped up following the president's 2007 reelection. His government expropriated 1,147 private companies between 2007 and 2012, with catastrophic effects.

Companies in once-productive industries were shut down and replaced by inefficient state-owned enterprises, scaring off investors. As production sank, Venezuela turned to relying heavily on imports. Coupled with a series of government interventions involving foreign reserves and price controls, disaster inevitably struck when the price of oil dropped. Some attributed this tragedy to the oil crisis, but according to data provided by the World Bank, seven countries that relied even more heavily on oil exports than Venezuela continued to experience economic growth from 2013 to 2017. [37]

The root cause of Venezuela's dramatic failure was the socialist economic system. Venezuela's economic policy essentially marched to the tune of the ten revolutionary demands Marx proposed in *The Communist Manifesto,* starting with abolition of private ownership and high taxes and moving to a centralized economy and means of production. [38] Venezuela met its economic fate at the hands of the communist specter.

Zimbabwe: From Africa's Breadbasket to Land of Famine

After Zimbabwe's declaration of independence in 1980, it endeavored to build a socialist state according to Marxist-Leninist principles. Its first prime minister was a Marxist believer and his guerrillas, guided by Mao Zedong Thought, received unconditional assistance from the PRC. Unlike other African countries that implemented socialism, Zimbabwe did not immediately impose policies of nationalization.

Zimbabwe's economic woes began in 2000 following the start of land reform. Land belonging to white farmers was seized and redistributed among landless blacks, as well as politically connected individuals. Many were inexperienced in farming, and the result was a sharp decline in agricultural productivity. In an attempt to evade the crisis, the Reserve Bank of Zimbabwe printed more money, leading to endless hyperinflation. Figures from the central bank indicate that in June 2008, the country's annual inflation reached 231 million percent. By mid-November 2008, inflation peaked at nearly 80 billion percent, after which the authorities gave up publishing monthly statistics. [39]

In 2008, Zimbabwe was struck by a major famine. Of the country's sixteen million people, five million were threatened with starvation. Today, malnutrition is chronic and widespread.

Communism plagues the world in ways that can be observed or foreseen across all countries. Developed Western countries are beginning to experience crises brought on by excessive welfare and state interventionism. Meanwhile, the tragedy of socialism is already a reality in the developing world. This is the principle: The communist specter uses economics to promise comfort and satisfaction, then lures people into moral degradation and the abyss of poverty.

5. Marx's Theory of Exploitation: An Inversion of Good and Evil

Through a set of elaborate theories, Marxism deceives people into replacing traditional morals with its ersatz standards of utility that invert right and wrong. In the Marxian view, whether an individual is good or bad is based not on his morality and actions, but rather on his place in the (inverse) hierarchy of capital.

One who belongs to what Marxists call the "capitalist" class is guilty of exploiting the proletariat, and since the proletariat is supposedly the oppressed and exploited class, its members naturally occupy the moral high ground. No matter how they treat business owners, property owners, and the affluent, they can hold their heads high. Marxism turned the possession of property into a crime and advocated violent expropriation.

In Marxist theory, only labor creates value. If a company owner invests $10 million in a company in a year, and the revenue that year is $11 million, in the Marxian view, this $1 million in profit is "surplus value" created by the employees but unfairly expropriated by the "capitalist" company owner. Thus, Marx claimed that exploitation was the secret to how capitalists made money and, therefore, the "original sin" of the bourgeoisie. Marx concluded that to eliminate this sin, the entire capitalist society must be destroyed — that is, the bourgeoisie would be eliminated and their assets confiscated, while the vanguard of the party would collectivize property and institute communism.

Marx's theory of exploitation divides people into two opposing classes: the bourgeoisie with capital, and the proletariat without. But, in fact, class mobility has increased rapidly since industrialized societies came to the fore. The degree of class mobility in the first half of the nineteenth century was similar to that in the 1970s in both the United Kingdom and the United States. [40] The interchange between classes is a dynamic process; a supposed member of the proletariat is no longer among the proletariat if he buys public equity in a company, for example. If one's class assignment can be changed so easily, attempts at dividing people into groups like this have no other purpose than to incite class hatred.

In China, the Soviet Union, and the communist states of Eastern Europe, the communist parties stole land, lynched landlords, and robbed business owners of their factories. They murdered "class enemies" and confiscated generational wealth, waging campaigns of state terrorism against the people. All this evildoing was the result of communism's hate-filled theories. Meanwhile, traditional moral standards, as well as belief in the divine, saints, and classical sages, were branded as belonging to "the exploiting classes" and were to be attacked and eradicated.

Marx's theories have long been discredited in economic and philosophical circles. Below are merely a few examples that illustrate the absurdity of Marx's theory of exploitation. According to Marxism, it is labor that creates value, and that value is determined by the labor time necessary for production. This is a ridiculous theory, because the value of a commodity is not an intrinsic property. For almost every good, there is a subjective human element, resulting in natural and largely unpredictable patterns of supply and demand.

Many economists have explored the process of valuation, and unlike Marx's narrow doctrine, most agree that numerous factors are involved in the creation of value — including land, capital, labor, science and technology, management, the risk of investment, and so on. Economic activities form a complex system, involving different links in the chain of production. Different factors of production have certain managerial requirements, and different people play different roles, which are indispensable to the whole chain and contribute t o the creation of "residual value."

For example, a business owner plans to spend $1 million hiring two designers to produce a new toy. A marketer also is hired to promote the product. Two years later, the new toy gains popularity and earns a profit of $50 million. Is it the labor of the designers and marketer that created the residual value of $50 million? Of course not. The reason the new toy earned millions is that people wanted it. The business owner's insight into the market, ability to organize and manage others, and courage to take a risk all contributed to the value of the toy. Suppose the creativity in the toy came from one of the designers — then, does the residual value of the $50 million come from the fact that the business owner exploited the designer's creativity without giving anything in return? Of course not. If the designer thought his creativity was not being adequately rewarded, he could have found another company that offered higher pay.

In a free market, a balance will ultimately be struck in matching skills and ambition with capital. Business owners who demand unreasonable profits will lose to the competition or be unable to attract talent. In addition, since waiting for a return on invested capital delays spending or other enjoyment of that capital, the profits are also due to the efforts of the investor. Therefore, it's normal that an additional sum will be gained in return. The principle is no different than lending at interest.

There also are many "accidental" factors involved in deciding the value of a commodity. Such factors can only be reasonably explained by a frame of reference founded on traditional beliefs and culture.

In certain situations, the creation and destruction of value can be entirely unrelated to labor. A diamond worth $10 million today may have been worthless five thousand years ago because no one wanted it. A barren patch of land inherited from a grandfather could suddenly be one hundred times more valuable due to the growth of a nearby city or the discovery of rare-earth metals underground. Here, such vast, unexpected wealth is simply a matter of good fortune; the increase in value involves no labor. Both Western and Eastern cultural traditions recognize that fortune is a form of divine blessing.

In order to demonstrate the "rationality" and "necessity" of state ownership, Marx concocted the exploitation theory based on surplus value, which turned the economic activities that people engage in as a normal part of life into negative and unethical behavior. His theory poured hatred and scorn on the existing economic order as part of his attempt to undermine and overthrow it.

In fact, the employers and the workers, the landlords and the peasants, form a community of shared interests. Their relationship should be one of cooperation and interdependence; each group supports the other to survive. Marx deliberately exaggerated the differences between classes, seeing them as absolutes — like the antagonism between mortal enemies.

There are good and bad people among employers, just as there are among workers. In economic exchange, what should really be exposed and sanctioned is anyone who violates ethical standards. The basis of judgment should be moral character, not wealth.

People can change their economic and social status through their own efforts. Workers can become investors through the accumulation of wealth. Investors can become workers due to failures in their investments. The role of labor and investors in modern society often changes. Most people also play both roles — putting the profits they made into future productive capacity, thus creating employment, increasing social wealth, and benefitting the general public. Even the founder of the US labor union movement said, "The worst crime against working people is a company which fails to operate at a profit." [41]

The absurd "surplus value theory" affixes the label of "exploitation" to the normal activities of landowners and capitalists. This has incited incalculable hatred and struggle, and muddled thinking, while destroying the lives of millions.

6. Hatred and Jealousy: The Origin of Absolute Egalitarianism

Communism advocates absolute egalitarianism. Superficially, this may sound like a high-minded aim, leading many to blindly believe it is righteous. In reality, absolute egalitarianism evokes hatred and jealousy, as people believing in it can't tolerate the success of others, or others being wealthier and having better lives, easier work, or more luxurious living conditions. Believers say, "I should have what you have, and I can get what you get." In such a worldview, everyone is equal and the whole world is the same.

Absolute egalitarianism manifests in at least two main ways. First, when people are not yet equal, they are encouraged to be dissatisfied with their economic status. People come to covet what others have and even seek it through improper or violent means. In extreme cases, they destroy others' property and even kill to get rich.

The worst manifestation of these tendencies is violent revolution. In order to provoke dissatisfaction, Marx divides society into two opposite classes: those who own the means of production, and those who don't. In the countryside, this was the landlord and the peasant; in the city, it was the business owner and the worker. The aim was to incite class hatred and use the supposedly disenfranchised members of society to carry out violent revolution. The peasants are poor, but the landlords are rich — seize their wealth! Everyone should be rich! Thus, the CCP called on peasants to engage in "land reform" — that is, attacking landlords and dividing up their land. If the landlords refused to comply, they were killed. The Party did this by first inciting hooligans to start trouble, then encouraging the peasantry to join them in rising up and attacking the landlord class. During the 1950s, the "land reform" movement turned into a terror campaign that claimed the lives of millions across China.

Second, once groups have basically achieved a state of "equality" — in which any benefits are divided up among everyone — anyone who stands out is penalized. Everyone is treated the same whether one works more, works less, or doesn't work at all. This fails to acknowledge a universal principle: While people may appear to be the same on the surface, in truth, each individual's personality, intellect, physical strength, morality, occupation, role, education, living conditions, endurance and perseverance, inventiveness, and so on are all different, and what one contributes to society is also different. Why should the same outcome be applied to all? In this sense, the "inequality" railed against by communists is actually true equality, while the equality pursued by them is true inequality and true injustice.

The ancients in China said that heaven will reward a person according to the effort he or she puts in. Absolute egalitarianism is impossible in the real world.

Under the cover of egalitarianism, the lazy benefit while the capable and the hardworking are penalized and even resented or hated. Everyone slows their pace to match the speed of the slowest. This causes everyone to become lazy, waiting for someone else to contribute so that one can take advantage and jump on for the ride, gaining something for nothing or stealing from another. The result is widespread moral decline.

The hatred and jealousy that drive absolute egalitarianism are the poisonous roots of communism's economic perspective. Human nature has both good and evil inherent in it. Western faiths refer to the seven deadly sins, while Eastern culture teaches that man has both Buddha nature and demon nature. Buddha nature manifests itself as kindness, the ability to endure hardship, and consideration for others. Demon nature manifests as selfishness, laziness, jealousy, malice, hatred, rage, lust, and tyranny, as well as having a disregard for life, inciting discord, spreading rumors, getting something for nothing, and so on.

The economic perspective adopted by communism deliberately stimulates demon nature, amplifying people's jealousy, greed, laziness, and other evil factors, causing people to lose their humanity and forsake the traditional values held for thousands of years.

In *The Theory of Moral Sentiments*, eighteenth-century economist and philosopher Adam Smith said that morality is the foundation of mankind's prosperity. Observing common rules of morality "is required for the very existence of human society, which would crumble into nothing if mankind were not generally impressed with a reverence for those important rules of conduct." [42]

Lawrence Kudlow, director of the US National Economic Council, believes that morality must exist alongside economic prosperity. He wrote in 1997 that if the United States could abide by the "foremost principle" — to adhere to the moral values the nation was founded on — the development of the United States would be limitless. [43]

a. Economic Egalitarianism: A Stepping Stone to Communism

Under the influence of absolute egalitarianism, vigorous calls ring out in the West for "social justice," as well as minimum-wage laws, affirmative action, and other demands. What lies behind these is a desire for equality of outcome, of which communist elements can take advantage. From the communist perspective, it doesn't matter whether these vulnerable groups obtain equality or if their social status improves. They are merely pawns for inciting resentment, and eventually revolution.

When communists succeed in their advocacy, they simply make

an unending stream of new demands. If they don't succeed, they strengthen people's notions about the justice of equality and turn this into a major platform upon which to gain more influence. Because communism incites resentment in multiple fields and via so many different means, if it's allowed to spread unchecked, the inevitable result is social turmoil. Communists will always be able to find vulnerable groups and demand financial or social equality for them, repeating the process until the path toward communism is paved.

Moreover, the implementation of these policies often results in the opposite of what is promised. Those who are supposed to be protected by these policies instead lose out. Take minimum-wage laws, for example: On the surface, its goal is to protect the rights of workers, but the effect is that many businesses simply stop hiring because it is uneconomical for them to do so. As a result, workers lose their jobs. Eliminating lower-wage jobs also means the loss of skill-building, as young people and those new to an occupation then have few opportunities to be trained and work their way up to higher-paying jobs. The one-size-fits-all approach also violates economic principles and results in excessive government intervention.

People use the excuse of "equal pay for equal work" to demand social revolution based on fighting racism and sexism. They cite statistics that, for example, the average wage of black males is less than the average wage of white males, that the average female wage is less than the average male wage, and that these discrepancies are the result of racism and sexism. In reality, such comparisons are not appropriate; when comparing apples to apples, the results are different. Research has found that college-educated, married black couples earn slightly more than their white counterparts. [44] After decades of communist tactics to destroy the traditional family and promote welfare, there are relatively fewer black families of this type, and this is the main reason why there are overall discrepancies between the races regarding income. Making meaningful and accurate comparisons should be common sense, but communist elements, by inciting discord and struggle, lead people to look at things irrationally.

Communism does not care about the well-being of vulnerable groups. It is simply interested in slogans that drag people down the road to destruction.

b. Communism's Use of Unions to Undermine Free Societies

The loss of US manufacturing jobs in the past few decades is a well-known phenomenon, but many people don't realize that unions, hijacked by leftist causes, are one of the main culprits. Many of today's unions claim to help obtain benefits for the working class, but they often do the opposite. This is evident in the history of unions and the transformation of their mission.

Trade unions were initially founded by members of the working class with few or no skills, for the purpose of negotiating with management. To a certain extent, a trade union is able to broker and resolve conflicts between workers and owners. But communist elements took unions and turned them into tools to promote communist policies and movements. The unions became a powerful weapon for destroying free enterprise and carrying out political struggle.

Friedrich Engels wrote on the topic, "The time also is rapidly approaching when the working class will have understood that the struggle for high wages and short hours, and the whole action of Trades Unions as now carried on, is not an end in itself, but a means, a very necessary and effective means' but only one of several means towards a higher end: the abolition of the wages system altogether." [45]

Lenin believed that the formation and legalization of trade unions was an important means for the working class to wrest control from the "capitalist" class, and that the unions would become the pillar of the Communist Party and a key force in class struggle.

In a speech, Lenin proposed that trade unions become "a school of administration, a school of economic management, a school of communism," and a link between the Communist Party and the masses. The daily work of the trade union was to convince the masses to transition from capitalism to communism. "The trade unions are a 'reservoir' of the state power," he wrote. [46]

In the mid-to-late nineteenth century, communist and left-wing forces used trade unions to incite workers to go on large-scale strikes, make harsh demands on owners, and even take violent measures, such as destroying machinery and factories. In October 1905, more than 1.7 million workers in Russia participated in a nationwide political strike that paralyzed the country's economy. During this time, a particularly aggressive union, the Central Workers' Group, was formed and became the main precursor to the Petrograd Soviet, a "council" of workers and soldiers that played a central role as the vehicle for the Russian Revolution. [47]

Trade unions in Western and developed countries also have been widely infiltrated and used by communist elements. The relationship between employers and employees is a symbiotic one, yet communists try to provoke, expand, and intensify discord between them. Unions are used to escalate conflicts during the bargaining process between management and workers. Additionally, unions rationalize and intensify the confrontational side of the management–worker relationship and use this to legitimize their own existence. From there, they inflame workers' dissatisfaction and blame the "capitalists" for any problems. This has been key to unions' survival.

On the surface, trade unions are fighting for the interests of workers, but in reality, they are undermining industrial competitiveness. There are two reasons for this. First, under the pretext of protecting workers' rights and interests, unions make it difficult for enterprises to lay off employees who don't perform well and who achieve little. This gives rise to a culture of laziness. Not only is this unfair to employees who work diligently, but it also makes them less proactive. The most important factor in the growth of a company is its workers, but with the unions' umbrella of protection over employees who fail to perform, enterprises lose their competitiveness. Enterprises that fail to meet union demands are then the targets of struggle, including strikes and protests, which further hinder business. The powerful United Auto Workers union routinely called for strikes in Detroit. Prior to the 2008 financial crisis, the union demanded $70 an hour in wages and benefits. Consequently, the US automobile manufacturing industry was driven to the brink of bankruptcy. [48]

Second, under the pretext of protecting employees' welfare (including pensions, health insurance, and the like), unions constantly raise costs for enterprises. This forces companies to curtail growth and to cut their investment in research and development, which hurts competitiveness. It also results in companies having to increase product prices, which harms consumer interests. Studies show that this is why companies without unions, such as Toyota and Honda, were able to produce high-quality cars at a lower cost, and why Detroit-based automobile factories with labor unions became less competitive. [49]

As Edwin Feulner, founder of US think tank The Heritage Foundation, said of unions, "They function like an albatross around a company's neck — making it less flexible, less able to react wisely to the demands of a changing marketplace." [50]

While the loss of job opportunities in the US manufacturing industry has been recognized and discussed for decades, many people don't know that unions are a key driver behind the job losses. Unionized manufacturing jobs fell by 75 percent between 1977 and 2008, while nonunion manufacturing employment increased by 6 percent over that time, according to a report by The Heritage Foundation.

The situation in the construction sector is similar. Heritage Foundation research fellow James Sherk wrote: "Unlike the manufacturing sector, the construction industry has grown considerably since the late 1970s. However, in the aggregate, that growth has occurred exclusively in nonunion jobs, expanding 159 percent since 1977. Unionized construction jobs fell by 17 percent." [51]

In addition, labor unions are the tools employed by communist elements to promote egalitarianism in enterprises. Sherk notes that unions demand that companies pay wages according to the length of service of the employee (the same is done in socialist countries), without regard to the employee's contribution to the company or performance. "Union contracts compress wages: They suppress the wages of more productive workers and raise the wages of the less competent," he wrote. [52] The idea at work here is the same as absolute egalitarianism under communism, which is effectively the redistribution of wealth among employees within the enterprise. The interference in the internal decision-making of enterprises and the monopoly of the labor market erodes the free market.

Unions' aggressive advocacy for what they describe as workers' welfare ends up favoring some workers over others and puts a drag on individual companies and the economy as a whole. A survey conducted in 2005 showed that "most union households disapprove of American unions" and that "the main reason for their disapproval is never openly discussed in union media or addressed at union conventions." [53]

Labor unions infiltrated by communism, and under the guidance of the progressive movement, have often become tools to wage struggle against the free market, rather than pushing for and safeguarding employees' rightful interests. Corruption and vested interests are common among union leaders. Their single-minded battle against what they call injustice in the workplace creates a burden on industry and productivity, preventing corporate reform and rational attempts to streamline manufacturing, services, education, government bureaucracy, and other fields. Politically, the Left draws support from unions to promote their social movements and drive wedges in society.

7. Communist 'Ideals': Tempting Man Toward His Own Destruction

Although communist theory is full of loopholes and contradictions, many are still deceived by it. This is because Marx described a utopian communist paradise that people all over the world could enjoy. This is the central fantasy and delusion. His depiction included "overwhelming material abundance" in a new utopian society. Each person would work "according to his ability" and receive "according to his need." There would be no private ownership, no gap between the rich and the poor, no ruling class, and no exploitation. There would be freedom and equality for all, and each person would be able to develop his or her particular talents. Life would be wonderful.

This set of deceitful arguments, repackaged in so many ways, has attracted many to fight for it. Many Westerners today have never experienced or learned about the tragedies of life under a totalitarian state. They continue to harbor an illusory hope for a communist paradise, and therefore fan the flames by advocating communist and socialist ideas.

All the ideas put forward by Marx are dangerous illusions. Marxism claims that a communist society will enjoy a superabundance of material goods. However, human desires and human wants are endless. Under the constraints of limited human knowledge, limited working hours, and limited resources, shortages and deprivations are inevitable. The scarcity principle is the starting point for all economic studies. Without these constraints, people wouldn't have to explore which kind of production method was most efficient, as the supposed superabundance would provide for all and could be squandered at will.

Marxism also claims that moral standards would be greatly improved in a communist society. However, as good and evil coexist in each person, the improvement of moral standards in a society requires the guidance of upright beliefs and values, as well as personal efforts in spiritual cultivation. What Marxism preaches is atheism and class struggle, which enlarge the evil side of humans. People are denied freedom of belief, and religion is twisted into a political tool used by communist parties to distort and persecute true faith. Without righteous belief in the divine and self-discipline, morality can only decline. Moreover, once in power, all communist leaders prove to be tyrants — arrogant, lewd, and completely unethical. To expect their followers to be so vastly improved in moral standards runs counter to reason.

Marxism also proclaims there will be equality for all. But as discussed earlier, socialism inevitably leads to tyranny. Power is the basis of resource distribution, yet the distribution of power under a totalitarian state is most unjust. Therefore, resource distribution under totalitarianism also will be most unjust. In all countries where socialism rules or has ruled, people see a privileged stratum form, as well as extreme gaps between the rich and the poor and the suppression of people by the state. Resources are exhausted for military purposes, and people's belongings are robbed to make the privileged class more powerful, while the majority are left to labor in poverty.

Marxism deceives with the promise of "from each according to his ability, to each according to his need." [54] Communism promises that every member of society can give full play to his or her abilities. But in reality, under socialist economies, people are unable to act at will according to their own abilities because they do not have basic freedoms.

Marxism says that the division of labor creates alienation. But in fact, division of labor is necessary for any society. Smith argues in *The Wealth of Nations* that a division of labor can greatly increase productivity and promote prosperity. The differences created by the division are not necessarily conflicts, nor do they necessarily lead to alienation and depersonalization. People from all walks of life, regardless of their station, can contribute to society, elevate their morals, and help to bring happiness to their families and communities.

However, communism uses individuals' pursuit of goodness to mislead them into becoming religious fanatics for communist ideology. It uses the pursuit of goodness as its banner to pull people away from the divine. It pollutes people's minds, strengthens their evil nature, and leads them to commit all manner of crimes. Under this influence, people indulge in material enjoyment, casting aside loftier and nobler beliefs in the higher purpose of life. Communism poisons everything it touches and slaughters people by the millions, as seen in every country where it comes to power. If the world's people do not wake up now, they will face horrifying consequences.

8. Morality, Prosperity, and Peace

Pursuing happiness is part of human nature. A prosperous economy can bring happiness, yet the economy does not exist in a vacuum. When the path of economic development deviates from ethics and morality, an economic crisis may follow. A society that is merely wealthy is not only incapable of bringing joy and happiness, but its prosperity will also be short-lived. As the foundation of ethics and morality crumbles, a disastrous outcome awaits.

In 2010, *People's Daily*, a mouthpiece for the Chinese regime, reported that despite economic development, China had been declining for years on the Forbes' Gross National Happiness Index. The world's second-largest economy is plagued with corruption, environmental pollution, and food-safety incidents, making the Chinese people extremely insecure about their livelihood. In this case, wealth has increased as morality and happiness have declined.

This reflects the fatal flaw in communism: Human beings are composed not only of flesh, but, far more so, of mind and spirit. The divine laid down the path that man's life would take. The Chinese say "every bite and every sip is preordained," which is analogous to the Western spiritual belief in the concept of fate or predestination. People who believe in the divine understand that wealth is a grace bestowed upon them by their Creator. They value having a humble and thankful heart, and hence they are content and happy.

Among those aboard the doomed Titanic as the ship sank in 1912 was millionaire John Jacob Astor IV, whose fortune was enough to build thirty Titanics. Yet when facing death, he did what he thought was morally correct and protected women and children — he gave his spot in the final lifeboat to two terrified children. [55] Similarly, Isidor Straus, co-owner of Macy's department store, said, "I will not go before the other men." His wife, Ida, also refused to get on a lifeboat, giving her place to Ellen Bird, their new housemaid. Ida chose to spend her final moments with her husband. [56]

These people of great wealth chose to put traditional values and faith before the opportunity to save their assets and lives. Their sense of morality and justice reflected the highest state of human civilization and human nature: A noble character is more valuable than life, which is yet more valuable than wealth.

Mr. Li Hongzhi, the founder of Falun Gong, wrote in "Wealth With Virtue":

It is the duty of the ruler and officials to bring wealth to the populace, yet promotion of money-worship is the worst policy one could adopt. Wealth without virtue (de) will harm all sentient beings, while wealth with virtue is what all people hope for. Therefore, one cannot be affluent without advocating virtue.

Virtue is accumulated in past lives. Becoming a king, an official, wealthy, or nobility all come from virtue. No virtue, no gain; the loss of virtue means the loss of everything. Thus, those who seek power and wealth must first accumulate virtue. By suffering hardships and doing good deeds one can accumulate virtue among the masses. To achieve this, one must understand the principle of cause and effect. Knowing this can enable officials and the populace to exercise self-restraint, and prosperity and peace will thereby prevail under heaven. [57]

If humankind maintains the aforementioned values for wealth and life, the economic challenges rooted in human beings' greed, sloth, and jealousy will be reduced considerably. The more humanity is able to suppress its selfish desires, the less the specter of communism will be able to lure the human heart, and moral standards will remain inviolate.

The communist specter has made intricate arrangements to destroy mankind. Its economic arrangements are only one part of the story. To free ourselves from the control of communist "ideals," we need to expose the conspiracy, identify the fraudulent messaging, and stop putting hope in this bankrupt creed. Civilization will regain its vitality when mankind rediscovers traditional values and recovers morality and virtue. Only then will humanity be able to obtain true peace and embrace everlasting prosperity and happiness.

CHAPTER TEN

Corrupting the Legal System

1. Law and Faith

LAW IS THE IRON FORCE of fairness and justice that affirms
good and punishes evil. What is good and what is evil must be understood by those who write laws. From the perspective of faith, these
criteria come from the divine. The teachings of sages and religious
scriptures provided the basis for the laws that govern human society.

The Code of Hammurabi, enacted in ancient Babylon, is one of
the earliest sets of written laws that have been found. Engraved in
the stone tablet above the code itself is a powerful scene: Shamash,
god of the sun and justice, bestowing the laws upon King Hammurabi. This is the depiction of a god granting a human sovereign the
authority to govern his people using the rule of law.

For Hebrews, the Ten Commandments in the Old Testament
were considered to be both divine and secular law simultaneously
— a tradition that became the foundation of Western legal culture.

From the time of the fourth-century Roman emperors, to the East Roman Justinian I and his successors, to Alfred the Great, the first of Britain's Anglo-Saxon kings, the legal system took the Ten Commandments and Christian doctrine as its inspiration. [1]

Followers of religion believe that in order to be considered legitimate, the law must accommodate divine standards of good and evil, as well as religious teachings. The thinking behind nonviolent civil disobedience in the United States can be traced back to early Christian doctrine. When Roman emperor Gaius Caligula commanded that his statue be erected within the Temple of Jerusalem and that Christians worship Roman gods, Christians opted to face crucifixion or be burned at the stake rather than obey. To have followed the command would have meant violating the first two Commandments — in other words, the emperor demanded that secular law take precedence over divine commandment, which is sacred and inviolable.

The Ten Commandments can be divided into two categories. The first four describe the relationship between man and God — that is, what constitutes appropriate reverence for God. The other six govern relationships between people and reflect the teaching to love others as you love yourself. Reverence for God is an imperative that enables humanity to maintain, unchanged, the principles of fairness and justice.

The same was true in ancient China, where historically the law was promulgated by imperial decree. The emperor, or "Son of Heaven," was required to follow providence and the principles of heaven and earth. This is the "Tao," or Way, imparted by Lao Tzu and the Yellow Emperor. The Han Dynasty Confucian scholar Dong Zhongshu said: "The greatness of Tao originates from heaven. Heaven never changes, and neither does the Tao." [2] In ancient

Chinese usage, "heaven" is not an abstraction of natural forces, but refers to the divine. Faith in the Tao of heaven forms the moral bedrock of Chinese culture. The imperial legislative systems derived from this belief influenced China for thousands of years.

Twentieth-century American legal scholar Harold J. Berman believed that the law coexists with the overall principles of social morality and faith. Even under the separation of church and state, the two are mutually dependent. In any society, the concepts of justice and legality must have their roots in what is considered holy and sacred. [3] The modern legal system retains many facets of religious ceremony that enhance its power.

2. Law Under Communist Tyrannies

Communist parties are anti-theist cults. They aim to sever a society's links to its ancestral culture and traditional values, and they will never follow the teachings of righteous gods in their legislative principles. It was never realistic to expect that communist parties would make any sincere attempts to maintain fairness or justice.

a. Extralegal Policies of State Terror

Traditionally, Christians talk about loving others as we love ourselves, and Confucian teachings say that the benevolent man loves others. Here, love is not limited to the narrow concept of love between a man and a woman, or the love that exists among family members or friends. Love also encompasses benevolence, mercy, justice, selflessness, and other virtues. With this cultural foundation, not only is the law sacred, but it also embodies the spirit of love in human society.

No legal system can hope to account for any and all possible forms of conflict and provide judgments for each. Thus, laws must factor in the subjectivity of all parties. A judge must follow the spirit of the law to give a verdict that abides by the principle of benevolence.

In the Temple of Jerusalem, Jesus admonished the Pharisees for their hypocrisy, for despite strictly adhering to the words of Moses, they had ignored virtues required by the code, such as justice, mercy, and truthfulness. Jesus himself healed on the Sabbath and sat with gentiles, for what he cared about was the spirit of kindness embodied within the doctrines, not only their literal meanings.

By contrast, communism is rooted in hatred. It not only hates God, but also hates the culture, lifestyle, and traditions that the divine established for humanity. Karl Marx did not mince words in expressing his desire to doom himself to ruin and bring the world down with him. He wrote to his future wife, "Jenny, if we can but weld our souls together, then with contempt shall I fling my glove in the world's face, then shall I stride through the wreckage a creator!" [4]

Sergey Gennadievich Nechayev, a communist terrorist in czarist Russia, wrote in his pamphlet *The Revolutionary Catechism* that the revolutionary should break "all the bonds which tie him to the social order and the civilized world with all its laws, moralities, and customs, and with all its generally accepted conventions." The revolutionary, according to Nechayev, should see himself as the archenemy of this world and its conventions, and "if he continues to live with them it is only in order to destroy them more speedily." [5] Nechayev's use of the clerical term "catechism" for his lawless vision hints at the cult-like disdain that communism harbors for humanity and the divine. "He is not a revolutionary if he has any sympathy for this world," Nechayev wrote.

Lenin expressed a similar view: "Dictatorship is rule based directly upon force and unrestricted by any laws. The revolutionary dictatorship of the proletariat is rule won and maintained by the use of violence by the proletariat against the bourgeoisie, rule that is unrestricted by any laws." [6]

Wielding political power to kill, torture, and mete out collective punishment in the absence of legal restraints is nothing other than state terrorism, and it is the first step taken by communist regimes when they come to power.

In the months following the Bolshevik overthrow of the Russian government in 1917, hundreds of thousands of people were killed in the course of the political struggle. The Bolsheviks established the All-Russian Extraordinary Commission for Combating Counter-revolution and Sabotage, abbreviated Cheka, and endowed it with powers of summary execution. From 1918 to 1922, the Chekists killed no less than two million people without trial. [7]

Alexander Nikolaevich Yakovlev, former propaganda minister of the Central Committee and member of the Politburo and Secretariat of the Communist Party of the Soviet Union, wrote that in the 20th century alone, sixty million people in Russia had died as a result of war, hunger, and repression. Using public archives, Yakovlev estimated that the number of people killed in Soviet persecution campaigns was twenty million to thirty million. In 1987, the Politburo of the Soviet Union set up a committee, of which Yakovlev was a member, to review miscarriages of justice under Soviet rule. After reviewing thousands of files, Yakovlev wrote: "There's a feeling that I've long been unable to shake. It seems that the perpetrators of these atrocities are a group of people who are mentally deranged, but I fear that such an explanation runs the risk of oversimplifying the problem." [8] To put it more plainly, Yakovlev saw that the atrocities committed in the communist era were not the result of mere impulses, but rather careful planning. These crimes were committed not for the greater good of the world, but from a deep hatred of life itself. The drivers of communism commit atrocities not out of ignorance, but out of malice.

b. Ever-Changing Standards of Right and Wrong

While communism ignores the rule of law to perpetrate acts of state terror, it puts on a show in front of Western countries by claiming it's committed to upholding the law. It does this so that it can engage, infiltrate, and subvert free societies through the avenues of trade and economic partnerships, cultural exchange, and geopolitical cooperation. For instance, at the onset of China's reform and opening up in 1979, the Chinese Communist Party passed a "criminal procedure law," ostensibly to strengthen the judiciary. But this law has never been seriously enforced.

According to Marx, the law is a product of "class contradiction" and a tool that embodies the will of the ruling class. The laws of a communist party come neither from God, nor from a genuine love of the people, nor from a desire to maintain a fair and just society. The interests of the ruling group, that is, the communist party of a given country, are all that matter. As the goals and interests of the party change, so change its laws.

Naturally, once the CCP seized power, it adopted class struggle as its guideline and proceeded to rob the entire citizenry. It promulgated laws against the crime of "counter-revolutionary activity," which applied to everyone who opposed the Party's policies of theft. The CCP punished counter-revolutionaries with incarceration or death.

After completing the process of mass robbery to implement public ownership, the CCP needed a way to keep what it had stolen. It shifted its priorities toward economic development and imple-

288

mented laws that protected private property. In essence, this means little more than protecting the Party's vested interests. For example, the widespread compulsory demolition of Chinese people's homes to make way for development projects illustrates the regime's continued infringement on the right to private property.

In March 1999, the CCP announced the need to "rule the country according to law." [9] Yet, only a few months later, it began the nationwide persecution of Falun Gong and established a Gestapo-like extrajudicial body, the 610 Office, to carry out the brutal campaign. To fulfill its mission, the 610 Office was given the authority to bypass all laws and judicial procedures, allowing it to manipulate the public security apparatus and judicial system to suppress Falun Gong.

The Party periodically conjures up new enemies so as to renew its tyrannical rule over the Chinese people. The targets of persecution are ever-changing — from landlords and capitalists in the 1950s and 1960s, to the students protesting for democracy in 1989, to Falun Gong practitioners and other Chinese of faith, to the human rights lawyers who dare take up their cases.

Accordingly, the law must be changed frequently. In seventy years of rule, the Party has promulgated four constitutions, the last of which has undergone four revisions since its introduction in 1982. Gaining experience from multiple political campaigns, the CCP has used the law to adjust and disguise its motives and actions. Sometimes it does not even bother to apply this camouflage.

c. Ignoring the Constitution

The Constitution of the People's Republic of China is replete with verbose language in an effort to show that the CCP is committed to the rule of law and civilized international norms. In practice, however, the constitution is never strictly followed, and basic rights such as freedom of speech, belief, and association are not actually protected.

According to Marxist theory, law reflects the will of the ruling class, rather than objective justice. For a communist party, then, passing and amending laws to suppress its enemies and impose its will on society follow as a matter of course. Under this kind of system, anyone who dares to challenge the "will of the ruling class" — that is, anyone who opposes the interests of the communist party — is subject to legal persecution as a class enemy, whether they are unemployed workers, demobilized soldiers, farmers whose land was expropriated, human rights lawyers, or simply people struggling to make ends meet.

In communist countries, the laws on the books always make way for the interests of the regime. If a lawyer tries to cite the law and argue in favor of justice, the judge and prosecution will shut him down by talking about the supposed spirit of the law. They even blatantly say that the court is run by the communist party and must follow its orders. Whatever the thoughts of these individual court workers, what they say indeed reflects the spirit of law that exists under communist regimes.

English philosopher Francis Bacon once wrote of the harm that is done when the law is used to dictate commands rather than offer impartial judgment: "One foul sentence doth more hurt than many foul examples. For these do but corrupt the stream, the other corrupteth the fountain." [11]

In the Chinese court system, during hearings involving persecuted Falun Gong practitioners, the judges may say things like the following: "Why are you bringing up the law? I care only about politics." "The Party doesn't allow defense. The leaders' words are the law." "The Communist Party leads the court, so we need to follow the Party line." "No legal procedure is necessary for Falun Gong issues." "Don't talk to me about conscience." [10]

The laws created under communism, ever-malleable and only selectively practiced, hold no sanctity from which to derive legitimate authority. Over the past century, the spirit of the law that governs the Party's legal system has brought about countless injustices and has overseen the deaths of one hundred million innocent people — a debt of blood for which no representative of the communist cause can ever atone.

"A murderer must pay with his life, just as a debtor with money," a Chinese proverb says. Were the Communist Party to truly enforce the law, it would become liable for its bloody history.

3. How Communism Warps the Law in the West

As with politics, economics, education, and other facets of society, Western rule of law has not escaped infiltration and subversion by the communist specter. In communist countries, the law is manipulated as an instrument for maintaining the regime's rule, reinforcing communist party ideology, and suppressing the people. In free countries, the specter's aim is to use the law to distort the standards of good and evil, to subvert traditional faith and the law's moral foundations, and to seize the powers of legislation and enforcement, thus putting demonic norms into practice.

The communist specter's influence over the rule of law can be found all across the West. As the United States is the leader of the free world, this section focuses on the erosion of US legal institutions.

a. Subverting the Moral Foundations of the Law

As communist parties and their various followers around the world promoted atheism and the theory of evolution, the connection between the law and divine principles was gradually rejected. The spirit of the law began to shift from its divine role of maintaining fairness and justice to expressing the will of political interests and radical ideology. The law has been largely reduced to an instrument of revenge, arbitration, bargaining, and the allocation of benefits. This opened the door for those poisoned by communism to pass laws to undermine society and move humanity closer to destruction.

Liberalism and progressivism reject traditional faith and moral judgment, seeing morality as a secular agreement that changes according to the development of society. Marriage, for example, is regarded as a simple contract between two people who are willing to state their commitment to each other, rather than a vow made before the divine. Recognition of same-sex marriage is based on the ostensible premise of freedom and progress — a premise that is malleable and will inevitably result in the corruption of the law. The separation of traditional morality from justice was reflected in an abortion case that reached the Supreme Court in 1992. Three justices stated: "Some of us as individuals find abortion offensive to our most basic principles of morality, but that cannot control our decision. Our obligation is to define the liberty of all, not to mandate our own moral code." [12]

Put another way, the law prioritizes freedom over morality, and the values of liberty and morality are separate. But liberty, as established by the American Founding Fathers, is a "self-evident" principle, that is, it is bestowed by God — or as the Declaration of Independence puts it, "their Creator." Rejecting the universal standards set by the Creator in order to increase the range of so-called freedoms is a method the devil uses to distort the law and lead humanity to its downfall.

b. Seizing the Powers of Legislation and Promulgation

Before a new law takes effect, it goes through multiple stages, including its drafting, endorsement by politicians, passage by the legislature, and implementation by law enforcement officials. There also may be court rulings over its legality. During this process, individuals or groups in academia, media, legal circles, and even the entertainment industry exert influence over the preparation and enactment of the law. The communist specter has found representatives across society to help it take control of the legislative process. Various lobbyists have done their best to fill government agencies with leftists. In the judicial branch, they became judges, prosecutors, and other officials responsible for the carriage of justice.

Presidents will do everything in their power to appoint like-minded justices to the Supreme Court, or use executive powers to circumvent the legal system. Historically, liberal US presidents have tended to grant more pardons. In a recent administration, the president commuted the sentences of 1,385 convicts and granted a total of 212 pardons, the greatest number since the administration of President Harry Truman. [13] In one of his final acts before leaving the White House, the president commuted the sentences of 209 individuals and granted pardons to 64 others. Most of those who received pardons were nonviolent drug offenders, but one exception was a man who had been charged and found guilty of leaking 700,000 classified military documents. With presidential clemency, this man's sentence was reduced, and he served less than 7 years of his 35-year sentence. [14]

While the president has the constitutionally ordained power to grant pardons, overuse of this power works against the function and purpose of the law, which is to punish wrongdoing and support upstanding citizens. In 1954, then-Sen. Lyndon B. Johnson of Texas, who later served as the 36th president of the United States, introduced the Johnson Amendment, a provision in the tax code that prohibits nonprofit organizations, including churches, from engaging in certain activities. Violators can have their tax exemptions revoked. Wary of this, some Christian churches have instructed their ministers to avoid certain topics when speaking at the pulpit, including controversial social issues such as abortion, homosexuality, euthanasia, stem cell research, and so on.

The communist specter has also manipulated all political groups in an attempt to change law enforcement, through prosecutorial elections. One district attorney, sent to his position by progressive patrons and political groups, fired thirty-one prosecutors during his first week on the job. Calling for an end to "mass incarceration," he also ordered the remainder of his staff to stop prosecuting people for marijuana possession. Similar situations exist in other states. The president of the union for deputy district attorneys in Los Angeles County said that it was as if prosecutors were being called on to "pick and choose" which laws to enforce. In her opinion, it's a "slippery slope" when elected officials are asked to ignore the laws they swore to uphold. [15]

Judges also have jurisdiction to cancel orders from administrative departments. For instance, US immigration law gives the president the right to deny entry to foreigners in emergency situations. However, some judges influenced by liberalism considered a travel ban issued by the 45th president to be religious discrimination. Their rulings delayed the ban for over four months until the executive action was upheld by the Supreme Court.

Since lawyers greatly influence court rulings, the political lean-ings of a legal association can have a direct impact on whether the spirit of the law can be followed. The founder of one lawyers' asso-ciation with a nationwide presence was a self-avowed socialist who believed in public ownership and said that his ultimate goal was to establish communism. [16] The association boasts a membership in the tens of thousands across the country and an annual budget in the hundreds of millions. It files lawsuits to support causes such as abortion rights, same-sex marriage, and the right of homosexuals to adopt children.

Followers of liberalism and progressivism occupy key political positions across the United States and dominate academia, the media, and social movements. This has allowed the communist specter to wield unprecedented power over the legislative and judicial processes.

c. Twisted Court Interpretations

Traditional religions emphasize the importance of personal account-ability. In the Bible, the book of Ezekiel uses father and son as a parable to depict good and bad. Though they are father and son, they bear the consequences of their respective conduct and are not personally responsible for each other's actions. As the Bible says, "For whatsoever a man soweth, that shall he also reap." Likewise, the Chinese believe that goodness begets goodness and that evil will be punished by heaven.

Liberty means responsibility. A person has the right and free-dom to choose his ideas, speech, and actions. He also needs to be responsible for his own choices. Once a person has committed a crime, he should be punished accordingly. This is the principle of justice. Liberal judges, however, encourage people to shirk their responsibilities and shift accountability to prevailing social conditions, such as their economic or racial background, physical and mental health, education, and other demographic parameters, allowing criminals to escape legal punishment.

Prohibiting Public Expressions of Faith

God is everywhere in American life. The nation's motto is "In God We Trust," which is even written on the dollar bill. The US Declaration of Independence states that human rights are what the Creator has given us. All US government officials, including the president and judges, say "So help me God" when they are sworn in. The most common ending to presidential speeches is "God bless America." The Pledge of Allegiance, recited in public schools, describes the United States as "one nation under God."

Some of these traditions have lasted for more than two hundred years, almost as far back as the founding of the United States. But in the past sixty years, they have been constantly challenged by the Left.

One national lawyers' association aims to remove the Ten Commandments from public display across the United States. The most famous case occurred in Montgomery, Alabama. In 2001, the association called for the removal of a slate bearing the Ten Commandments that was located in the rotunda of the state court. The group found a judge who had been appointed by a Democratic president to hear the case. In a seventy-six-page verdict, the judge ruled in favor of the lawyers' association.

The specifics of the ruling may sound ridiculous. For example, the judge claimed that the "solemn ambiance of the rotunda," the frescoes behind the slate, and the atmosphere created by a picture window featuring a waterfall constituted sufficient reason to have the Ten Commandments removed. The judge also said that the slate's "sloping top" resembled an open Bible and gave viewers cause to "feel as though the State of Alabama is advancing, endorsing, favoring or preferring, Christianity." [17]

As early as 1980, the Supreme Court had banned the Ten Commandments from being displayed in public schools. This decision was the catalyst for an overall movement across the country to have the Ten Commandments removed from public view. In Utah, the national lawyers' association even offered a reward to anyone willing to report those plaques and slates that had not yet been taken down. [18]

One US Circuit Court ruled on June 26, 2002, that public schools were prohibited from holding "sworn oaths" because they included the words "under God." This decision was overturned by the Supreme Court on June 14, 2004. [19]

This is an ongoing legal battle. The American national anthem, motto, Pledge of Allegiance, school prayers, and the like are under siege by atheists and leftist activists. References to "God," or the Creator, as seen in the Declaration of Independence, reflect the divine principles underpinning the US Constitution, and do not violate America's principle of religious freedom. The public display of the Ten Commandments and other religious plaques underscores the deep faith of the American people. In a nation based on strong spiritual traditions, the rise of political movements attempting to prohibit the public expression of belief in the divine indicates the extent to which communism has penetrated the legal system.

Altering the Spirit of the Constitution Through Interpretation and Case Law

In the drafting of the US Constitution, the Founding Fathers established the separation of powers, with the judicial branch originally having the least power. Congress (the legislative branch) is responsible for passing laws; the president (the executive branch) is responsible for executing and enforcing the laws created by Congress; and the Supreme Court (the judicial branch) has neither the power to pass laws nor to govern.

In 2002, while the Supreme Court was hearing a case concerning the Pledge of Allegiance, polls indicated that 90 percent of Americans supported retaining the phrase "under God." In the House of Representatives, there were 416 votes in favor of retention versus just three against. [20] In the Senate, the result was 99 to zero. [21] The congressional votes reflected the genuine opinion of the American public.

As elected representatives of the people, members of Congress and the president serve terms that range from two to six years before coming up for reelection. As long as the public and mainstream society are guided by divine standards of morality, the extent to which the president and members of Congress can fall toward the left is limited. On the other hand, Supreme Court justices don't need to heed public opinion, since they hold their positions for life. Furthermore, there are only nine justices. It is comparatively easier to influence the decisions made by these nine individuals than it is to alter public opinion.

In the United States, amending the Constitution requires support from two-thirds of Congress and three-quarters of the states. These strict measures make it difficult to amend the Constitution outright. Therefore, the progressive strategy is not to amend the Constitution directly, but to reinterpret it. They regard the Constitution as a "living" and continually "evolving" document. Using precedent set by the Supreme Court, they encode the views of the Left into law. In this way, they covertly exert their will over the Constitution, which is tantamount to undermining it.

Divine commandment is no longer the highest principle. The Constitution has taken a heavy beating under the gavels of liberal Supreme Court justices, since their rulings are final and must be respected by even the president. The judicial branch is taking an ever-increasing share of authority among the three branches established by the Founding Fathers. In practice, Supreme Court justices have acquired partial legislative and even executive powers.

Liberal Supreme Court justices have brought a number of consequences upon American society that are severe and difficult to remedy. As things stand, the Supreme Court can, through case hearings, order the removal of the Ten Commandments from public schools and spaces, rewrite criminal procedures, raise taxes, recognize rights to abortion and same-sex marriage, allow the publication and display of pornography, and so on.

The growing supremacy of the judiciary combined with the ruling of liberal judges has given the specter of communism an important tool for achieving its designs.

Promoting Obscene Content in the Name of Freedom

The 1960s was an era of deep transformation across American society. Left-wing students drove the anti-war movement, rock 'n' roll, hippie culture, the feminist movement, sexual liberation, and other anti-traditional currents, raising chaos throughout the country.

The chief justice of the Supreme Court in this period was the liberal Earl Warren. During Warren's term as chief justice, the Supreme Court made very influential and far-reaching rulings. This included the prohibition of prayers in public school and the allowance of publications featuring sexually explicit material. [22][23]

In the book *The Supremacists: The Tyranny of Judges and How to*

Stop It, constitutional law expert Phyllis Schlafly provided statistics showing that from 1966 to 1970, the Supreme Court made thirty-four rulings that overruled lower-level court decisions to prohibit obscene content. [24] The Supreme Court's rulings were not signed, and the majority opinion consisted of just one or two lines. Put another way, even the justices themselves didn't bother to rationalize their decisions.

In 1968, Hollywood abandoned its Motion Picture Production Code, lifting its restrictions on obscene content in film. A profusion of various kinds of pornographic works soon followed, and today they have saturated every corner of society.

The First Amendment of the Constitution guarantees freedom of speech. It was intended to guarantee the right to express political opinions, not to manufacture and disseminate pornography.

Legalizing Drug Abuse

As the world got ready to welcome the new year on December 31, 2017, cable news channel CNN broadcast footage with multiple shots of a female reporter smoking marijuana. Visibly under the influence, she appeared disoriented and unaware of her surroundings. The broadcast received widespread criticism. [25]

In 1996, California became the first US state to legalize medical marijuana, and many states soon followed suit. By 2012, Colorado and Washington had legalized marijuana for "recreational use." In these two states, planting, manufacturing, and selling marijuana to adults is completely legal. It has also since been legalized in California. In October 2018, the Canadian government legalized marijuana use.

Aside from causing serious damage to the human body, drugs are psychologically addictive. Once dependent, people can abandon moral inhibitions in order to obtain more of the drug. On the other hand, those who support legalizing drugs believe it would be an effective way to reduce drug trafficking. They say that legalization allows stricter regulation over the drug, and accordingly a reduction in drug-related crime.

Governments anticipate that legalizing drugs would generate billions of dollars in revenue. But it's not hard to see that as greater numbers of people become addicts, lose their desire to work, and suffer poor health, productivity will fall, and the aggregate wealth created by society will shrink. It is self-evident that legalizing drugs cannot increase government revenue in the long term. Furthermore, judging what is right or wrong shouldn't be based on economic profit, but on divine standards. Traditional morality sees the human form as sacred and created in the divine likeness. Western religions believe the body is the temple of the Holy Spirit, while in the East, it was believed that the body can be improved through cultivation to become a Buddha or a Tao. Drug abuse, then, is an act of desecration.

According to a report by the *Los Angeles Times*, one of the important figures lobbying for the legalization of marijuana in the United States is a wealthy progressive. [26] In March 2017, six senators wrote a letter to the US State Department requesting that this individual be investigated for using his foundation to promote progressivism abroad and subvert conservative governments. [27]

The legalization of drugs is an additional step toward encouraging people to lose their inhibitions and cut themselves off from the divine. As society experiences turmoil and economic downturns, communists seize opportunities to gain political power.

Legalizing Same-Sex Marriage

Schlafly listed twelve methods judges use to undermine morality: rewrite the Constitution, censor acknowledgment of God, redefine marriage, undermine US sovereignty, threaten property rights, promote pornography, foster feminism, handicap law enforcement, invite illegal immigration, interfere with elections, take over parental rights, and impose taxes. [28]

The book of Genesis describes the destruction of Sodom. One of the sins the doomed city's residents indulged in was homosexuality. This is the origin of the term "sodomy," meaning sexual relations between men. Those with basic knowledge of the Bible know that homosexuality goes against the will of God.

In June 2015, the Supreme Court ruled in a 5–4 decision that same-sex marriage is a right guaranteed by the Constitution. [29] When the ruling was passed, the US president at the time changed the banner on the White House's official Twitter account to the rainbow flag in support of LGBT rights. The Supreme Court's ruling prohibited the thirteen states that still banned same-sex marriage from enforcing their laws. In August 2015, a clerk in Rowan County, Kentucky, refused to issue marriage certificates for same-sex couples due to her beliefs. She was later jailed for five nights for defying a US federal court order to issue the documents. [30] In fact, the court had violated her constitutional right to freedom of belief. Commenting on the clerk's case, former governor of Arkansas and former Republican presidential candidate Mike Huckabee called the Supreme Court's ruling on marriage "judicial tyranny." [31]

As of 2019, twenty-eight countries and territories had officially acknowledged or accepted same-sex marriage, including the United States, the United Kingdom, France, Germany, Spain, Norway, Denmark, Finland, Sweden, Portugal, Belgium, Australia, New

Zealand, and Canada. The law has the power to reinforce morality or influence its movement in a new direction. To legalize behavior that deviates from traditional moral values is the same as having the government and laws train the people to betray morality and disobey divine commandments.

Under the influence of political correctness, criticism of the chaos that our society finds itself in — whether from the people, civil associations, or religious groups in particular — can easily be escalated to the level of politics or law, and result in restrictions on free speech or other punishments. Following the legalization of immoral behavior, those who make any comments or criticisms on related issues are often accused of violating laws, such as those concerning gender discrimination. The law has been twisted into a means of strangling people's ability to make moral judgments. It is essentially promoting homosexuality and encouraging people to give themselves to endless desire and degeneracy.

d. Restricting Law Enforcement

Under liberal influence, many judges or legislative agencies deliberately curtail the legitimate power of law enforcement, effectively turning a blind eye to crime. The communist specter's aim in doing this is to paralyze the state apparatus in order to stir up social turmoil, which in turn creates excuses either for the expansion of government, or the necessary conditions for a coup or revolution.

Many states have passed far-left laws, a typical example being "sanctuary" policies. Among other provisions, sanctuary cities often prohibit federal immigration officials from arresting illegal immigrants in local prisons, including those with outstanding warrants for arrest. Local police are barred from cooperating and communicating with federal agents to enforce immigration laws.

This poses a serious security risk for the public. In July 2015, illegal immigrant José Inez García Zárate shot and killed a young woman who was walking along a pier in San Francisco. Zárate had a history of crime: He had been charged with seven felonies involving drugs and robbery, and possession of weaponry, and had been deported five times. Under San Francisco's sanctuary laws, officials released Zárate from custody three months before the fatal shooting, rather than transferring him to federal immigration authorities, who had requested custody of him for deportation.

When a criminal stands trial, extremely strict standards are placed on the prosecution. This is ostensibly to protect the legitimate rights of the suspect, but often the result is that criminals are able to take advantage of loopholes in the law. Cunning suspects — or those who enjoy status or privileges, who understand the law and regulations, or who hire capable attorneys — can drag out the legal process, at great cost to the judicial system. It can be very difficult to bring guilty suspects to justice.

Influenced by the spread of "sexual liberation," verdicts in cases involving sex crimes often cite findings in research by Alfred Kinsey or activists who follow him to argue that the damage caused by sex abuse is little or nonexistent. Many cases have been settled by reducing the sentences of sexual predators. [32] Many ordinary criminals also have had their original sentences reduced, ostensibly owing to budget shortages or on account of prisoners' rights. The real motivation, though, is to use political correctness to weaken the power of the law, disturb social order, and pave the way for further expansion of government.

For the law to be fair, it must administer strict punishments to those who commit unpardonable crimes. Since antiquity, murder has been punishable by death. But today, some countries and territories have abolished capital punishment on such grounds as "humanity," "tolerance," or a supposed respect for life.

Under the influence of twisted liberalism and progressivism, some people give undue weight to prisoners' rights — no matter the severity of their crimes — while remaining strangely silent regarding the victims. If a murderer is fed and housed by taxpayer money, his loss of freedom is hardly a fair trade for the death of the victim and the trauma it causes for loved ones.

Many researchers in the United States have found that capital punishment is effective in deterring crime. In the 1990s, three professors, including Paul Rubin at Emory University, examined 20 years of crime statistics from 3,000 cities and towns across the United States and concluded that "each execution results, on average, in 18 fewer murders — with a margin of error of plus or minus 10." [33]

Even scholars who are against capital punishment must concede that it has a deterrent effect. By pushing the concepts of freedom and legality to extremes, the Left has distorted the law and robbed it of its sanctity.

e. Using Foreign Laws to Weaken US Sovereignty

When liberal judges can't find wording in the US Constitution to support their personal opinions, they use laws passed in other countries to sustain their arguments.

For instance, in the Supreme Court case of *Lawrence v. Texas* (2003), the liberal justices wanted to repeal a Texas statute banning consenting homosexual adults from engaging in sexual acts, but they could not find anything from the Constitution to support this case. They then quoted an "authoritative" agency outside of the United States as saying that homosexuality was "an integral part of human freedom in many other countries," and successfully repealed the law. This case resulted in repeals of similar statutes in thirteen other states. [34]

Communist thought has spread around the world in different forms. The socialist trend throughout Asia and Europe is plain to see, and it has great influence in Africa and Latin America as well. Countries such as Zimbabwe and Venezuela are openly socialist countries. America's neighbors, Canada and Mexico, slant to the political left.

Commerce and globalization have brought the United States in closer connection with other countries. In order to introduce elements of socialism domestically, liberal judges leverage the excuse of conforming to international convention and then use case law to alter the spirit of the Constitution. If even the United States, as the leader of the free world, can't maintain basic, traditional standards, the entire globe will be lost to communism.

4. Restoring the Spirit of the Law

Today, the law has been turned against the divine teachings that originally inspired it. Legality has become a tool the communist specter uses to trample upon the moral foundation of human society, bringing it to the brink of destruction. Anti-traditional and immoral legislation has weakened the ability of the law to maintain social order, leaving the expansion of state power as the only "solution" to the malaise.

Under a legal system controlled by the communist specter, Americans would be left with only two options: Either refuse to follow the authorities and their degenerate laws, or betray their morality in order to comply. The former would mean the destruction of law in practice, for as jurist Harold Berman put it, "The law must be believed in; otherwise, it exists in name only." [35]

The 1958 book *The Naked Communist* lists forty-five goals pursued by communism in order to infiltrate and undermine the United States. Seven of them concern the legal system. [36]

The sixteenth goal consists of using the courts' technical decisions to weaken important US institutions by claiming that their conduct infringes upon civil rights.

The twenty-fourth is to abolish all laws restricting indecent content by portraying them as censorship that violates free speech and expression.

The twenty-ninth is to challenge the Constitution as flawed, obsolete, or incompatible with international practice.

The thirty-third is to abolish all laws that interfere with the communist apparatus.

The thirty-eighth is to make it legal for non-police agencies to carry out arrests. All behavioral problems are to be delegated to mental health workers.

The thirty-ninth is to gain control over the field of psychiatry and impose mental health laws to control individuals who oppose communist aims.

The forty-fifth is to abolish the Connally Reservation, also known as the Connally Amendment. This regulation gives the United States the right to favor domestic jurisdiction over rulings by international courts. The purpose of this goal is to prevent the United States from protecting its domestic sovereignty and to instead have international bodies such as the International Court of Justice overrule the US judiciary.

Looking at the goals listed above and comparing them with what has already been implemented, it is apparent that communism is well-placed to continue undermining US law and justice.

Be it state-sponsored policies of hatred in countries controlled by communist regimes, or regulation in Western countries where communist ideology has hollowed out the legislative and judicial institutions, in both cases the target is the spirit of the law — that is, reverence for the divine and traditional morality.

If we are unable to maintain the moral standards dictated by divine commandment as our criteria for recognizing ultimate good and evil, society will continue to pass laws that conform to communist ideology, favoring the wicked and suppressing the righteous. Society will lose its divine principles of justice and liberty and succumb to the communist specter's tyranny.

CHAPTER ELEVEN

Desecrating the Arts

1. Art: A Gift From the Divine

OVER THE MANY YEARS of human civilization, man has contemplated what constitutes true beauty. People of faith know that all the wonders of the world come from the divine. Profound art is an attempt to emulate and display the beauty of heaven in the human world. Inspiration comes from the divine, and artists can become outstanding figures in their fields if they receive divine blessings and wisdom.

During the Renaissance, great artists plumbed their ingenuity and deep faith to create works in praise of God. Artists in the mid-Renaissance period, including Leonardo da Vinci, Michelangelo, and Raphael, grasped techniques that far exceeded those of their predecessors and their peers, as if by miracle. Their masterpieces — including paintings, statues, and architecture — became timeless classics.

For centuries, these works of art set a noble example for humanity. By appreciating this art, not only can the artists of later generations learn pure artistic technique, but members of the public can truly feel and see the presence of the divine. When these works, the techniques that created them, and the spirit that infused the artists are all preserved, human society is able to maintain a connection with the divine. Then, even as humanity goes through its periods of decadence and decline, there will be hope for a return to tradition and a path to salvation.

The same principles prevail in the sphere of music. As the saying (reportedly from a German opera house) goes: "Bach gave us God's word. Mozart gave us God's laughter. Beethoven gave us God's fire. God gave us music that we might pray without words." For his entire life, Johann Sebastian Bach considered devotion to God and the praise and worship of God to be the highest principles in the creation of his music. On all of his important musical scores, the letters SDG can be seen — an abbreviation of "Soli Deo gloria," meaning "glory to God alone."

The highest level an artist can reach is to perceive heavenly phenomena by means of divine revelation and depict it in a tangible medium. The great paintings and statues, and the most sublime scores in the early, baroque, and classical canon, were all created by religious believers and represent the pinnacle of artistic work attained by man.

The three most important elements in artistic creation are representation, creation, and communication. All artistic creations contain a theme, that is, the message the artist seeks to communicate, regardless of the form the work takes — whether it be a poem, painting, statue, photograph, novel, play, dance, or film. The artist delivers the theme to the hearts of the reader, listener, or viewer.

This process is the communication — the transmission of the artist's mind to the recipient.

To achieve the goal of communication, artists must possess a superb ability to imitate and represent, with the object of imitation being the world of gods or of man, or even the underworld. Artistic creation is a process of refining the deeper or more essential elements of an object of representation. It requires artists to strengthen their own ability to communicate and to touch people's hearts. If the artist possesses righteous faith and is a person of high moral character, the divine will endow him with the inspiration to create. Such works will be pure, benevolent, and divine — beneficial to both the artist and society.

On the other hand, when the artist abandons moral standards, negative elements hijack the creative process, with evil forces exerting influence and using the artist to depict hideous creations and grotesqueries from the underworld. Works of this kind harm their author and the wider society.

The value of the orthodox, traditional arts thus becomes clear. Divine culture and art in the East and the West were connections woven between the divine and human civilization, and were meant to bring them into contact. The ideas and messages transmitted through this art are beauty, benevolence, light, and hope. On the other hand, corrupt works of "art" are created by those under the control of evil elements. They drive a wedge between man and the divine, and drag humans closer to evil.

2. Art's Immense Influence on Humanity

Great works of art transmit heritage, disseminate knowledge and wisdom, and fortify character. They hold exalted positions in the great civilizations of the West and the East.

The ancient Greek mathematician and philosopher Pythago-ras believed that the secret of music was in its imitation of the harmony of the heavenly bodies, which itself reflects the harmony of the universe.

The Chinese held similar views. The *Treatises on Music and Harmony* discuss music's correspondence with the five elements (metal, wood, water, fire, and earth), and how musical instruments are constructed to represent and emulate the patterns of heaven and earth. Only in this way can "music of the grandest style" be composed, that which exhibits "the same harmony that prevails between heaven and earth." [1] This kind of music is able to not only attract divine birds like the crane and phoenix, but also serve as an invitation to deities to grace the occasion with their presence.

Confucius taught that humanity should learn from the Western Zhou Dynasty (1045 – 771 B.C.), a kingdom whose rulers empha-sized the importance of proper rites, and thus brought order to the country without the need for harsh laws or coercion. He said: "[The Zhou Dynasty] surveyed the two dynasties that went before; its ways are refined and elegant. I follow Zhou." [2] He admired how the legendary Chinese rulers governed with ritual and music: "The Sage-Emperor Shun invented a five-stringed musical instrument, which he called qin, sang to its tune about the gentle summer breeze from the south, and lo and behold, his empire ran smoothly [under the influence of his music]." [3] These examples illustrate the edify-ing effects of pure, upright music.

The "Symphony of the Qin Prince Breaking Up the Enemy's Front," an autobiographical piece composed by the great Tang Dynasty emperor Li Shimin, won the deep respect of ethnic groups living on the periphery of the Tang realm. The *New Book of Tang* recorded that on the journey to seek Buddhist scriptures from the

West, monk Xuanzang was told by a king in a remote Indian state, "Your emperor must be a saint, for he composed the 'Symphony of the Qin Prince Breaking Up the Enemy's Front.'" [4]

During the reign of Louis xiv, the French royal court displayed great elegance through dance and art. Dance contains not only technique, but also social etiquette and norms. Louis xiv inspired Europe through the art and culture of his court, which were emulated by other courts and the population at large in Europe.

Not only was Frederick the Great of Prussia an outstanding king, but he was also an accomplished musician, composer, and flautist. He ordered the construction of the Berlin opera house, personally supervised the opera, and opened it to a wider set of social classes. To this day, opera remains an important part of German culture. These few examples make clear the long-lasting influence that orthodox art can exert on society.

Upright art conforms to natural law, imitates divine wisdom, and brings with it special energy and effects. It benefits people by feeding both the senses and the soul. The greatest artists work not only on the physical, technical level, but also, more importantly, on the spiritual level, in their communion with the theme of the work. Such artists sometimes express a sense of experiencing a higher force beyond this physical world. The effect is similar to that of singing an ode to God — a solemn and divine experience that transcends human language. Behind true art lies the accumulated wisdom of a people, their creativity, and their inspiration. There are often profound meanings that go far beyond what is seen on the surface. Some works transmit a special kind of spiritual energy. All of this has an effect on viewers at a deeper level. The effect is singular and irreplaceable by any other means.

A superb artist can influence the morality of society by instilling values into people's hearts through poignant stories and images. Even people without deep learning or education can gain insight, inspiration, and moral lessons from traditional art. In traditional Western societies, consider how many learned right from wrong, good from evil, through the medium of folk tales such as "Hansel and Gretel" and "Snow White."

In China, many generations learned from the four great novels (*Water Margin, Journey to the West, Romance of the Three Kingdoms*, and *Dream of the Red Chamber*) and from the traditional arts of storytelling and drama. Such works allow people to feel divine greatness and make them yearn to assimilate to heavenly principles.

Degenerate values also exert an invisible influence through art. Screenwriting lecturer Robert McKee wrote in his book *Story: Substance, Structure, Style and the Principles of Screenwriting*: "Every effective story sends a charged idea out to us, in effect compelling the idea into us, so that we must believe. In fact, the persuasive power of a story is so great that we may believe its meaning even if we find it morally repellent." [5]

Art can have a tremendous impact — both positive and negative — on human morality, thought, and behavior.

"The Mozart effect," for instance, has attracted worldwide attention, with the scientific community conducting a number of studies on the positive influence of Wolfgang Amadeus Mozart's music on people and animals. In 2016, a more in-depth study of the Mozart effect found that the composer's music can boost human cognitive function and behavior. Surprisingly, playing Mozart's music in reverse has the opposite effect. Austrian composer Arnold Schoenberg's modern atonal music has an effect similar to that of playing Mozart backwards, which demonstrates its negative qualities. [6]

Compared with atonal music, rock 'n' roll can have an even greater negative impact. One researcher compiled data from two similar cities and found that the city in which more rock songs were broadcast via radio and television saw 50 percent more cases of pregnancy out of wedlock, dropouts, youth deaths, crimes, and so on. [7] Some rock music even glorifies suicide. One commentator, referring to a song by a famous rock star who faced several lawsuits from parents of young listeners, wrote, "Its dark rhythms and depressing lyrics certainly can be taken as an encouragement for suicide, and it is an irrefutable fact that young people have snuffed out their lives while listening to it repeatedly." [8] It is not uncommon for teens who commit suicide to do as described in rock lyrics, and numerous rock musicians have themselves descended into depression and drug abuse, or taken their own lives.

Another well-known example of art put to negative use is the Nazi propaganda film *Triumph of the Will*. Despite director Leni Riefenstahl's argument that she had merely created a documentary, the film exhibits superb artistic mastery. The grand scenes and displays of strength made audiences resonate with the energy and power behind it. Her many innovative shooting techniques and technical prowess influenced film for decades to come. Yet the work also became a crucial piece of propaganda for Hitler and Nazi Germany and is regarded as one of the most successful works of propaganda in history. An obituary for Riefenstahl published in the British newspaper *The Independent* in 2003 stated, "*Triumph of the Will* seduced many wise men and women, persuaded them to admire rather than to despise, and undoubtedly won the Nazis friends and allies all over the world." [9]

Understanding the great power of art can help us better understand the importance of traditional art and why evil elements want to undermine and sabotage it.

3. Communism's Sabotage and Abuse of Art

Since art has such a tremendous effect on society, it's not surprising that communism uses art to achieve its aim of socially engineering humans and leading them toward destruction.

a. Art in Communist Countries

Communist parties know the power of art and they turn all art forms into tools for advancing their brainwashing. Many people have ridiculed the Chinese Communist Party for having singers and actors become military generals. They wonder how civilians who have never been trained in arms or warfare could be qualified to be generals. The CCP believes that these people are just as important as trained military personnel in promoting and upholding the communist cult — or perhaps even more crucial. In this sense, its military ranks conform perfectly with Party principles. As Mao Zedong said, "We must also have a cultural army, which is absolutely indispensable for uniting our own ranks and defeating the enemy." [10]

Artistic performances in communist countries are designed to have people forget the miseries they suffer under communist rule and to cultivate their loyalty to the communist party through art. This propaganda effect — called "thought work" — cannot be achieved by mere martial power.

One can compare the CCP's grand opening ceremony at the Beijing Olympics, which was put on at enormous cost to the taxpayer, to North Korea's large-scale song and dance festival Arirang and the former Soviet Union's ballet troupes. All served the needs of the party.

In September 2011, the CCP's Ministry of Culture held a so-called Chinese culture festival, China: The Art of a Nation, at the John F.

Kennedy Center for the Performing Arts in Washington, DC. It included the CCP's signature propaganda piece, the ballet *Red Detachment of Women*, which promotes class hatred and violent revolution.

If upright art that was close to the divine and promoted traditional values were allowed to exist simultaneously with party-controlled art used for brainwashing the public, then the latter would lose its monopoly and have no effect. This is why all communist countries maintain strict censorship over the arts and the publishing industry.

b. Communist Elements Behind the Avant-Garde Movement

For centuries, classical art has been passed down from generation to generation. This tradition continued until the twentieth century, when it came to an abrupt end. The transmission and inheritance of art were disrupted by a radical avant-garde movement and began to quickly degenerate. As artist Robert Florczak said: "The profound, the inspiring, and the beautiful were replaced by the new, the different, and the ugly. ... Standards declined until there were no standards. All that was left was personal expression." [11] Humanity thus lost its universal sense of the aesthetic.

The source of this battery of new artistic movements is closely connected to ideological trends influenced by communism. Many of these artists were either avowed communists or para-communists of one kind or another, or they were subject to the sway of these ideologies.

Georg Lukács, the Hungarian cultural commissioner of the Communist International and founder of Western Marxism, created the Frankfurt School. One of its tasks was to establish a "new cultural form" by abandoning traditional culture. This new cultural form set about excluding art that sought to represent the divine. As Herbert Marcuse, a German socialist and a representative of the Frankfurt School, wrote: "Art both protests these [existing social] relations, and at the same time transcends them. Thereby art subverts the dominant consciousness, the ordinary experience." [12] That is, Marxists enlist art in the revolt against the divine and the subversion of morality. Views of this sort dominate the direction of modern art.

Gustave Courbet, the founder of the French realist school, was a participant in the Paris Commune. He was elected as a committee member of the Commune and the chairman of the radical Federation of Artists. Courbet devoted himself to transforming the old system and establishing new artistic directions. He ordered the Federation to demolish the intricate neoclassical Vendôme Column (which was later rebuilt). Courbet denied that human beings were created by God, and he was determined to use art to express the worldview of the proletariat, as well as materialism. He is known for saying, "I have never seen either angels or goddesses, so I am not interested in painting them." [13]

Courbet believed that reforming the arts was really waging a revolution. In the name of painting what he called "reality," he replaced beauty with ugliness. His nude paintings, for instance, focused in particular on depicting the female genitalia — a supposedly revolutionary act — as a way of rebelling, transgressing against tradition, and somehow further inciting communist activism. The thinking and life of Courbet illustrate the close link between the communist ideology of revolution and modern art.

Under the influence of modernist thought, the revolutionary fervor of artists from the late nineteenth century brought about a series of movements in the art world. Unlike traditional schools of artistic expression, these were avant-garde movements that explicitly sought to break tradition. The term "avant-garde" was first used by socialist scholars to describe artistic movements that matched their own political aspirations.

In the late nineteenth century, these influences brought about impressionism. Since then, modern artists have abandoned the demands of traditional oil painting, including precision, proportion, structure, perspective, and transitions between light and shade. Neoimpressionism (pointillism) and postimpressionism then emerged, centering their works on the exploration of the personal feelings of the artist. Representative figures in this school include Georges-Pierre Seurat and Vincent van Gogh, both of whom were inclined toward socialism. Van Gogh abused alcohol and suffered mental illness later in life, and his paintings appeared to reflect the world that people experience while on drugs.

Works of art contain the messages their creators wanted to convey. Artists during the peak of the Renaissance conveyed compassion and beauty to their audiences. Compare this to contemporary artists, who exude negative and dark messages. Modern artists abandon their own thoughts and allow themselves to come under the control of low-level and ghostly entities. They themselves are often incoherent and confused, and their works are similar — dark, negative, hazy, gray, depressed, decadent, and disordered.

After impressionism came expressionism and fauvism, followed by Pablo Picasso's cubism. In 1944, Picasso joined the French Communist Party. In his letter *Why I Became a Communist*, he wrote: "My joining the Communist Party is a logical step in my life, my work and gives them their meaning. ... In my own ways I have always said what I considered most true, most just and best and, therefore, most beautiful. But during the oppression and the insurrection, I felt that that was not enough, that I had to fight not only with painting but with my whole being." [14]

Picasso encouraged a break with the classical methods of painting. For him, everything was a piece of dough to be picked up and shaped as he pleased. The eerier his works became, the happier he appeared to be. The process of creating monstrous images is the process of destroying an image, to the point where no one can understand it. Even Georges Braque, the modern artist who co-founded cubism with Picasso, on viewing Picasso's *Les Demoiselles d'Avignon,* was "horrified by its ugliness and intensity." Picasso had been "drinking turpentine and spitting fire," acting more like a carnival performer than an artist, he said. [15]

Marcel Duchamp, an early member of the dada art movement, also sought to subvert and rebel against tradition with his display and use of readymade objects. He repurposed found or factory-made items and turned them into so-called art installations. Duchamp, who was called the father of conceptual art, advocated the idea that anything could be called art. The dadaist movement is itself a communistic project, as evidenced by the manifesto of the Berlin dadaists, who called for an "international revolutionary union of all creative and intellectual men and women on the basis of radical Communism," as well as "the immediate expropriation of property (socialization) and the communal feeding of all" and "the erection of cities of light, and gardens which will belong to society as a whole and prepare man for a state of freedom." [16]

Dadaism's criticism of tradition evolved into surrealism in France, as represented by the communist André Breton, who advocated revolution. He was against the supposed suppression brought by reason, culture, and society — a view typical of the modern artists in Europe at the time.

The artistic movements that extended these principles include abstractism, minimalism, pop art, and postmodernism. Abstractism is about the emotional expression of rebellion, disorder, emptiness, and escapism. The ugly trampling of moral values is evident in these "-isms" in the arts today. At their most outrageous, these artists create works that openly desecrate religious figures like Jesus Christ.

Not all modern artists support leftwing politics, but there is a clear ideological commonality with communist thought — that is, the rejection of the divine, and the aim to replace the divine as the starting point for understanding human life. These "-isms" came to exert increasing influence in the public sphere and ultimately have led to the complete marginalization of classical art.

c. The Inversion of Traditional Aesthetics: The Ugly as Art

The numerous schools of modern art that have appeared and developed share several things in common: They invert conventional aesthetics; they take ugliness as beauty; and they aim to shock, even to the point of being as ghastly as the artist's imagination allows.

Duchamp signed his name on a urinal and named it *Fountain*, to be put on display for the public in New York. Though the object was never shown publicly, Duchamp's action was considered a clever joke among his peers in the art world, and later artists and academics have thought it the height of creativity. This is the environment in the art world, whereby classical easel painting has been marginalized and installation art has risen to prominence. In 1958, Yves Klein held his exhibition *The Void* at the Iris Clert Gallery in Paris. The displayed "works" turned out to be empty, white walls.

A major figure of the postwar German avant-garde, Joseph Beuys, covered his head with honey and gold leaf and murmured nonstop for three hours to a dead hare in his arms in the 1965 work *How to Explain Pictures to a Dead Hare*. In Beuys's view, anyone could be an artist. One anecdote goes that a frustrated questioner once shouted at him, "You talk about everything under the sun, except art!" Beuys reportedly responded, "Everything under the sun is art!" [17]

In 1961, Piero Manzoni, a key figure of the avant-garde, claimed he had put his own feces in ninety cans, called them artwork, and put them up for sale under the name *Merda d'artista* ("Artist's Shit"). In 2015, one of the cans was sold in London for a record price of 182,500 pounds, or about $240,000 — more than a hundred times the price of its weight in gold. He also signed his name on the bodies of nude women as part of a series he called *Sculture viventi* ("Living Sculpture").

In China, there was a nude "artist" who coated his body with honey and fish oil to attract flies. Such desecration of the body seems intended to communicate the idea that life is cheap, ugly, and disgusting. In the BBC documentary *Beijing Swings,* about "extreme artists" in China, so-called performance art included the performative consumption of a human fetus. Amidst public condemnation that such acts were "hideous," art critic Waldemar Januszczak, the presenter of the documentary, inadvertently revealed its true nature in saying, "It is worth trying to understand why China is producing the most outrageous and darkest art, of anywhere in the world." [18] In fact, this is the result of the pursuit of the demonic. Some of these modern works of so-called art are so filthy and shameless that they exceed the mental endurance of normal people. Such aspects of the avant-garde movement amount to a Cultural Revolution in the art world.

Those who support modernism have taken to the trend like ducks to water, but painters truly proficient in the technical skill of painting have a tough time. Painters and sculptors who adhere strictly to tradition, who master their craft through painstaking practice, have been squeezed out of the art world. John William Godward, the English Victorian neoclassicist painter associated with the Pre-Raphaelite Brotherhood, felt that he was being edged out of relevance as his style of realistic classical painting fell out of favor with the rise of Picasso's modernist works. In 1922, he committed suicide and was said to have written in his suicide note, "The world is not big enough for myself and a Picasso." [19]

Similar methods were adopted to ruin music. Authentic music conforms with musical theory and order. Musical tuning and the keys and modes it produces are all derived from harmonious natural patterns. The universe created by the divine is harmonious. Humans are able to appreciate and participate in the harmony of the universe, and thus create beauty, since humans are also created by the divine.

Modern atonal music rejects ideas like tonality, chords, and melody, and lacks order in its structure. It is a revolt against divinely imparted classical music, and it violates the harmony in the universe, which is why many audiences find it unpleasant. Modernist musicians argue, based on their warped theories of aesthetics, that audience members must train their ears to get used to such music so that they can enjoy it.

Schoenberg, one of the founders of modern music, introduced his "twelve-tone system," a fundamentally atonal structure that marked the creation of anti-classical musical technique. Schoenberg's music was considered the negation of all German musical culture up to then — a betrayal of taste, feeling, tradition, and all aesthetic principles. His music was called "cocaine" by Germans at the time: "To perform Schoenberg means the same as to open a cocaine bar for the people. Cocaine is poison. Schoenberg's music is cocaine." [20] One later music critic assessed his work thusly: "It is a measure of the immensity of the man's achievement that, fifty years after his death, he can still empty any hall on earth." [21]

What led to the widespread acceptance of Schoenberg were the musical theories of Theodor W. Adorno, an important figure in the Frankfurt School. In Adorno's 1949 work *Philosophy of Modern Music,* he portrayed Schoenberg as the "quintessential exponent of modernism in music" and explained Schoenberg's twelve-tone compositional method as the culmination of the attempt to grant music "an autonomous status and structural self-sufficiency in response to the omnipresent domination of capitalistic ideology." Adorno's philosophical support for Schoenberg set the stage for the widespread acceptance of the latter's system by later generations of composers and music critics. [22] Since then, numerous musicians have emulated Schoenberg, and his avant-garde style has had a major impact on the postwar music world.

After destroying tradition with modern music, avant-garde art used rock 'n' roll to supplant the role of classical music in people's lives. Sidney Finkelstein, the leading music theorist of the Communist Party USA, openly declared that the boundaries between classical and popular music should be eliminated. At around the same time, strongly rhythmic rock music was gaining an increasing foothold in the United States, as classical and traditional music were squeezed out and marginalized.

The characteristics of rock 'n' roll include inharmonious sounds, unstructured melodies, strong rhythmic beats, and emotional conflict — quite similar to the communist idea of struggle. According to the *Records of the Grand Historian* by China's foremost ancient historian, Sima Qian, only when sound conforms to morality can it be called music. Typically, the lives and compositions of rock 'n' roll musicians are centered around sex, violence, and drugs.

Rock 'n' roll, along with other modern sounds such as rap and hip-hop, continued to gain popularity in the United States. Rappers flaunt their rebellion against tradition and society with their casual use of drugs, obscene language, and unruly, violent behavior. As the morality of society as a whole declines, such "art forms," previously regarded as the product of subcultures, have made their way into the wider society and are even sought-after by mainstream performance venues.

So far, we have focused mainly on the current circumstances in the worlds of art and music. In fact, the entire artistic world has been greatly impacted, and the influence of the modern art movement can be seen in the deviation from traditional ideas, methods, and skills in areas like architecture, dance, decoration, design, photography, film, and more. For example, the founder of modern dance, Isadora Duncan, was openly bisexual and an atheist. She objected to ballet, calling it ugly and unnatural. In 1921, she and 150 children with barely any dance training performed her work "Internationale," set to the communist anthem, in Moscow for Communist Party elites, including Vladimir Lenin. [23]

As for why these deviations exist and become trendy, or even mainstream, it is closely related to communism's corruption of divinely inspired traditional arts. On the surface, of course, this is not apparent, and the situation seems to be a form of self-deception that has been widely accepted — the notion that if there's a theory behind it, then it's art.

If people look closely at the differences between avant-garde and traditional art, they will find that the artists of the Renaissance not only used art to praise God, but also presented beauty in an uplifting manner that engendered feelings of truth and goodness in the human heart. In doing so, their art helped maintain the morality of society.

On the other hand, the various mutated forms of avant-garde try to upend all the achievements of the Renaissance, "to destroy the uplifting — therefore, bourgeois — potential of art, literature, and music, so that man, *bereft of his connection to the divine*, sees his only creative option to be political revolt." Ugliness that is "so carefully nurtured by the Frankfurt School [has] corrupted our highest cultural endeavors," and popular culture in turn, becomes "openly bestial," wrote one academic. [24] Admiring and idolizing such ugliness brings forth the dark side of people; decadent, depraved, violent, evil, and other negative kinds of thoughts gain ascendancy. The pursuit of such ugliness has led to deconstructing and uglifying scenes of the divine and of humanity's own divine nature, as well as acts of direct blasphemy against the divine. This has alienated people not only from the divine, but also from their innate divine nature and traditional values.

d. The Perversion of Literature

Literature is a special art form. It uses language to pass on the wisdom that the divine has bestowed upon humankind, as well as to record the formative experiences of humankind. The two great epics of ancient Greece, *The Iliad* and *The Odyssey*, both portray the complex series of events surrounding the Trojan War, vividly depicting a historical epic of gods and men. The virtues of courage, generosity, wisdom, justice, and temperance that were praised in the epics became an important source of values for the Greek world and all of Western civilization.

Due to the great influence literature has, evil elements use it to control people, concocting and promoting written works that impart the ideology of communism, slander traditional culture, destroy people's morality, and spread pessimism and an attitude of passivity and meaninglessness toward life. Literature has become one of the key tools communism uses to control the world.

The communist parties of the Soviet Union and the CCP, in order to brainwash the general public, both instructed their intellectuals to portray the lives of the proletariat and the concept of class consciousness using traditional techniques, in order to explain communist ideology and policies. This gave rise to a large number of propagandistic literary works, including the Soviet novels *The Iron Flood* and *How the Steel Was Tempered* and the CCP works *The Song of Youth, The Sun Shines on the Sanggan River*, and others, all of which had an enormous impact. Communist parties call this style of work "socialist realism." Mao generalized its function as "serving the workers, peasants, and soldiers" and serving "the proletariat." [25] The ability of this type of literature to instill ideology is obvious and well-understood. However, communism's use of literature to destroy humanity is not limited to this.

The following summarizes some of the major aims and effects of communist-influenced literature.

Using Literature to Destroy Tradition

A major step in the destruction of humanity has been to slander the traditional civilizations that the divine bestowed on mankind. Communist elements use intellectuals with modern thoughts to create and promote works that distort traditional culture.

In Europe in 1909, Italian poet Filippo Tommaso Marinetti published the *Futurist Manifesto*, calling for the total rejection of tradition and the celebration of machinery, technology, speed, violence, and competition. Russian poet and communist Vladimir Mayakovsky published the manifesto *A Slap in the Face of Public Taste* in 1913, in which he expressed his resolve to break away from traditional Russian literature.

During China's New Culture Movement, author Lu Xun became famous for viciously attacking tradition and denouncing Chinese antiquity. In his first novel, *A Madman's Diary*, he had the protagonist declare that all of Chinese history could be summed up in two characters: "man eating." Lu was praised by Mao as "the greatest and most courageous standard-bearer of this new cultural force" and "the chief commander of China's Cultural Revolution." Mao also said, "The road he took was the very road of China's new national culture." [26]

Defending Hideous Portrayals as 'Reality'

Today, intellectuals and artists use literature and the arts to portray things or scenes that are ugly, strange, and terrifying, using the excuse that they are merely showing things as they really are.

Traditional art conveys harmony, grace, clarity, restraint, propriety, balance, universality, and ideals, which require selection and choice. In the view of modern artists, such works cannot be considered authentic. This view, however, comes from a misunderstanding of the origin and function of art. Art originates from everyday life, but it should transcend everyday life so that it may both delight and instruct. Because of this, during the creative process, artists must select, refine, and process what to portray.

Blindly focusing on this understanding of realism artificially restricts the boundaries of life and art. If this type of realism is art, then what everyone sees and hears is all art — in which case, why spend time and money training artists?

Corrupting Moral Values

Pretexts such as "expressing one's true self" and giving free rein to one's "stream of consciousness" have led people to abandon traditional moral standards and indulge in the demonic side of human nature.

French communist and poet André Breton defined surrealism as "psychic automatism in its pure state, by which one proposes to express — verbally, by means of the written word, or in any other manner — the actual functioning of thought. Dictated by thought, in the absence of any control exercised by reason, exempt from any aesthetic or moral concern." [27]

"Stream of consciousness" writing and surrealist "automatic writing" are closely related. Influenced by Sigmund Freud's psychopathology, some writers in the West started to experiment with stream-of-consciousness writing from the beginning of the twentieth century. Such writings usually have simple storylines and focus on the inner and private thought processes of insignificant characters (anti-heroes) through narratives composed of meandering thoughts.

Human beings simultaneously contain the potential for both kindness and evil. A life should be dedicated to the constant elevation of moral standards and cultivation of virtue through self-restraint. In modern society, many people experience ill thoughts and desires. Putting them on display for public consumption is equivalent to polluting society.

Unleashing Man's Dark Side as 'Criticism' and 'Protest'

Writers and artists in the Western free world, under the influence of anti-traditionalist sentiment, consider all laws, regulations, and moral codes to be restrictive and suppressive. They see problems with modern society and the weaknesses of human nature, but instead of dealing with them rationally, they promote extreme individualism via criticism and protest, indulging in their personal desires.

They use degenerate means to express so-called resistance, while strengthening the dark side of their nature, indulging in hatred, laziness, desire, lust, aggression, and the pursuit of fame. A lack of moral self-restraint won't solve any social issues; it can only worsen them.

During the counterculture movement of the 1960s, American poet Allen Ginsberg became the representative of the Beat Generation and is still venerated today by those who wish to rebel against society. His poem "Howl" depicts extreme lifestyles and mental states, including alcoholism, sexual promiscuity, drugs, sodomy, self-mutilation, prostitution, streaking, violent assault, theft, vagabonding, and madness.

As the counterculture movement became institutionalized, "Howl" came to be regarded as a literary classic and was included in numerous literary collections. Ginsberg admitted that he was a communist when he "was a kid" and held no regrets. [28] He idolized Fidel Castro and other communist dictators and widely promoted homosexuality and pedophilia. Ginsberg is a clear representative of the common ground between communism and extreme individualism.

Spreading Pornography

From the beginning of the twentieth century, explicit sexual content began to appear in literary works, some of which were filled with such content yet were still praised as classics. Many commentators and scholars abandoned their social responsibilities and praised such pornographic works as real, artistic masterpieces. Much of traditional morality is based on proper relations between the sexes and self-restraint. Breaking such restrictions — with whatever noble-sounding justification — undermines and destroys morality.

Dehumanizing People

Over the past several decades, as the culture became more and more confused, a great deal of genre fiction surfaced, including thrillers and works of horror and fantasy. Through such works, low-level elements can control people's minds and bodies, resulting in the dehumanization of human beings.

A three-foot block of ice does not result from only one day of coldness, as a saying goes. It takes a long period of time, and the involvement of many fields, for literature to degrade so far that it becomes a tool for evil. Romanticism widened literature's coverage of people's private and inner lives, and some ugly and bizarre phenomena — including extreme and insane human mental states — were presented for public consumption. Several British Romantic poets were collectively dubbed "the Satanic School" because of the immoral content of their poems.

Realism uses the excuse of presenting reality to express the degenerate side of human nature. Thus, certain works emphasize warped thoughts and immoral conduct. One critic called realism "romanticism going on all fours." [29] The philosophy of naturalism, as promoted by Jean-Jacques Rousseau, attributed the decline in human morality to the social environment and family genetics, thus removing the individual's moral responsibility. Aestheticism calls for "art for art's sake," claiming that art is meant to simply provide sensory stimuli and carries no moral imperative.

In fact, all art has subtle, profound, and long-lasting effects on the moral compass. To deny the moral responsibility of art is to

331

open the door for immorality to creep in. While some contemporary authors have generated high-quality works, what many others have produced is simply dreck. The negative elements are obviously the result of declining moral standards, and they effectively paved the road for communist ideology to destroy mankind via literature.

When a person writes, his or her moral standard and mental state are reflected in his or her work. With the overall decline of human morality, the negative mindset of writers takes a dominant stance. This has created numerous works that, instead of seeking to bring out the goodness in people, pull people down toward hell.

4. Reviving True Art

The power of art is enormous. Good art can rectify the human heart, elevate morality, harmonize yin and yang, and even enable humans to connect with heaven, earth, and divine beings.

In the past century, the specter of communism took advantage of man's demon nature and malice, prompting the creation of an enormous variety of so-called "art." People were led to revolt against and blaspheme the divine, oppose tradition, and overturn morality. This had the ultimate effect of turning large parts of society demonic, to a degree that would have been deeply shocking to anyone living in a previous era.

Compared to the beauty of traditional arts, modern works are extremely ugly. Humanity's aesthetic standards have been destroyed. The avant-garde has become mainstream and commands vast sums of money, while traditional, upright arts have been denigrated.

Arts have been manipulated into a vehicle for people to indulge in their desires and vent their demon nature. The boundary between beauty and ugliness, grace and vulgarity, goodness and evil, has been blurred or even erased. Grotesquerie, chaos, and darkness have taken the place of universal values. Human society is filled with demonic messages, and human beings are being steered along a path of decadence and destruction.

Only by elevating morality and returning to faith and tradition will humankind be able to see another renaissance in the arts. Only then will we all see the beauty, nobility, and splendor of what art can be and is meant to be.

Notes

Chapter Two: Communism's European Beginnings

1. KARL MARX, "Invocation of One in Despair," in *Early Works of Karl Marx: Book of Verse,* Marxists Internet Archive, accessed August 28, 2019, https://www.marxists.org/archive/marx/works/1837-pre/verse/verse11.htm.

2. KARL MARX, "Letter From Marx to His Father in Trier," in *The First Writings of Karl Marx,* Marxists Internet Archive, accessed August 28, 2019, https://www.marxists.org/archive/marx/works/1837-pre/letters/37_11_10.htm.

3. KARL MARX, "The Pale Maiden," in *Early Works of Karl Marx: Book of Verse,* Marxists Internet Archive, accessed August 28, 2019, https://www.marxists.org/archive/marx/works/1837-pre/verse/verse24.htm.

4. HEINRICH MARX, as quoted in Richard Wurmbrand, *Marx & Satan* (Westchester, Ill.: Crossway Books, 1986), 21.

5. ELEANOR MARX-AVELING, "Biographical Notes on Marx's Literary Interests," in *Marx and Engels on Literature and Art,* Marxists Internet Archive, accessed April 18, 2020, https://marxists.catbull.com/archive/marx/bio/marx/eleanor-literature.htm.

6. KARL MARX, "The Fiddler," in *Early Works of Karl Marx: Book of Verse,* Marxists Internet Archive, accessed August 28, 2019, https://www.marxists.org/archive/marx/works/1837-pre/verse/verse4.htm.

7. ROBERT PAYNE, *Marx* (New York: Simon and Schuster, 1968).

8. ERIC VOEGELIN, *From Enlightenment to Revolution,* ed. John H. Hallowell (Durham, NC: Duke University Press, 1975), 298–299.

9. KARL MARX, "Human Pride," in *Early Works of Karl Marx: Book of Verse,* Marxists Internet Archive, accessed August 28, 2019, https://www.marxists.org/archive/marx/works/1837-pre/verse/verse20.htm.

10. MARX, as quoted in Wurmbrand, *Marx & Satan,* 2.

11. WURMBRAND, *Marx & Satan,* 28.

12. KARL MARX, "On Hegel," in *Early Works of Karl Marx: Book of Verse,* Marxists Internet Archive, accessed August 28, 2019, https://www.marxists.org/archive/marx/works/1837-pre/verse/verse15.htm.

13. LUDWIG FEUERBACH, "Essence of Religion in General," in *The Essence of Christianity,* Marxists Internet Archive, accessed August 28, 2019,

https://www.marxists.org/reference/
archive/feuerbach/works/essence/
ec01_1.htm.

14. KARL MARX, as quoted in I. Bernard
Cohen, *Revolution in Science*
(Cambridge, Mass.: The Belknap
Press of Harvard University Press,
1985), 345.

15. FRIEDRICH ENGELS,
"On Authority," in *The Marx-Engels
Reader*, Marxists Internet Archive,
accessed April 18, 2020, https://
www.marxists.org/archive/marx/
works/1872/10/authority.htm.

16. "Robespierre's Epitaph,"
The Tomahawk (January 9,
1796), Romantic Circles, accessed
September 6, 2019, https://
www.rc.umd.edu/editions/
warpoetry/1796/1796_2.html.

17. JACQUES GODECHOT, "The Internal
History of France During the Wars,
1793–1814," in *The New Cambridge
Modern History*, ed. C. W. Crawley
(Cambridge, UK: Cambridge
University Press, 1965), 9:280–281.

18. MIGUEL A. FARIA JR., "The
Economic Terror of the French
Revolution," Hacienda Publishing,
July 1, 2003, accessed April 18, 2020,
https://haciendapublishing.com/
articles/economic-terror-french-
revolution.

19. GREGORY FREMONT-BARNES,
*Encyclopedia
of the Age of Political Revolutions
and New Ideologies, 1760–1815*
(Westport, CT: Greenwood Press,
Inc., 2007), 119.

20. WILLIAM HENLEY JERVIS, *The
Gallican Church and the Revolution*
(London: Kegan Paul, Trench, & Co.,
1882).

21. W. CLEON SKOUSEN,
"The Founders of Communism,"
in *The Naked Communist* (Salt
Lake City, UT: Ensign Publishing
Company, 1962).

22. JOHN M. MERRIMAN, *Massacre:
The Life and Death of the Paris
Commune* (New York: Basic Books,
2014).

23. LOUIS-AUGUSTE BLANQUI,
"Speech Before the Society of the
Friends of the People," in *Selected
Works of Louis-Auguste Blanqui*
(Scotts Valley, CA: CreateSpace
Independent Publishing Platform,
2011), 15.

24. KARL MARX, "The Paris Commune,"
in *The Civil War in France*, Marxists
Internet Archive, accessed April 19,
2020, https://www.marxists.org/
archive/marx/works/1871/civil-war-
france/index.htm.

25. ZHANG DEYI 張德彝, *San shu qi* 三
述奇 *[The Third Diary]*, (Shanghai:
Shanghai Guji Chubanshe, 1995).
[In Chinese]

26. MERRIMAN, *Massacre*.

27. VLADIMIR LENIN, "Frederick
Engels," in *Lenin Collected Works*,
vol. 2 (Moscow: Progress Publishers,
1972), Marxists Internet Archive,
accessed April 19, 2020, https://
www.marxists.org/archive/lenin/
works/1895/misc/engels-bio.htm.

28. ERIC HOBSBAWM,
*How to Change the World:
Reflections on Marx and Marxism*
(New Haven, CT, and London: Yale
University Press, 2011), 214.

29. WINSTON CHURCHILL, "The
Sinews of Peace ('Iron Curtain
Speech')" (speech, Westminster
College, Fulton, MO, March 5, 1946),

International Churchill Society, accessed April 19, 2020, https://winstonchurchill.org/resources/speeches/1946-1963-elder-statesman/the-sinews-of-peace.

Chapter Three: Tyranny in the East

1. US CONGRESS, HOUSE, "Remembering the Victims of Communism," remarks by Rep. Christopher Smith, 115th Congress, 1st sess., *Congressional Record* 163 (November 13, 2017) https://www.congress.gov/congressional-record/2017/11/13/extensions-of-remarks-section/article/E1557-2.

2. STÉPHANE COURTOIS et al., eds., *The Black Book of Communism: Crimes, Terror, Repression,* trans. Jonathan Murphy and Mark Kramer (Cambridge, MA: Harvard University Press, 1999).

3. RICHARD PIPES, *The Russian Revolution* (New York: Vintage Books, 1991), 411.

4. WINSTON CHURCHILL, *The World Crisis, Vol. 5: The Unknown War* (London: Bloomsbury Academic, 2015).

5. ROBERT SERVICE, *Lenin, a Biography* (Cambridge, MA.: Harvard University Press, 2000), 365.

6. COURTOIS et al., eds., *The Black Book,* 177.

7. ROBERT GELLATELY, *Lenin, Stalin, and Hitler: The Age of Social Catastrophe* (New York: Knopf Publishing Group, 2007), 75.

8. "Zhongguo Gongchandang da shiji. 1945 nian" 中國共產黨大事記·1945 年 ["A Chronicle of Key Events of the Chinese Communist Party 1945"], *News of the Communist Party of China,* accessed April 16, 2020, http://cpc.people.com.cn/GB/64162/64164/4416000.html. [In Chinese]

9. FRANK DIKÖTTER, *The Tragedy of Liberation: A History of the Chinese Revolution 1945–1957* (London: Bloomsbury Press, 2013).

10. MARTIN AMIS, *Koba the Dread: Laughter and the Twenty Million* (New York: Vintage Books, 2003).

11. ROY MEDVEDEV, *Let History Judge: The Origins and Consequences of Stalinism,* trans. George Shriver (New York: Columbia University Press, 1989), 240–245.

12. ALEKSANDR SOLZHENITSYN, *The Gulag Archipelago 1918–1956: An Experiment in Literary Investigation, Books I–II,* trans. Thomas P. Whitney (New York: Harper & Row, 1973).

13. MEDVEDEV, *Let History Judge,* 396.

14. REUTERS, "4.2 Million Were Victims of Purges, KGB Chief Says," *LA Times,* June 15, 1991, https://www.latimes.com/archives/la-xpm-1991-06-15-mn-496-story.html.

15. ALEXANDER YAKOVLEV, *Yakeliefu fangtan lu 1992–2005* 雅科夫列夫訪談錄（1992—2005）*[Alexander Yakovlev: Selected interviews (1992–2005)],* trans. Chinese Academy of Social Sciences, 234. [In Chinese]

16. WEN YULUO 遇罗文, "Daxing

tusha diaocha" 大兴屠杀调查 ["An Investigation of the Beijing Daxing Massacre"] in *Wen Ge da tusha* 文革大屠殺 *[Massacres in the Cultural Revolution],* ed. Song Yongyi 宋永毅 (Hong Kong: Kaifang zazhishe, 2002), 13–36. [In Chinese]

17. R. J. RUMMEL, *China's Bloody Century: Genocide and Mass Murder Since 1900* (New York: Routledge, 2017), 253.

18. DONG BAOXUN 董宝训 AND DING LONGJIA 丁龙嘉, *Chen yuan zhao yun—pingfan yuan jia cuo an* 沉冤昭雪一平反冤假錯案 *[Exonerate the Innocent: Rehabilitate the Wrongly Accused and Sentenced]* (Hefei: Anhui Renmin Chubanshe, 1998), 1. [In Chinese]

19. ORIANA FALLACI, "Deng: Cleaning Up Mao's 'Feudal Mistakes,'" *The Washington Post,* August 31, 1980, https://www.washingtonpost.com/archive/opinions/1980/08/31/deng-cleaning-up-maos-feudal-mistakes/4e684a74-8083-4e43-80e4-c8d519d8b772.

20. DING LONGJIA 丁龙嘉 AND TING YU 听雨, *Kang Sheng yu Zhao Jianmin yuan'an* 康生与赵健民冤案 *[Kang Sheng and the Unjust Case of Zhao Jianmin]* (Beijing: Renmin Chubanshe, 1999), as referenced in Hu Angang, *Mao and the Cultural Revolution,* ed. W. H. Hau (Honolulu: Enrich Professional Publishing, INC., 2016), 2:98.

21. DAVID MATAS AND DAVID KILGOUR, *Bloody Harvest: The Killing of Falun Gong for Their Organs* (Ontario: Seraphim Editions, 2009), 13.

22. US CONGRESS, HOUSE, *Expressing concern regarding persistent and credible reports of systematic, state-sanctioned organ harvesting from non-consenting prisoners of conscience in the People's Republic of China, including from large numbers of Falun Gong practitioners and members of other religious and ethnic minority groups,* HR 343, 114th Cong., 2nd sess., introduced in House June 25, 2015, https://www.congress.gov/bill/114th-congress/house-resolution/343.

23. CHINA TRIBUNAL: Independent Tribunal into Forced Organ Harvesting from Prisoners of Conscience in China, "China Tribunal: Final Judgment 17th June," March 1, 2020, https://chinatribunal.com/final-judgment.

24. COURTOIS et al., eds., *The Black Book,* 4.

25. THOMAS SPOORENBERG AND DANIEL SCHWEKENDIEK, "Demographic Changes in North Korea: 1993–2008," *Population and Development Review,* March 21, 2012, accessed via Wiley Online Library, https://onlinelibrary.wiley.com/doi/abs/10.1111/j.1728-4457.2012.00475.x.

Chapter Four: Exporting Revolution

1. CHONGYI FENG, "How the Chinese Communist Party Exerts Its Influence in Australia," *ABC News* (Australia), June 5, 2017, http://www.abc.net.au/news/2017-06-06/how-china-uses-its-soft-power-strategy-in-australia/8590610.

2. JUNG CHANG AND JON HALLIDAY,

"Lukewarm Believer (1920–25; age 26–31)," *Mao: The Unknown Story* (New York: Anchor Books, 2006).

3. HARRY TRUMAN, "Statement on Formosa" (speech, White House, January 5, 1950), USC US–China Institute, accessed April 19, 2020, https://china.usc.edu/harry-s-truman-%E2%80%9Cstatement-formosa%E2%80%9D-january-5-1950.

4. "US Enters the Korean Conflict," National Archives, last modified September 7, 2016, https://www.archives.gov/education/lessons/korean-conflict.

5. QIAN YAPING 錢亞平, "60 nian lai Zhongguo de dui wai yuanzhu: zui duo shi zhan guojia caizheng zhichu 7%" 60年來中國的對外援助：最多時佔國家財政支出7% ["Sixty Years of China's Foreign Aid: Up to 7 Percent of the National Fiscal Expenditure"], in *People's Daily*, May 27, 2011, http://history.people.com.cn/BIG5/205396/14757192.html. [In Chinese]

6. CHEN XIANHUI 陳憲輝, "Di 38 zhang kang Mei yuan Chao" 第38章 抗美援朝 ["Chapter 38: Resist US, Aid Korea"], in *Geming de zhenxiang. Ershi shiji Zhongguo jishi* 革命的真相.二十世紀中國記事 *[The Truth of the Revolution: 20th Century Chronology of China]* (December 2014), https://www.bannedbook.net/forum2/topic6605.html. [In Chinese]

7. ZHONG SHANLUO 鐘山洛, *Dangshi mimi* 黨史秘密 *[Secrets of Party History]* (Taiwan: Ha Ye chubanshe, 2016). [In Chinese]

8. CHEN XIANHUI 陳憲輝, "Di 52 zhang Wen Ge wai jiao: duiwai shuchu geming" 第52章文革外交與輸出革命 ["Chapter 52: The Cultural Revolution Diplomacy and Export Revolution"], in *Geming de zhenxiang. Ershi shiji Zhongguo jishi* 革命的真相.二十世紀中國紀事 *[The Truth of the Revolution: 20th Century Chronology of China]* (December 2014), https://www.bannedbook.net/forum2/topic6605.html. [In Chinese]

9. LI SU 李肅, "Jie mi shi ke: taoli Chaoxian wangming Zhongguo (wanzhengban)" 解密时刻：逃離朝鮮 亡命中國（完整版） ["Leaking Moment: Escaping North Korea, Dying in China" (complete version)], *Voice of America*, October 8, 2012, https://www.voachinese.com/a/hm-escaping-north-korea-20121007/1522169.html. [In Chinese]

10. SONG ZHENG 宋征, "1965 Yinni '9.30' zhengbian shimo" 1965印尼『9.30』政變始末 ["The 9.30 Coup in Indonesia in 1965"], *China in Perspective*, modified September 20, 2017, http://www.chinainperspective.com/ArtShow.aspx?AID=183410. [In Chinese]

11. WANG NAN 王南, "Shuo gu lun jin: Miandian de Zhongguo chongjidui bo", 說古論今：緬甸的中國衝擊波 ["Talking About History: China's Shock Wave in Myanmar"], *Voice of America*, February 24, 2012, https://www.voachinese.com/a/article-2012024-burma-china-factors-iv-140343173/812128.html. [In Chinese]

12. CHENG YINGHONG 程映虹, "Xiang shijie shuchu geming—'Wen Ge' zai Ya Fei La de yingxiang chutan" "向世界輸出革命--'文革'在亞非拉的影響初探" ["Exporting

Revolution to the World: An Early Exploration of the Impact of the Cultural Revolution in Asia, Africa and Latin America"], *Modern China Studies*, vol. 3 (2006). [In Chinese]

13. CHEN YINAN 陳益南, "She zai Zhongguo de Ma Gong diantai", 設在中國的馬共電台 ["MCP Radio Station in China"], *Yanhuang Chunqiu*, vol. 8, 2015. [In Chinese]

14. CHENG YINGHONG, "Xiang shijie shuchu geming."

15. Ibid.

16. CHEN, "Di 52 zhang Wen Ge wai jiao."

17. HANSHAN 寒山, "Jin shi zuo fei: Xiong Xiangshi he Zhonggong zai La Mei shuchu geing de lishi" 今是昨非 : 熊向暉和中共在拉美輸出革命的歷史 ["Xiong Xianghui and the CCP's history of exporting revolution to Latin America"], *Radio Free Asia*, November 17, 2005, https://www.rfa.org/cantonese/features/history/china_cccp-20051117.html. [In Chinese]

18. CHENG, "Xiang shijie shuchu geming."

19. CHEN KUIDE 陳奎德, *Jindai xianfa de yanhua* 近代憲政的演化 [*The Evolution of Contemporary Constitutionalism*], *The Observer* (2007), chap. 60. [In Chinese]

20. Ibid., chap. 67.

21. Ibid., chap. 77.

22. WANG HONGQI, "Zhongguo dui Aerbaniya de yuanzhu" 中國對阿爾巴尼亞的援助 ["China's Aid to Albania"], *Yanhuang Chunqiu*,

accessed April 16, 2020, http://www.yhcqw.com/36/3172.html#. [In Chinese]

Chapter Five: Infiltrating the West

1. JOSEPH (JAKE) KLEIN, "An Interview With Trevor Loudon," Capital Research Center, February 24, 2017, accessed on April 16, 2020, https://capitalresearch.org/article/an-interview-with-trevor-loudon.

2. KARL MARX AND FRIEDRICH ENGELS, "Manifesto of the Communist Party," in *Marx & Engels Selected Works*, vol. 1, trans. Samuel Moore, ed. Andy Blunden (Moscow: Progress Publishers, 1969), vol. 1, chap. 4, Marxists Internet Archive, accessed April 17, 2020, https://www.marxists.org/archive/marx/works/1848/communist-manifesto/ch04.htm.

3. "Our History," Fabian Society, accessed March 6, 2020, https://fabians.org.uk/about-us/our-history.

4. MARY AGNES HAMILTON, *Sidney and Beatrice Webb: A Study in Contemporary Biography* (London: Sampson Low, Marston & Co., 1932).

5. VLADIMIR LENIN, '*Left Wing*' *Communism: An Infantile Disorder.* (Moscow: Foreign Languages Publishing House, 1952), 47.

6. GEORGE BERNARD SHAW, *The Intelligent Woman's Guide to Socialism and Capitalism* (New York: Brentano's Publishers, 1928), 470.

7. US CONGRESS, HOUSE, Committee on Un-American Activities, *Communist Legal Subversion: The Role of the Communist Lawyer: Report*, 86th Cong., 1st sess., February 16, 1959.

8. JOHN EARL HAYNES AND HARVEY KLEHR, *Venona: Decoding Soviet Espionage in America* (New Haven: Yale University Press, 1999), 138–145.

9. M. STANTON EVANS AND HERBERT ROMERSTEIN, *Stalin's Secret Agents: The Subversion of Roosevelt's Government* (New York: Threshold Editions, 2012).

10. WHITTAKER CHAMBERS, *Witness* (New York: Random House, 1952).

11. TOMAS SCHUMAN (YURI BEZMENOV), *Love Letter to America* (Los Angeles: Maxims Books, 1984), 21–46.

12. ION MIHAI PACEPA AND RONALD J. RYCHLAK, *Disinformation: Former Spy Chief Reveals Secret Strategies for Undermining Freedom, Attacking Religion, and Promoting Terrorism* (Washington, DC: WND Books Inc., 2013).

13. BUREAU OF THE CENSUS, "Historical Statistics of the United States: Colonial Times to 1970, Part 2," accessed on April 16, 2020, https://www.census.gov/history/pdf/1930-39unemployment.pdf.

14. DINESH D'SOUZA, *The Big Lie: Exposing the Nazi Roots of the American Left* (Washington, DC: Regnery Publishing, 2017).

15. JIM POWELL, *FDR's Folly: How Roosevelt and His New Deal Prolonged the Great Depression* (New York: Crown Forum, 2003).

16. MILTON FRIEDMAN, as quoted in Powell, *FDR's Folly*, back cover.

17. NICHOLAS EBERSTADT, "The Great Society at 50: What LBJ wrought," American Enterprise Institute, May 9, 2014, accessed on April 16, 2020, https://www.aei.org/articles/the-great-society-at-50.

18. ELMER T. PETERSON, "This Is the Hard Core of Freedom," *The Daily Oklahoman*, December 9, 1951.

19. WILLIAM S. LIND, 'Political Correctness:' A Short History of an Ideology* (Washington, DC: Free Congress Foundation, 2004), 4–5.

20. Ibid., 10.

21. LIN BIAO, "Defeat US Imperialism and Its Lackeys by People's War," in *Long Live the Victory of People's War!* (Beijing: Foreign Language Press, 1965).

22. MIKHAIL SUSLOV, "The Defense of Peace and the Struggle Against the Warmongers" (New Century Publishers, February 1950), Marxists Internet Archive, accessed April 17, 2020, https://www.marxists.org/archive/suslov/1949/11/x01.htm.

23. VLADIMIR BUKOVSKY, "The Peace Movement & the Soviet Union," *Commentary Magazine*, May 1982, accessed April 17, 2020, https://www.commentarymagazine.com/articles/the-peace-movement-the-soviet-union.

24. US CONGRESS, *Congressional Record: Proceedings and Debates*, 88th Cong., 1st sess., Vol. 109, Part 1, January 9, 1963–January 30, 1963.

25. STANISLAV LUNEV AND IRA WINKLER, *Through the Eyes of the Enemy: The Autobiography of Stanislav Lunev* (Washington, DC:

Regnery Publishing, 1998).

26. RONALD RADOSH, as quoted in
Robert Chandler, *Shadow World:
Resurgent Russia,
the Global New Left, and Radical
Islam* (Washington, DC.: Regnery
Publishing, 2008), 389.

27. "AIM Report: Communists Run
Anti-War Movement," Accuracy
in Media, February 19, 2003,
https://www.aim.org/aim-report/
aim-report-communists-run-anti-
war-movement.

28. JOHN PEPPER (JOSEPH POGANI),
American Negro Problems (New
York: Workers Library Publishers,
1928), Marxists Internet Archive,
accessed April 17, 2020, https://www.
marxists.org/history/usa/parties/
cpusa/1928/nomonth/0000-pepper-
negroproblems.pdf.

29. JAMES W. FORD AND JAMES S.
ALLEN, *The Negroes in a Soviet
America* (New York: Workers
Library Publishers, 1935), 24–30.

30. LEONARD PATTERSON, "I Trained
in Moscow for Black Revolution,"
Speakers Bureau of the John Birch
Society, YouTube video, posted
by Swamp Yankee, August 20,
2011, https://www.youtube.com/
watch?v=GuXQjk4zhZs.

31. G. LOUIS HEATH, ed., *Off the Pigs!
The History and Literature of the
Black Panther Party* (Metuchen, NJ:
Scarecrow Press, 1976), 61.

32. THURSTON POWERS,
"How Black Lives Matter Is Bringing
Back Traditional Marxism," *The
Federalist*, September 28, 2016,
http://thefederalist.com/2016/09/28/
black-lives-matter-bringing-back-
traditional-marxism.

33. DAVID HOROWITZ, *Barack Obama's
Rules for Revolution: The Alinsky
Model* (Sherman Oaks, CA: David
Horowitz Freedom Center, 2009),
6, 16.

34. SAUL ALINSKY, *Rules for Radicals:
A Pragmatic Primer for Realistic
Radicals* (New York: Vintage Books,
1971), 125–164.

35. SANFORD D. HORWITT,
*Let Them Call Me Rebel: Saul
Alinsky, His Life and Legacy* (New
York: Alfred A. Knopf, Inc., 1989),
xv–xvi.

36. ERIC NORDEN, "Playboy Interview
with Saul Alinsky: A Candid
Conversation with the Feisty Radical
Organizer," *New English Review*,
accessed April 17, 2020, https://www.
newenglishreview.org/custpage.
cfm?frm=189050&sec_id=189050.

37. RYAN LIZZA, "The Agitator,"
The New Republic, March 19,
2007, https://newrepublic.com/
article/61068/the-agitator-barack-
obamas-unlikely-political-
education.

38. NORDEN,
"Playboy Interview."

39. DAVID HOROWITZ AND RICHARD
POE, *The Shadow Party: How
George Soros, Hillary Clinton, and
Sixties Radicals Seized Control of
the Democratic Party* (Nashville,
Tennessee: Nelson Current, 2006),
110–114.

40. VLADIMIR LENIN, "Draft Theses
on the Role and Functions of
The Trade Unions Under the
New Economic Policy," in *Lenin
Collected Works*, vol. 42 (Moscow:
Progress Publishers, 1971), 374–386,
Marxists Internet Archive,

accessed April 17, 2020, https://www.marxists.org/archive/lenin/works/1921/dec/30b.htm.

41. TREVOR LOUDON, "Communism/Socialism: The Enemies Within," *The Schwarz Report*, vol. 54, no. 7, July 2014, http://www.schwarzreport.org/uploads/schwarz-report-pdf/schwarz-report-2014-07.pdf

42. NATHAN PINKOSKI, "Jordan Peterson Is a Fulcrum for Right and Left's Switch on Free Expression," *The Federalist*, February 2, 2018, http://thefederalist.com/2018/02/02/jordan-peterson-marks-fulcrum-right-lefts-side-switch-free-expression.

43. STANLEY KURTZ, "Campus Chaos: Daily Shout-Downs for a Week," *National Review*, October 12, 2017, https://www.nationalreview.com/corner/campus-chaos-daily-shout-downs-week-free-speech-charles-murray.

44. ANDREW O'REILLY, "Antifa Protests Mean High Security Costs for Berkeley Free Speech Week, but Who's Paying the Bill?", *Fox News*, September 15, 2017, http://www.foxnews.com/us/2017/09/15/antifa-protests-mean-high-security-costs-for-berkeley-free-speech-week-but-whos-paying-bill.html.

45. "Outspoken Conservative Ben Shapiro Says Political Correctness Breeds Insanity," *ABC News*, October 20, 2017, https://www.youtube.com/watch?time_continue=3&v=vj5JXrpwsZs&feature=emb_logo.

46. JESSICA SCHLADEBECK, "Penn Law Professor Loses Teaching Duties for Saying Black Students 'Rarely' Earn Top Marks," *New York Daily News*, March 15, 2018, http://www.nydailynews.com/news/national/law-professor-upenn-loses-teaching-duties-article-1.3876057.

47. PAUL HOLLANDER, *Political Pilgrims: Travels of Western Intellectuals to the Soviet Union, China, and Cuba* (New York: Oxford University Press, 1981).

48. J. EDGAR HOOVER, *Masters of Deceit: The Story of Communism in America and How to Fight It* (New York: Henry Holt and Co., 1958), 81–96.

49. THOMAS SCHUMAN (YURI BEZMENOV), *No 'Novosti' Is Good News* (Los Angeles: Almanac, 1985), 65–75.

50. FRED SCHWARZ AND DAVID NOEBEL, *You Can Still Trust the Communists ... to Be Communists (Socialists, Statists, and Progressives Too)* (Manitou Springs, CO: Christian Anti-Communism Crusade, 2010), 44–52.

51. PAUL JOHNSON, *Intellectuals: From Marx and Tolstoy to Sartre and Chomsky* (New York: Harper Perennial, 2007), 225.

Chapter Six: The Revolt Against God

1. KARL MARX, as quoted in Dimitry V. Pospielovsky, *A History of Marxist-Leninist Atheism and Soviet Anti Religious Policies: History of Soviet Atheism in Theory and Practice, and the Believer, Vol. 1* (London: Palgrave Macmillan, 1987), 80.

2. US LIBRARY OF CONGRESS,

"Translation of Letter from Lenin," Revelations from the Russian Archives, accessed April 17, 2020, https://www.loc.gov/exhibits/archives/trans-ae2bkhun.html.

3.   PATRIARCH ALEXY II as quoted in Nathaniel Davis, trans., *A Long Walk to Church: A Contemporary History of Russian Orthodoxy* (Oxford: Westview Press, 1994), 89.

4.   CHOEKYI GYALTSEN, Tenth Panchen Lama, as quoted in Central Tibetan Administration: Department of Information and International Relations, *From the Heart of the Panchen Lama* (Dharamsala, India: Central Tibetan Administration, 2003 edition), accessed April 17, 2020, http://tibet.net/wp-content/uploads/2015/04/FROM-THE-HEART-OF-THE-PANCHEN-LAMA-1998.pdf.

5.   TSERING WOESER, *Forbidden Memory: Tibet During the Cultural Revolution*, Susan T. Chen, trans., Robert Barnett, ed. (Lincoln, NE: Potomac Books, April 2020)

6.   US CONGRESS, HOUSE, Committee on Un-American Activities. *Investigation of Communist Activities in the New York City Area.* 83rd Cong., 1st sess., July 8, 1953. https://archive.org/stream/investigationofcnyc0708unit/investigationofcnyc0708unit_djvu.txt.

7.   MOMCHIL METODIEV, *Between Faith and Compromise: The Bulgarian Orthodox Church and the Communist State (1944–1989)* (Sofia: Institute for Studies of the Recent Past/Ciela, 2010).

8.   CHRISTOPHER ANDREW, "KGB Foreign Intelligence from Brezhnev to the Coup," in Wesley K. Wark, ed., *Espionage: Past, Present, Future?* (London: Routledge, 1994), 52.

9.   METODIEV, "Between Faith."

10. W. CLEON SKOUSEN, *The Naked Communist* (Salt Lake City: Ensign Publishing Co., 1958).

11. "Zhongguo Fojiao xiehui fuhuizhang: 'Shijiu Da Baogao shi dangdai Fojing Wo yijing shouchao san bian'" 中國佛教協會副會長：十九大報告是當代佛經　我已手抄三遍 ["Chinese Buddhist Association Deputy Chairman: 'The Chinese Communist Party's 19th Congress Report Is the Contemporary Buddhist Scripture, I Have Hand-copied It Three Times'"], *Stand News*, December 13, 2017. [In Chinese]

Chapter Seven: The Destruction of the Family

1.   FRIEDRICH ENGELS, *Origins of the Family, Private Property, and the State*, trans. Alick West, (1884), chap. 2, part 4, accessed via Marxists Internet Archive on April 17, 2020, https://www.marxists.org/archive/marx/works/1884/origin-family/ch02d.htm.

2.   W. BRADFORD WILCOX, "The Evolution of Divorce," *National Affairs*, no. 1 (Fall 2009), https://www.nationalaffairs.com/publications/detail/the-evolution-of-divorce.

3.   US CENTERS FOR DISEASE CONTROL AND PREVENTION, National Center for Health

Statistics, "Table 1–17. Number and Percent of Births to Unmarried Women, by Race and Hispanic Origin: United States, 1940–2000," https://www.cdc.gov/nchs/data/statab/t001x17.pdf.

4. JOHN ELFLEIN, "Percentage of births to unmarried women in the US from 1980 to 2018," Statista, December 3, 2019, https://www.statista.com/statistics/276025/us-percentage-of-births-to-unmarried-women/.

5. Genesis 2:23, American Standard Version Bible.

6. ROBERT OWEN, "Critique of Individualism (1825–1826)," Indiana University–Bloomington, July 4, 1826, accessed April 17, 2020. https://web.archive.org/web/20171126034814/http://www.indiana.edu:80/~kdhist/H105-documents-web/week11/Owen1826.html.

7. ENGELS, *Origins*, chap. 2.

8. Ibid.

9. ALEXANDER MELNICHENKO Александр Мельниченко, "Velikaya oktyabr'skaya seksual'naya revolyutsiya" Великая октябрьская сексуальная революция ["The Great October Sexual Revolution"], *Russian Folk Line*, August 20, 2017, http://ruskline.ru/opp/2017/avgust/21/velikaya_oktyabrskaya_seksualnaya_revolyuciya. [In Russian]

10. Ibid.

11. Ibid.

12. MADAME SMIDOVICH Смидович, as quoted in Natal'ya Korotkaya

Наталья Короткая, "Eros revolyutsii: Komsomolka, nye bud' myeshchankoy — pomogi muzhchinye cnyat' napryazheniye!" Эрос революции: "Комсомолка, не будь мещанкой — помоги мужчине снять напряжение!" ["Eros of the Revolution: 'Komsomol Girl, Do Not Be a Bourgeois — Help a Man Relieve Tension!'"], Tut.By Online, November 10, 2012, https://lady.tut.by/news/sex/319720.html?crnd=68249. [In Russian]

13. PAUL KENGOR, *Takedown: From Communists to Progressives, How the Left Has Sabotaged Family and Marriage* (Washington, DC: WND Books, 2015), 54.

14. MELNICHENKO, "The Great."

15. XIA HOU 夏侯, "Gongchanzhuyi de yinluan jiyin—xingjiefang" 共產主義的淫亂基因——性解放 ["The Promiscuous Gene of Communism: Sexual Liberation"], *The Epoch Times* (Chinese edition), April 9, 2017, http://www.epochtimes.com/gb/17/4/9/n9018949.htm. [In Chinese]

16. CLARA ZETKIN, "Lenin on the Women's Question," *The Emancipation of Women: From the Writings of V. I. Lenin*, Marxists Internet Archive, accessed April 17, 2020, https://www.marxists.org/archive/zetkin/1920/lenin/zetkin1.htm.

17. HUANG WENZHI 黃文治, "'Nuola zou hou zen yang': Funü jiefang, hunyinziyou ji jiejigeming—yi E Yu Wan Suqu wei zhongxin de lishikaocha (1922–1932)" "娜拉走後怎樣":婦女解放、婚姻自由及階級革命——以鄂豫皖蘇區為中心的歷史考察 (1922–1932) ["'What Happened after Nora Left': Women's

Liberation, Freedom of Marriage, and Class Revolution—A Historical Survey of the Hubei-Henan-Anhui Soviet Districts (1922–1932)"], *Open Times* no. 4 (2013). This source draws on information in *E Yu Wan Suqu geming lishi wenjianhuiji* 鄂豫皖苏区革命历史文件汇集, *[Collection of Revolutionary Historical Documents in the Hubei-Henan-Anhui Soviet Districts]*. [In Chinese]

18. JUDITH A. REISMAN et al., *Kinsey, Sex and Fraud: The Indoctrination of a People* (Lafayette, LA: Lochinvar-Huntington House, 1990).

19. LAWRENCE B. FINER, "Trends in Premarital Sex in the United States, 1954–2003," *Public Health Reports*, vol. 122, issue.1 (January 1, 2007): 73–78.

20. NICHOLAS H. WOLFINGER, "Counterintuitive Trends in the Link Between Premarital Sex and Marital Stability," Institute for Family Studies, June 6, 2016, https://ifstudies.org/blog/counterintuitive-trends-in-the-link-between-premarital-sex-and-marital-stability.

21. BETTY FRIEDAN, *The Feminine Mystique* (New York: W.W. Norton & Company, 1963).

22. JOANNE BOUCHER, "Betty Friedan and the Radical Past of Liberal Feminism," *New Politics*, vol. 9, no.3 (Summer 2003).

23. DAVID HOROWITZ, "Betty Friedan's Secret Communist Past," *Salon*, January 19, 1999, https://www.salon.com/1999/01/18/nc_18horo.

24. KATE WEIGAND, *Red Feminism: American Communism and the Making of Women's Liberation* (Baltimore, MD, and London: The Johns Hopkins University Press, 2002).

25. Ibid.

26. SIMONE DE BEAUVOIR, *The Second Sex*, trans. Constance Borde and Sheila Malovany-Chevallier (New York: Vintage Books, 2011).

27. LAWRENCE SUMMERS, "Harvard President Summers' Remarks About Women in Science, Engineering," *PBS NewsHour*, February 22, 2005, https://www.pbs.org/newshour/science/science-jan-june05-summersremarks_2-22.

28. ALAN FINDER, "Harvard Will Spend $50 Million to Make Faculty More Diverse," *The New York Times*, May 17, 2005, https://www.nytimes.com/2005/05/17/education/harvard-will-spend-50-million-to-make-faculty-more-diverse.html.

29. C. P. BENBOW AND J. C. STANLEY, "Sex Differences in Mathematical Ability: Fact or Artifact?" *Science*, 210, issue 4475 (December 1980): 1262–1264, https://science.sciencemag.org/content/210/4475/1262.

30. C. P. BENBOW, "Sex Differences in Ability in Intellectually Talented Preadolescents: Their Nature, Effects, and Possible Causes," *Behavioral and Brain Sciences* 11, no. 2 (June 1988): 169–183. https://www.cambridge.org/core/journals/behavioral-and-brain-sciences/article/sex-differences-in-mathematical-reasoning-ability-in-intellectually-talented-preadolescents-their-

nature-effects-and-possible-causes/
CoBC8628A056CB9B38
A3464D2DF5FA44.

31. C. P. BENBOW et al, "Sex Differences
in Mathematical Reasoning Ability
at Age 13: Their Status 20 Years
Later," *Psychological Science* 11,
no. 6 (November 2000): 474-480,
https://my.vanderbilt.edu/smpy/
files/2013/02/
SexDiffs.pdf.

32. ALEXIS DE TOCQUEVILLE, as quoted
in Friedrich A. Hayek, *The Road to
Serfdom* (London: Profile Books,
2005), 47.

33. SUSAN EDELMAN,
"Woman to Become NY Firefighter
Despite Failing Crucial Fitness Test,"
New York Post, May 3, 2015. https://
nypost.com/2015/05/03/woman-
to-become-ny-firefighter-despite-
failing-crucial-fitness-test.

34. UNA BUTORAC,
"These Female Firefighters Don't
Want a Gender Quota System,"
Special Broadcasting Service, March
24, 2017, https://www.sbs.com.
au/news/the-feed/these-female-
firefighters-don-t-want-a-gender-
quota-system.

35. COMMONWEALTH COURT OF
PENNSYLVANIA, *Commonwealth
of Pennsylvania by Israel Packel,
Attorney General, v. Pennsylvania
Interscholastic Athletic Association,*
334A.2d 839, 18 Pa. Commw. 45
(March 19, 1975).

36. CHRISTINA HOFF SOMMERS, *The
War Against Boys: How Misguided
Feminism Is Harming Our Young
Men* (New York: Simon
& Schuster, 2001).

37. JAMIE DOWARD,

"'Take These Children Seriously':
NHS Clinic in the Eye of Trans
Rights Storm," *The Guardian,*
November 18, 2017, https://www.
theguardian.com/society/2017/
nov/19/nhs-clinic-trans-rights-
storm-gender-identity-specialist-
centre-transgender.

38. VIVIAN GORNICK, as quoted in *The
Daily Illini,* University of Illinois,
April 25, 1981.

39. ROBIN MORGAN,
ed., *Sisterhood Is Powerful: An
Anthology of Writings From the
Women's Liberation Movement* (New
York: Vintage Books, 1970), 537.

40. DARLENA CUNHA,
"The Divorce Gap," *The Atlantic,*
April 28, 2016, https://www.
theatlantic.com/business/
archive/2016/04/the-divorce-
gap/480333.

41. DAVID W. PURCELL
et al., "Estimating the Population
Size of Men Who Have Sex with Men
in the United States to Obtain HIV
and Syphilis Rates," *Open AIDS
Journal* 6 (September 2012): 98–107,
https://www.ncbi.nlm.nih.gov/pmc/
articles/PMC3462414.

42. R. S. HOGG et al., "Modelling the
Impact of HIV Disease on Mortality
in Gay Men," *International Journal
of Epidemiology* 26, no. 3
(June 1997): 657–661.

43. UNITED NATIONS, "Programme
of Action of the International
Conference on Population and
Development," *The International
Conference on Population and
Development (ICPD) in Cairo,
Egypt* (New York: United
Nations, 1995), 59, https://www.
un.org/en/development/desa/

population/events/pdf/expert/27/
SupportingDocuments/A_
CONF.171_13_Rev.1.pdf.

44. The Vice Chairman's Staff of the
Joint Economic Committee at the
Request of Senator Mike Lee, "Love,
Marriage, and the Baby Carriage:
The Rise in Unwed Childbearing,"
Social Capital Project no. 3–17
(December 2017), https://www.
lee.senate.gov/public/_cache/
files/3a6e738b-305b-4553-b03b-
3c71382f102c/love-marriage-and-
the-baby-carriage.pdf.

45. ROBERT RECTOR, "How Welfare
Undermines Marriage and What
to Do About It," The Heritage
Foundation, November 17, 2014,
https://www.heritage.org/welfare/
report/how-welfare-undermines-
marriage-and-what-do-about-it.

46. PHYLLIS SCHLAFLY, *Who Killed The
American Family?* (Washington,
DC: WND Books, 2014), chap. 1.

47. RON HASKINS, "Three Simple
Rules Poor Teens Should Follow to
Join the Middle Class," Brookings
Institution, March 13, 2013, https://
www.brookings.edu/opinions/
three-simple-rules-poor-teens-
should-follow-to-join-the-middle-
class.

48. RECTOR, "How Welfare
Undermines."

49. MARK REGNERUS,
"Cheap Sex and the Decline
of Marriage," *The Wall Street
Journal*, September 29, 2017,
https://www.wsj.com/articles/
cheap-sex-and-the-decline-of-
marriage-1506690454.

50. YANG MEILING 楊美鈴, "Guniang
ye neng xuehui sha zhu" 姑娘也
能學會殺豬 ["Girls Can Slaughter

Pigs Too"], *People's Daily*, October
1, 1966.

51. YU LUOWEN 遇羅文, *Wo jia: wo
de gege Yu Luoke* 我家：我的哥哥
遇羅克 [*My Family: My Brother Yu
Luoke*], (Beijing: World Chinese
Publishing Co., Ltd, 2016).

52. YE, ZHOU 葉舟, "Ye Yuqin de
zuihou shinian" 葉以群的最後十
年 ["The Last Decade of Ye Yiqun"],
Wenhui Monthly, no. 12 (1989).

53. PANG XIANZHI 逢先知 AND JIN
CHONGJI 金冲及, *Mao Zedong
zhuan (1949–1976)* 毛澤東傳 (1949–
1976) [*Biography of Mao Zedong
(1949–1976)*] (Beijing: Central Party
Literature Press, 2003).

Chapter Eight:
How Communism Sows Chaos in Politics

1. JULES-ANTOINE CASTAGNARY,
Philosophie du Salon de 1857, as
quoted in Franklin L. Baumer,
*Modern European Thought:
Continuity and Change in Ideas,
1600–1950* (New York: Macmillan,
1977), 335.

2. KARL MARX AND FRIEDRICH
ENGELS, "Manifesto of the
Communist Party," in *Marx &
Engels Selected Works*, vol. 1, trans.
Samuel Moore, ed. Andy Blunden,
Marxists Internet Archive,
accessed April 17, 2020, https://
www.marxists.org/archive/marx/
works/1848/communist-manifesto/
ch02.htm.

3. FRANK NEWPORT, "Democrats
More Positive About Socialism
Than Capitalism," Gallup, August
13, 2018, https://news.gallup.com/
poll/240725/democrats-positive-
socialism-capitalism.aspx.

4. "Little Change in Public's Response to 'Capitalism,' 'Socialism,'" Pew Research Center, December 28, 2011, https://www.people-press. org/2011/12/28/little-change-in-publics-response-to-capitalism-socialism.

5. MILTON FRIEDMAN, *Free to Choose: A Personal Statement* (Boston: Mariner Books, 1990), 148.

6. MATTHEW VADUM, "Soros Election-Rigging Scheme Collapses: The Secretary of State Project's death is a victory for conservatives," *FrontPage Mag*, July 30, 2012, https://www. frontpagemag.com/fpm/139026/ soros-election-rigging-scheme-collapses-matthew-vadum.

7. RACHEL CHASON, "Non-Citizens Can Now Vote in College Park, Md.," *The Washington Post*, September 13, 2017, https://www. washingtonpost.com/local/ md-politics/college-park-decides-to-allow-noncitizens-to-vote-in-local-elections/2017/09/13/2b7adb4a-987b-11e7-87fc-c3f7ee4035c9_story. html?utm_term=.71671372768a.

8. Mao Zedong, "Analysis of the Classes in Chinese Society," in *Selected Works of Mao Tse-tung: Vol. 1*, Marxists Internet Archive, accessed April 17, 2020, https://www. marxists.org/reference/archive/mao/ selected-works/volume-1/index.htm.

9. BILVEER SINGH, *Quest for Political Power: Communist Subversion and Militancy in Singapore* (Singapore: Marshall Cavendish International [Asia] Pte Ltd, 2015).

10. LEONARD PATTERSON, "I Trained in Moscow for Black Revolution," Speakers Bureau of the John Birch Society, YouTube video, posted by Swamp Yankee, August 20, 2011, https://www.youtube.com/ watch?v=GuXQjk4zhZs.

11. WILLIAM F. JASPER, "Anarchy in Los Angeles: Who Fanned the Flames, and Why?" *The New American*, June 15, 1992, https:// www.thenewamerican.com/usnews/ crime/item/15807-anarchy-in-los-angeles-who-fanned-the-flames-and-why.

12. Ibid.

13. US CONGRESS, HOUSE, Committee on Un-American Activities, *Soviet Total War, 'Historic Mission' of Violence and Deceit* (Washington, DC: US Government Printing Office, 1956).

14. MARX AND ENGELS, "Manifesto."

15. VLADIMIR LENIN, *The State and Revolution* (1918), 381–492, Marxists Internet Archive, accessed April 17, 2020, https://www.marxists.org/ archive/lenin/works/1917/staterev/ ch01.htm.

16. ALEXIS DE TOCQUEVILLE, *Democracy in America*, vol. 2, Henry Reeve, trans., (London: Longmans, Green, and Co., 1889), 289.

17. ALBERT VENN DICEY, *Lectures on the Relation Between Law & Public Opinion in England, During the Nineteenth Century* (London: Macmillan and Co., 1919), xxxviii, Online Library of Liberty, accessed April 17, 2020, http://oll.libertyfund. org/pages/dicey-on-the-rise-of-legal-collectivism-in-the-20thc.

18. PAUL B. SKOUSEN, *The Naked Socialist* (Salt Lake City, UT: Izzard Ink, 2014), Kindle edition.

19. PETER VINTHAGEN SIMPSON, "Jonas, 32, Sewed Up His Own Leg after ER Wait," *The Local,* August 3, 2010, https://www.thelocal. se/20100803/28150.

20. JUANA SUMMERS, "AP-NORC Poll: Most Americans See a Sharply Divided Nation," *The Associated Press,* http://www.apnorc.org/ news-media/Pages/AP-NORC-Poll-Most-Americans-see-a-sharply-divided-nation.aspx.

21. RONALD REAGAN, "First Inaugural Address of Ronald Reagan" (speech, US Capitol, Washington, DC, January 20, 1981), The Avalon Project, accessed April 17, 2020, https://avalon.law.yale. edu/20th_century/reagan1.asp.

22. DONALD TRUMP, "Remarks by President Trump at the 2017 Values Voter Summit" (speech, Omni Shoreham Hotel, Washington, DC, October 13, 2017), White House, accessed April 17, 2020, https:// www.whitehouse.gov/briefings-statements/remarks-president-trump-2017-values-voter-summit.

Chapter Nine: The Communist Economic Trap

1. THOMAS JEFFERSON et al., "United States Declaration of Independence," July 4, 1776, National Archives, accessed April 20, 2020, https:// www.archives.gov/founding-docs/ declaration-transcript.

2. KARL MARX AND FRIEDRICH ENGELS, "Manifesto of the Communist Party," in *Marx & Engels Selected Works,* vol. 1, trans. Samuel Moore, ed. Andy Blunden (Moscow: Progress Publishers, 1969), Marxists Internet Archive, accessed April 20, 2020, https:// www.marxists.org/archive/marx/ works/1848/communist-manifesto/ ch04.htm.

3. FRED SCHWARZ, *You Can Trust the Communists (to Be Communists)* (New Jersey: Prentice-Hall, 1960), 26–27.

4. FRIEDRICH A. HAYEK, *The Fatal Conceit: The Errors of Socialism,* W. W. Bartley III, ed. (Chicago: University of Chicago Press, 1991).

5. THOMAS SOWELL, *Intellectuals and Society,* Revised and Expanded Edition (New York: Basic Books, 2012), chap. 2.

6. LUDWIG VON MISES, "Economic Calculation in the Socialist Commonwealth," Mises Institute, accessed April 20, 2020, https://mises.org/library/ economic-calculation-socialist-commonwealth.

7. SHI SHAN 石山, "Zhongguo guoqi gaige de kunjing" 中国国企改革的困境 ["Quagmire in the Reform of China's State-Owned Enterprises"], Radio Free Asia, September 22, 2015, https://www. rfa.org/mandarin/yataibaodao/ jingmao/xql-09222015103826.html. [In Chinese]

8. LINETTE LOPEZ, "Zombie Companies Are Holding China's Economy Hostage," *Business Insider,* May 24, 2016, https:// www.businessinsider.com/ chinas-economy-is-being-held-hostage-2016-5.

9. MARX AND ENGELS, "Manifesto."

10. MAX GALKA, "The History of US Government Spending, Revenue, and Debt (1790–2015)," Metrocosm (blog), February 16, 2016, http://metrocosm.com/history-of-us-taxes.

11. ORGANIZATION FOR ECONOMIC COOPERATION AND DEVELOPMENT, "OECD Tax Rates on Labour Income Continued Decreasing Slowly in 2016," November 4, 2017, http://www.oecd.org/newsroom/oecd-tax-rates-on-labour-income-continued-decreasing-slowly-in-2016.htm.

12. RACHEL SHEFFIELD AND ROBERT RECTOR, "The War on Poverty After 50 Years," The Heritage Foundation, September 15, 2014, https://www.heritage.org/poverty-and-inequality/report/the-war-poverty-after-50-years.

13. ROBERT RECTOR, "The War on Poverty: 50 Years of Failure," The Heritage Foundation, September 23, 2014, https://www.heritage.org/marriage-and-family/commentary/the-war-poverty-50-years-failure.

14. ALEXIS DE TOCQUEVILLE, *Memoir on Pauperism*, trans. Seymour Drescher (London: Civitas, 1997).

15. SHEFFIELD AND RECTOR, "The War on Poverty."

16. NIMA SANANDAJI, *Scandinavian Unexceptionalism: Culture, Markets, and the Failure of Third-Way Socialism* (London: Institute for Economic Affairs, 2015), Kindle edition, 75.

17. TOCQUEVILLE, *Memoir.*

18. Ibid, 31.

19. "A National Sport No More," *The Economist,* November 3, 2012, https://www.economist.com/europe/2012/11/03/a-national-sport-no-more.

20. MARTIN HALLA, MARIO LACKNER, AND FRIEDRICH G. SCHNEIDER, "An Empirical Analysis of the Dynamics of the Welfare State: The Case of Benefit Morale," *Kyklos* 63, no.1 (2010): 55–74, Wiley Online Library, accessed April 20, 2020, https://onlinelibrary.wiley.com/doi/abs/10.1111/j.1467-6435.2010.00460.x.

21. NICHOLAS KRISTOF, "Profiting From a Child's Illiteracy," *The New York Times,* December 7, 2012, https://www.nytimes.com/2012/12/09/opinion/sunday/kristof-profiting-from-a-childs-illiteracy.html.

22. Ibid.

23. Ibid.

24. WILLIAM A. NISKANEN, "Welfare and the Culture of Poverty," *The Cato Journal* 16, no. 1 (1996), https://www.cato.org/sites/cato.org/files/serials/files/cato-journal/1996/5/cj16n1-1.pdf.

25. WALTER E. WILLIAMS, "The True Black Tragedy: Illegitimacy Rate of Nearly 75%," CNSNews.com, May 19, 2015, https://www.cnsnews.com/commentary/walter-e-williams/true-black-tragedy.

26. ORGANIZATION FOR ECONOMIC COOPERATION AND DEVELOPMENT, "General Government Debt (Indicator)," 2019, accessed April 27, 2020, https://data.oecd.org/gga/general-government-debt.htm.

27. RONALD COASE, as quoted in Thomas W. Hazlett, "Looking for

Results: An Interview With Ronald Coase," *Reason,* January 1997, https://reason.com/archives/1997/01/01/looking-for-results.

28. FRIEDRICH A. HAYEK, *The Road to Serfdom* (Chicago: University of Chicago Press, 1944).

29. M. SZMIGIERA, "Direct Investment Position of the United States in China from 2000 to 2018," Statistica.com, September 2, 2019, https://www.statista.com/statistics/188629/united-states-direct-investments-in-china-since-2000.

30. "Zhongguo waishang touzi baogao, 2016" 中国外商投资报告, ["Report on Foreign Investments in China, 2016"], in *Zhongguo washang zhijie touzi linian gaikuang* 中国外商直接投资历年概况 [*A General Summary of Direct Foreign Investments in China*], The Ministry of Commerce of China. [In Chinese]

31. US COMMISSION ON THE THEFT OF AMERICAN INTELLECTUAL PROPERTY, "Update to the IP Commission Report: The Theft of American Intellectual Property: Reassessments of the Challenge and United States Policy," (Washington DC: The National Bureau of Asian Research, February 2017), http://www.ipcommission.org/report/IP_Commission_Report_Update_2017.pdf.

32. CHRIS STROHM, "No Sign China Has Stopped Hacking US Companies, Official Says," *Bloomberg,* November 18, 2015, https://www.bloomberg.com/news/articles/2015-11-18/no-sign-china-has-stopped-hacking-u-s-companies-official-says.

33. KURT BIRAY, "Communist Nostalgia in Eastern Europe: Longing for the Past," Open Democracy, November 10, 2015, https://www.opendemocracy.net/can-europe-make-it/kurt-biray/communist-nostalgia-in-eastern-europe-longing-for-past.

34. JOHN POLGA-HECIMOVICH, "The Roots of Venezuela's Failing State," *Origins* 10, no. 9 (June 2017), http://origins.osu.edu/article/roots-venezuelas-failing-state.

35. JOSÉ NIÑO, "Venezuela Before Chavez: A Prelude to Socialist Failure," Mises Wire, May 4, 2017, https://mises.org/wire/venezuela-chavez-prelude-socialist-failure.

36. JOHN BISSETT, "Hugo Chavez: Revolutionary Socialist or Leftwing Reformist?" *Socialist Standard* 101, no. 1215 (November 2005), http://socialiststandardmyspace.blogspot.com/2015/05/hugo-chavez-revolutionary-socialist-or.html.

37. JULIAN ADORNEY, "Socialism Set Fire to Venezuela's Oil Crisis," Real Clear World, August 29, 2017, https://www.realclearworld.com/articles/2017/08/29/socialism_set_fire_to_venezuelas_oil_crisis_112520.html.

38. JOSÉ NIÑO, "John Oliver is Wrong About Venezuela — It's a Socialist Country," Mises Institute, May 30, 2018, https://mises.org/wire/john-oliver-wrong-about-venezuela-%E2%80%94-its-socialist-country.

39. CHRIS MCGREAL, "Zimbabwe's Inflation Rate Surges to 231,000,000%," *The Guardian,* October 9, 2008, https://www.theguardian.com/world/2008/oct/09/zimbabwe.

40. JASON LONG, "The Surprising Social Mobility of Victorian Britain,"

European Review of Economic History 17, no. 1 (February 1, 2013): 1–23, https://doi.org/10.1093/ereh/heso20.

41. MICHAEL ROTHSCHILD, *Bionomics: Economy as Ecosystem* (Washington, DC: Beard Books, 2004), 115.

42. ADAM SMITH, *The Theory of Moral Sentiments* (Malta: Gutenberg Publishers, 2011).

43. LAWRENCE KUDLOW, *American Abundance: The New Economic and Moral Prosperity* (New York: HarperCollins Publishers, 1997).

44. THOMAS SOWELL, *Economic Facts and Fallacies* (New York: Basic Books, 2008), 174.

45. FRIEDRICH ENGELS, "Trades Unions," *The Labour Standard*, May 28, 1881, Marxists Internet Archive, accessed April 20, 2020, https://www.marxists.org/archive/marx/works/1881/05/28.htm.

46. VLADIMIR LENIN, "The Trade Unions, The Present Situation and Trotsky's Mistakes," in *Lenin's Collected Works*, trans. Yuri Sdobnikov (Moscow: Progress Publishers, 1965), 32:19–42, Marxists Internet Archive, accessed April 20, 2020, https://www.marxists.org/archive/lenin/works/1920/dec/30.htm.

47. LÜ JIAMIN 呂嘉民, "Liening gonghuixueshuo shi" 列寧工會學說史 ["A History of Leninist Theory on Unions"], (Liaoning People's Press, 1987). [In Chinese]

48. JAMES SHERK, "What Unions Do: How Labor Unions Affect Jobs and the Economy," The Heritage Foundation, May 21, 2009, https://www.heritage.org/jobs-and-labor/report/what-unions-do-how-labor-unions-affect-jobs-and-the-economy.

49. Ibid.

50. EDWIN J. FEULNER, "Taking Down Twinkies," The Heritage Foundation, November 19, 2012, https://www.heritage.org/jobs-and-labor/commentary/taking-down-twinkies.

51. SHERK, "What Unions Do."

52. Ibid.

53. STEVE INSKEEP, "Solidarity for Sale: Corruption in Labor Unions," National Public Radio, February 6, 2007, https://www.npr.org/templates/story/story.php?storyId=5181842.

54. KARL MARX, "Critique of the Gotha Programme," in *Marx & Engels Selected Works* (Moscow: Progress Publishers, 1970), 3:13–30, Marxists Internet Archive, April 20, 2020, https://www.marxists.org/archive/marx/works/1875/gotha/cho1.htm.

55. KEITH WOOTTON, dir., *Children on the Titanic* (Marina Del Rey, CA: Vision Films, 2014).

56. WALTER LORD, *A Night to Remember: The Classic Account of the Final Hours of the Titanic* (United States: Henry Holt and Company, 2005), 50.

57. LI HONGZHI, "Wealth With Virtue," in *Essentials for Further Advancement*, January 27, 1995, https://www.falundafa.org/eng/eng/jjyzo2.htm.

Chapter Ten:
Corrupting the Legal System

1. HAROLD J. BERMAN, *The Interaction of Law and Religion* (Nashville: Abingdon Press, 1974), 51–55.

2. DONG ZHONGSHU 董仲舒, as quoted in Ban Gu 班固, "Dong Zhongshu zhuan" 董仲舒傳 ["Chronicle of Dong Zhongshu"] in *Han Shu* 漢書 [*The Book of Han*]. [In Chinese]

3. BERMAN, *The Interaction.*

4. KARL MARX, as quoted in W. Cleon Skousen, *The Naked Communist* (Salt Lake City: The Ensign Publishing Co., 1962), 13.

5. SERGEY NECHAYEV, *The Revolutionary Catechism* (1869), Marxists Internet Archive, accessed on April 20, 2020, https://www. marxists.org/subject/anarchism/ nechayev/catechism.htm.

6. VLADIMIR LENIN, "The Proletarian Revolution and the Renegade Kautsky: How Kautsky Turned Marx Into A Common Liberal," in *Lenin Collected Works*, trans. Jim Riordan (Moscow: Progress Publishers, 1974), 28:227–325, Marxists Internet Archive, accessed on April 20, 2020, https://www.marxists.org/archive/ lenin/works/1918/prrk/common_ liberal.htm.

7. LI YUZHEN 李玉貞, *Yi bu dianfuxing zhuzhuo: Ershi shiji Eguoshi* 一部 顛覆性著作：二十世紀俄國史 [*Work of Insurrection: 20th-Century Russian History*], (Beijing: Yanhuang Chunqiu, 2010). [In Chinese]

8. ALEXANDER NIKOLAEVICH YAKOVLEV, "Zhi Zhongguo Duzhe" 致中國讀者 ["To Chinese Readers"], in *Yibei kujiu—Eluosi de*

Buershiweikezhuyi he gaige yundong 一杯苦酒——俄羅斯的布爾什維 克主義和改革運動 [*A Bitter Cup: Bolshevism and the Reformation of Russia*], trans. Xu Kui 徐葵 et al., (Beijing: Xinhua chubanshe, 1999), 10. [In Chinese] The cited text is a preface written for the Chinese-language edition of Yakovlev's book.

9. AN LINXIAN 安霖賢, *Xianfa yuanze yu yi fa zhiguo* 宪法原则与依法 治国 [*Constitutional Principles and Governing the Country by Law*], People.com.cn, November 2, 2006, http://legal.people.com.cn/ GB/43027/73487/73490/ 4990833.html. [In Chinese]

10. OUYANG FEI 歐陽非, "Hongse huangtang huangyan lun" 紅 色荒唐言論 ["Red Nonsense"], Minghui.org, January 8, 2015, http://www.minghui.org/mh/ articles/2015/1/8/302850.html. [In Chinese]

11. FRANCIS BACON, "Of Judicature," in *The Essays or Counsels, Civil and Moral of Francis Bacon*, ed. Samuel Harvey Reynolds (Oxford: Clarendon Press, 1890), Internet Archive, accessed on April 20, 2020, https://archive.org/stream/ essaysorcounseloobacouoft/ essaysorcounseloobacouoft_djvu. txt.

12. *Planned Parenthood of Southeastern Pennsylvania v. Casey (Nos. 91–744, 91–902)*, Legal Information Institute, accessed on April 20, 2020, https:// www.law.cornell.edu/supct/html/91- 744.ZO.html.

13. NEIL EGGLESTON, "President Obama Has Now Granted More Commutations Than Any President in This Nation's History," The White House, January 17,

2017, https://obamawhitehouse.
archives.gov/blog/2017/01/17/
president-obama-has-now-granted-
more-commutations-any-president-
nations-history.

14. GREGORY KORTE, "Obama
Commutes Sentence of Chelsea
Manning in Last-Minute Clemency
Push,"
USA TODAY, January 17, 2017,
https://www.usatoday.com/story/
news/politics/2017/01/17/obama-
commutes-sentence-chelsea-
manning/96678814.

15. PAIGE ST. JOHN AND ABBIE
VANSICKLE, "Here's Why George
Soros, Liberal Groups Are Spending
Big to Help Decide Who's Your
Next DA," *Los Angeles Times*, May
23, 2018, http://www.latimes.com/
local/california/la-me-prosecutor-
campaign-20180523-story.html.

16. US CONGRESS, HOUSE, Affidavit of
Roger N. Baldwin, *Investigation of
Un-American Propaganda Activities
in the United States: Hearings
before a Special Committee on
Un-American Activities*, December
31, 1938, 3081–3082, Internet
Archive, accessed on April 20,
2020, https://archive.org/details/
investigationofu193804unit/
page/2448/mode/2up/search/
Baldwin.

17. MYRON H. THOMPSON, as quoted in
Phyllis Schlafly, *The Supremacists:
The Tyranny of Judges and How to
Stop It* (Minneapolis, MN: Richard
Vigilante Books, 2006), 26–27.

18. PHYLLIS SCHLAFLY, "Pots of
Gold Behind Crosses and Ten
Commandments," Eagle Forum,
June 23, 2004, http://eagleforum.
org/column/2004/june04/04-06-23.
html.

19. *Elk Grove Unified School District v.
Newdow*, 542 US 1 (2004).

20. US CONGRESS, HOUSE, *Expressing
the Sense of the House of
Representatives that Newdow v.
US Congress Was Erroneously
Decided, and for Other Purposes*,
HR 459, 107th Cong., 1st sess.,
introduced and agreed in House
June 27, 2002, https://www.congress.
gov/bill/107th-congress/house-
resolution/459.

21. US CONGRESS, SENATE,
*A Resolution Expressing Support
for the Pledge of Allegiance*, S. 292,
107th Cong., 1st sess., introduced
and agreed in Senate June 26,
2002, https://www.congress.
gov/bill/107th-congress/senate-
resolution/292.

22. SCHLAFLY,
The Supremacists, 30.

23. Ibid., 58.

24. Ibid., 60–61.

25. "CNN Revels in Pot Smoke
During New Year's Eve Report
From Denver," Fox News, January
1, 2018, http://www.foxnews.
com/entertainment/2018/01/01/
cnn-revels-in-pot-smoke-during-
new-years-eve-report-from-denver.
html.

26. PATRICK MCGREEVY, "Billionaire
Activists like Sean Parker and
George Soros Are Fueling the
Campaign to Legalize Pot," *Los
Angeles Times*, November 2, 2016,
http://www.latimes.com/politics/
la-pol-ca-proposition64-cash-snap-
20161102-story.html.

27. SEN. MIKE LEE, "GOP Senators
Call on Sec. Tillerson to Investigate
State Department Meddling,"

March 14, 2017, https://www.lee.
senate.gov/public/index.cfm/press-
releases?ID=B5BD5596-25C8-495F-
A8B1-A4D248649C04.

28. SCHLAFLY, *The Supremacists*.

29. *Obergefell v. Hodges*, 576 US 644
(2015).

30. TODD STARNES, "Kentucky
Clerk: 'This is a fight worth
fighting,'" Fox News, September
3, 2015, http://www.foxnews.com/
opinion/2015/09/03/kentucky-clerk-
am-prepared-to-go-to-jail.html.

31. MIKE HUCKABEE, as quoted in
"Attorney for Kim Davis Speaks
Out, Huckabee Blasts 'Judicial
Overreach' in Case," interview by
Sean Hannity, *Fox News*, September
8, 2015, http://www.foxnews.com/
transcript/2015/09/08/attorney-for-
kim-davis-speaks-out-huckabee-
blasts-judicial-overreach-in-case.
html.

32. STOP THE KINSEY INSTITUTE
COALITION, "Kinsey Helped
Undermine Laws Protecting Women
& Children," accessed on April 20,
2020, http://stopthekinseyinstitute.
org/more/undermining-laws.

33. PAUL RUBIN, et al., "Does Capital
Punishment Have a Deterrent
Effect? New Evidence From
Post-Moratorium Panel Data,"
Clemson University and Emory
University (October 2003),
https://cjlf.org/deathpenalty/
DezRubShepDeterFinal.pdf.

34. *Lawrence v. Texas*, 539 US 558 (2003).

35. BERMAN, *The Interaction*.

36. SKOUSEN, *The Naked Communist*.

Chapter Eleven: Desecrating the Arts

1. "Record of Music," in *Classic of
Rites*, trans. James Legge, Chinese
Text Project, accessed May 8, 2020,
https://ctext.org/liji/yue-ji?filter
=435370&searchmode
=showall#result.

2. CONFUCIUS 孔子, *Lun Yu* 論語 [*The
Analects of Confucius*] (New York:
Ballantine Books, 1999), 3.14. [In
Chinese]

3. SIMA QIAN, "A Treatise on Music,"
in *Records of the Grand Historian*,
trans. Burton Watson, vol. 24, 3rd
ed. (New York: Columbia University
Press, 1995).

4. OUYANG XIU 歐陽脩 and SONG QI
宋祁, *Xin Tang Shu* 新唐書 [*New
Book of Tang*], vol. 237 (1060). [In
Chinese]

5. ROBERT MCKEE, *Story: Style,
Structure, Substance, and the
Principles of Screenwriting* (New
York: ReganBooks, 1997), 129–130.

6. YINGSHOU XING et al., "Mozart,
Mozart Rhythm and Retrograde
Mozart Effects: Evidences from
Behaviours and Neurobiology
Bases," in *Scientific Reports*, vol.
6 (January 21, 2016), https://www.
nature.com/articles/srep18744.

7. DAVID NOEBEL, *The Marxist
Minstrels: A Handbook on
Communist Subversion of Music*
(Tulsa, OK: American Christian
College Press, 1974), 58–59.

8. DAVID CLOUD, "Rock Music and
Suicide," Way of Life Literature,
December 20, 2000, https://www.
wayoflife.org/reports/rock_music_
and_suicide.html.

9. VAL WILLIAMS, "Leni Riefenstahl: Film-maker Who Became Notorious as Hitler's Propagandist," *The Independent*, September 10, 2003, https://web.archive.org/web/20090830045819/http://www.independent.co.uk/news/obituaries/leni-riefenstahl-548728.html.

10. MAO ZEDONG, "Talks at the Yenan Forum on Literature and Art," in *Selected Works of Mao Tse-Tung* (Beijing: Foreign Languages Press), Marxists Internet Archive, accessed on April 23, 2020, https://www.marxists.org/reference/archive/mao/selected-works/volume-3/mswv3_08.htm.

11. PRAGERU, "Why Is Modern Art So Bad?", YouTube, September 1, 2014, https://www.youtube.com/watch?v=lNI07egoefc.

12. HERBERT MARCUSE, *The Aesthetic Dimension: Toward a Critique of Marxist Aesthetics* (Boston: Beacon Press, 1978), ix.

13. JACKSON SPIELVOGEL, *Western Civilization: Volume C: Since 1789* (United States: Cengage Learning, 2010), 698.

14. PABLO PICASSO, "Why I Became a Communist" (1945), as quoted in "Picasso, the FBI, and Why He Became a Communist," Meyer Schapiro Collection at Columbia University's Rare Book & Manuscript Library, February 24, 2010, accessed July 11, 2018, https://blogs.cul.columbia.edu/schapiro/2010/02/24/picasso-and-communism.

15. ROBERT HUGHES, *The Shock of the New: The Hundred-Year History of Modern Art—Its Rise, Its Dazzling Achievement, Its Fall* (London: Knopf, 1991), 24.

16. RICHARD HUELSENBECK AND RAOUL HAUSMANN, "What Is Dadaism and What Does It Want in Germany?", in Charles Harrison and Paul Wood, *Art in Theory, 1900–2000: An Anthology of Changing Ideas*, 2nd ed. (Malden, Mass, Oxford: Blackwell Pub, 2003).

17. JOSEPH BEUYS, as quoted in "Joseph Beuys: The Revolution Is Us," Tate.org, February 23, 1993, https://www.tate.org.uk/whats-on/tate-liverpool/exhibition/joseph-beuys-revolution-us.

18. WALDEMAR JANUSZCZAK, as quoted in Ben Cade, "Zhu Yu: China's Baby-Eating Shock Artist Goes Hyperreal," Culture Trip, October 5, 2016, https://theculturetrip.com/asia/china/articles/zhu-yu-china-s-baby-eating-shock-artist-goes-hyperreal.

19. JOHN WIILIAM GODWARD, as quoted in Brad Smithfield, "'The World Is Not Big Enough for Me and a Picasso': The Life and Artwork of John William Godward," The Vintage News, January 10, 2017, https://www.thevintagenews.com/2017/01/10/world-not-big-enough-picasso-life-artwork-john-william-godward.

20. WALTER FRISCH, ed., *Schoenberg and His World* (Princeton, NJ: Princeton University Press, 1999), 94.

21. NORMAN LEBRECHT, "Why We're Still Afraid of Schoenberg," *The Lebrecht Weekly*, July 8, 2001, http://www.scena.org/columns/lebrecht/010708-NL-Schoenberg.html.

22. GOLAN GUR, "Arnold Schoenberg and the Ideology of Progress

in Twentieth-Century Musical
Thinking," *Search: Journal for New
Music and Culture*, 5 (Summer
2009), http://www.searchnewmusic.
org/gur.pdf.

23. JULIA MICKENBERG, *American Girls
in Red Russia: Chasing the Soviet
Dream* (United States: University of
Chicago Press, 2017), 216–217.

24. MICHAEL MINNICINO, "The New
Dark Age: The Frankfurt School
and 'Political Correctness,'" in
Fidelio Magazine 1, no.1 (Winter
1992), accessed April 24, 2020, http://
archive.schillerinstitute.org/fid_91-
96/921_frankfurt.html.

25. MAO ZEDONG, "Talks at the Yenan
Forum."

26. MAO ZEDONG, "On New
Democracy," in *Selected Works of
Mao Tse-Tung* (Beijing: Foreign
Languages Press, 1942), Marxists
Internet Archive, accessed on April
24, 2020, https://www.marxists.org/
reference/archive/mao/selected-
works/volume-2/mswv2_26.htm.

27. ANDRÉ BRETON, *Manifestoes of
Surrealism*, trans. Richard Seaver
and Helen Lane (Ann Arbor, MI:
University of Michigan Press, 1969),
26.

28. ALLEN GINSBERG, "America,"
Selected Poems 1947–1995 (New York:
HarperCollins Publishers Inc.,
2001).

29. IRVING BABBITT, *Rousseau
and Romanticism* (Oxford, UK:
Routledge, 1991), 104.